D0516722

"What I love about *More Vegetables, Please!* is tha easy-to-make and tasty whole-food recipes. Nearly every page has cooking tips, and each recipe has a nutritional breakdown. While some recipes call for special ingredients, you'll be able to make many of these recipes from staple foods, herbs, and condiments that are already in your kitchen. This will soon be a dog-eared favorite!"

—Liz Lipski, Ph.D., CCN, CHN, director of doctoral studies at Hawthorn University and author of *Digestive Wellness*, *Digestive Wellness for Children*, and *Leaky Gut Syndrome*

"Everybody will do well by eating more vegetables, and this creative cookbook will show you how to do that in many different ways!"

—Annemarie Colbin, Ph.D., founder and CEO of The Natural Gourmet Institute for Health and Culinary Arts and author of *The Whole-Food Guide to Strong Bones*

"With their emphasis on fresh fruits and vegetables, eating what's in season, and smart food combinations, nutritionist Elson Haas and natural foods cooking expert Patty James combine forces to create an approach that makes it fun and easy to enjoy a health-promoting, delicious, and balanced diet."

—Lorna Sass, author of *Short-Cut Vegan* and *Great Vegetarian Cooking Under Pressure*

"*More Vegetables, Please!* is so much more than a cookbook; it's a guide to being your own nutritionist. Haas and James make it easy to know which vitamins and phytonutrients we're getting in each meal. They also show us how easy it is to cook a delicious variety of nature's gifts. *More Vegetables, Please!* is a reference and cookbook for anyone seeking optimum wellness."

—Judy Brooks, executive producer and cohost of *Healing Quest* on PBS Television Stations

More Vegetables, Please!

Over **100** Easy & Delicious
Recipes for Eating Healthy
Foods Each & Every Day

ELSON M. HAAS, MD
PATTY JAMES, MS

NEW HARBINGER PUBLICATIONS, INC.

Publisher's Note

This publication is designed to provide accurate and authoritative information in regard to the subject matter covered. It is sold with the understanding that the publisher is not engaged in rendering psychological, financial, legal, or other professional services. If expert assistance or counseling is needed, the services of a competent professional should be sought.

Distributed in Canada by Raincoast Books

Copyright © 2009 by Elson M. Haas and Patty James
New Harbinger Publications, Inc.
5674 Shattuck Avenue
Oakland, CA 94609
www.newharbinger.com

Cover design by Amy Shoup. Text design by Sara Christian and Amy Shoup. Illustrations by Jon Rubin. Acquired by Jess O'Brien. Edited by Marisa Solis.

ISBN 978-1-57224-453-5 Paperback
All Rights Reserved
Printed in Canada

Library of Congress Cataloging-in-Publication Data

Haas, Elson M., 1947-
  More vegetables, please! : over 100 easy & delicious recipes for
eating healthy foods each & every day / Elson M. Haas, Patty James.
      p. cm.
  Includes index.
  ISBN 978-1-57224-590-7 (alk. paper)
  1. Vegetables in human nutrition. 2. Cookery (Vegetables) 3.
Vegetables--Therapeutic use. I. James, Patty. II. Title.
  QP144.V44H334 2009
  641.6'5--dc22
                              2009027323

  11   10   09

  10   9   8   7   6   5   4   3   2   1

First printing

This book is printed with soy ink.

Mixed Sources
Product group from well-managed
forests, controlled sources and
recycled wood or fiber
www.fsc.org Cert no. SW-COC-000952
© 1996 Forest Stewardship Council

I wish to dedicate this book to the health of the family and home-cooked meals. It's so important to nourish ourselves and our loved ones, and we begin that with fresh foods, especially vegetables. I pray for Earth's well-being so that she can continue to provide wholesome food to all her people. And last, I dedicate this book to the family garden. Grow some fresh vegetables with your household and neighbors.

Blessings, Good Nourishment, and Stay Healthy,

—Dr. Elson

. . . . .

To my children—Olivia, Russell, and Kathryn—and my son-in-law, David. I am honored to be your mother and so proud of each of you. You are my life.

To my mother, Joan H. James, who has always nourished me physically and mentally and whose wisdom inspires me.

To my granddaughter Brealyn Rose Trujillo. You are what keeps me on my path. I will do whatever I can to make the world a healthier place for you.

To my big, wonderful family and my "girls." I can't imagine life without you.

To my dear friend Elson Haas, who has always believed in me and supported me, I simply say, thank you.

—Patty James

Contents

Acknowledgments

To all my students these past years, from my Summer Camp kids who truly made me feel like I was making a difference in the world, to the many folks who felt like family when they were in my kitchen, wherever that kitchen might be! Your health is my passion, and I feel so blessed to be part of your lives. Thank you all.

To all the people at New Harbinger whose enthusiasm for our book is infectious and who truly believe in this book's message, thank you. Marisa Solís, our wonderful editor, thank you for your never-ending patience and wise suggestions.

Introduction

"More vegetables, please," is what I found myself consistently telling waitstaff at restaurants. I couldn't help but notice that at all the restaurants I went to—from the fanciest ones to those that claimed to offer wholesome food—vegetables were in short supply on the menu.

There're too many simple carbohydrates and sweeteners added to most dishes, and entrées are generally very rich in fats and oils. All restaurants want their food to taste great, and, let's face it, too often that comes from added sugars, fats, and salt. It's no wonder that modern-day eaters have trouble maintaining a healthy weight.

As an author and a family physician, I am always asking myself, "What does the public, my readers, need to know that can improve their health? What will make a difference?" So, I mentioned my ideas to my good friend and colleague, Patty James, an inspired chef and educator. "I want to write a book called *More Vegetables, Please!* People need to eat more veggies, and yet, what they tell me is that they really don't know how to incorporate them well into their family meals, nor do they know how to prepare them so that they taste great. We especially need to get more veggies into mainstream family meals." Being the very enthusiastic person she is, Patty replied, "Let's do this. I can help, and I have lots of ideas." Patty teaches cooking and nutrition classes for adults and children—and she knows how to make preparing food fun and the end result healthy and very tasty.

Who is this book for? We believe that it's for everyone—individuals, couples, and families—since we all need to eat more vegetables, our most nutritious natural foods, which come in a wide variety of colors and flavors.

If you're eating a mainstream American diet, you will greatly benefit from following our suggestions and recipes in *More Vegetables, Please!* We believe that this dietary approach will be synonymous with *More Health, Please.* We even see vegetarians who do not eat enough veggies. Many vegetarians who I consult with in practice eat an overabundance of bread and cheese and do not include fresh salads and properly cooked veggie dishes in their diets. Whether you're a vegetarian or meat-eater, you need colors, nutrition, and vitality in your foods—and you'll find that in the vegetable kingdom.

It is very clear that we have a huge problem in this country—and in the Western world—with dietary balance. We are consuming too many calories, especially from refined sugars, and this is part of the obesity epidemic. In John Robbins's brilliant book *Healthy at 100*, he reviews civilizations in which people tended to live long and healthy lives, and he describes what it takes to live that way in this twenty-first century. Many people find their weight resolution in the latest high-protein, low-carbohydrate diet, yet that is not ideal because many of these programs suggest too much animal protein and fat, and this may well be linked to cardiovascular diseases and cancer. The solution lies in eating more natural foods, and this begins with nutritious and colorful vegetables, followed by high-fiber, whole-grain complex carbohydrates, and then fruits, nuts and seeds, legumes, and appropriate animal proteins.

Living a long and healthy life begins ideally in childhood. We suggest that, if applicable, you involve even the youngest family members in the experience of healthy cooking. But don't forget, it's never too late to start eating more vegetables. We want to contribute to a healthier way of eating; our objectives are to support you and your family in good, simple, and wholesome meals; to make the transition fun; and, clearly, to bring those vital veggies into your daily menu plans.

We believe that we have succeeded in making a simple, practical book that will help you make your diet richer in vegetables and healthier overall. We encourage you to experience and enjoy the recipes and suggestions in this book with your family and friends. Patty James and I know you will enjoy the process and the outcome. You will also be surprised at the simplicity of the recipes and the flattering responses you will get from the family.

Enjoy, and Stay Healthy,

—Dr. Elson Haas

How to Use This Book:
Making *More Vegetables, Please!* Work for You

We are truly excited to bring to you this book about adding more vegetables into any, and hopefully most, of your meals. In following our tips and recipes, you'll be improving your nourishment and adding colorful, nutritious foods to your diet—and incorporating new menus for yourself and your family. We are not putting a specific dietary label on this book or on the meals and recipe ideas we provide; it's not specifically vegan (eating no animal-derived products, so excluding all meats, eggs, and dairy), lacto-vegetarian (eating no meat or eggs but including dairy), vegetarian (eating no meat but including eggs and dairy), or omnivorian (eating anything). This book is appropriate for everyone wanting to eat a healthy diet while enjoying familiar foods and trying new dishes. Our goal is to help you be your own nutritionist and healthy chef. This doesn't need to be confusing or complicated.

Let us give you a few tips on making this book work for you. First, you can obviously look through it page by page, taking in information and being inspired by the ingredients and recipes that you want to incorporate into your diet. Many people plan the "main" dish or entrée first and go from there—and this book allows you to do just that in chapter 8, which is devoted to entrées. Most recipes in that chapter offer recommendations for side dishes with seasonal variations. A third way to use this book is to search for specific ingredients, such as tomatoes or zucchini, in our index, and begin your menu there with a dish you want to try. This book is also designed with the seasons in mind, so you can scour our Eating Seasonally sidebars for guidance when a vegetable is coming out your ears and you need new inspiration! And finally, we say use this book as a guide, meaning you don't have to follow it to the T. Use your imagination to get creative in the kitchen—enjoy the process and the food!

Many recipes have serving suggestions, so you don't have to think too hard about what to pair your dish with—we've done that for you. Many vegetable "side" dishes (we dislike calling them side dishes, as we think that many are hearty, nutritious, and fabulous enough to not be relegated to the "side" and instead to the "center," but we defer to cookbook standards here) have suggestions for entrée selections. Consider making up some new menu plans for the week and, if you have a family, involve them in this process. When kids in particular are part of the process, they are more likely to learn about and make good, healthy eating choices for the rest of their lives.

Chapter 1 provides an overview of what vegetables are and more than a dozen reasons why they are essential to a healthy eating routine. We discuss the chemical makeup of vegetables in very basic terms so that you really understand why they're fundamental to a healthy diet and properly functioning body. In chapter 2 we divide vegetables into categories so that you can understand which vegetables are related and what some of their group characteristics are. Then we list *every vegetable mentioned in this book*, giving nutrient info, cooking tips, pairing suggestions, and more. Chapter 3 gets you ready to bring more vegetables, please (MVP) into your diets with tips on produce shopping, transforming common unhealthy meals, getting children involved in meal preparation, and more. There's even a list of cooking terms used in this book for your reference.

Chapters 4 through 10 are filled with carefully selected recipes that are healthy, delicious, and, of course, contain at least one vegetable (though most average three or four). Each chapter opens with an introduction, followed by several scrumptious recipes. Many recipes feature highlighted information in the following categories:

- *Eating Seasonally*, which provides vegetable choices by the season so that you're always consuming the freshest local produce all year long

- *Variations*, which suggests ways to tweak the recipe for a slightly different flavor, for MVP, and more

- *Health Note*, which provides interesting nutritional facts

- *Cooking Tip*, which offers advice on food prep and cooking techniques

- *Kids in the Kitchen*, which provides simple ways to include children in the cooking experience

Our recipes can be used both as a step-by-step manual and as a base from which to experiment. Be creative! Try our Variations suggestions, or invent your own; they will change the spiciness or flavor or consistency of the dish, and this is what makes cooking—and eating—fun. Also, many recipes provide seasonal vegetable alternatives. So don't skip over a recipe because its name implies a winter dish—modify it to include whatever is local, fresh, and in season.

Understanding the Nutrient Data

Patty uses MasterCook, a recipe-management software, to calculate the nutrient information for each dish in this book. Oftentimes, after creating a recipe or changing an old recipe, Patty will examine the nutrition content only to find some imbalance: inadequate protein, or too much sodium. In these instances, Patty has recreated the recipe until the data is within healthy limits (Aren't you glad you didn't have to do this?) So, you can be sure that these recipes really have been tested (and retested) with your health in mind. We are pleased to offer this information to you to assist in planning your meals.

It's important, however, that you understand how to read the nutrition information. The percentage of fats noted on a nutrition label, or even in this book, for a given food can be confusing. What's important to keep in mind is that some foods, like vegetables, have few calories, so when a fatty ingredient like oil is added, the percentage can really climb. That is why some salads will show a high percentage of fat—it's all in the dressing. Another example is our Grilled Asparagus recipe; you'll read that 80.2% of calories are from fat. This doesn't mean that the recipe will immediately clog your arteries, it simply means that because asparagus have very few calories, the olive oil and cheese called for in the recipe are the major sources of calories and fats, thus the higher percentage. Although a recipe's data may show that it's high in fat, be sure to consider the amount of calories and whether the meal consists of mainly vegetables—it can still be incredibly nutritious and healthy.

Also be cognizant of your sodium amount, as Americans consume too much salt. Some vegetables have a naturally high sodium content and thus some recipes are higher than others in sodium even though there is no added salt. Please see the Health Note for the Split Pea Soup recipe (page 125) about recommended sodium intake.

Overall, we want to teach you to add MVP to recipes not as an afterthought but as a primary focus of every meal you eat. For vegetarians this might come easily, though not always. For meat-lovers it might take a little more thought, but we have revised many common meat-centered meals to include more veggies, so you don't have to do all the thinking.

Our hope is that this is the book that'll always be on your counter, the one that you refer to often. Moreover, we hope it will alter the way you think about and utilize food in your and your family's diet, supporting better health for all.

Enjoy!

Chapter 1
Why More Vegetables?

The word "doctor" comes from the Latin word *doctore*, which translates as *teacher*. So in that sense, we are both teachers, whether caring for patients or running a cooking school. We both make it our mission to inspire and guide people to live most healthfully, and we feel strongly that how you look and feel is a result of how you live. Thus, if you want to feel better, something has to change. Most often that is within your lifestyle—and especially in your diet.

Now and for decades, much of our work has focused on nutrition and the many facets of diet, epidemiology (what causes illness), and the wonderful world of nutritional and herbal supplements, an exciting and ever-advancing field. We have studied, cooked, and written recipes, often in collaboration with some of the most imaginative chefs out there. At the same time, we are very familiar with feeding families for fitness and health, as Elson did with his two children and Patty did with hers. Also, we have reviewed hundreds of new and old diets, programs, fads, and food fantasies that have traveled across the recent decades, from vegetarian to high protein to low carbs and high fiber. Interestingly, the universal message consistently professed by the physicians, nutritionists, and government employees who've authored the diet regimens is: *Eat more fresh foods and more vegetables and fruits.* Everyone says that!

We believe that the best current eating program to keep us healthy and more alkaline (we'll explain that later) is *50 percent vegetables* (by volume). This high-vegetable diet is especially helpful to maintain or even drop weight. It includes a focus on green veggies in particular and less of the more-caloric and starchy vegetables, like potatoes and carrots. This diet also provides consistent and lower-calorie, nutrient-rich vegetables that contain higher amounts of water than more-concentrated fats and protein foods; more veggies (and fruits) keep the body hydrated.

Healthy and Balanced Diet

Vegetables make up an important part of a healthy diet; we believe they're the most important part. If we are eating a sufficient amount of fresh veggies in our diet, then we are also consuming a diet that typically meets the criteria that Dr. Haas suggests are the qualities of a healthy diet. That includes:

- Natural foods fresh from nature
- Seasonal eating within our local, natural cycle
- Fresh foods and vegetables eaten right after being picked
- Nutritious foods, which means veggies, veggies, veggies
- Tasty and appealing veggies, which add flavor
- A variety of foods, which naturally creates a balanced diet
- Well-combined foods, which allows for better digestion and assimilation of nutrients

To balance our diet, we need to move from what we learned in school about eating meats and dairy products as part of every meal, which began as a marketing plan from the dairy and meat associations nearly a century ago. It takes a while to change habits, yet this is a valuable one to work on for the health and wellbeing of individuals and families. We must move toward the New Basic Four.

OLD BASIC FOUR	NEW BASIC FOUR
Animal meats	Vegetables
Dairy products	Fruits
Cereal grains	Whole grains and legumes (beans and peas)
Fruits and vegetables	Proteins and fats/oils (vegetarian: nuts and seeds; omnivorian: dairy, eggs, and meats)

The New Basic Four has a greater focus on fresh fruits and vegetables instead of the higher animal food intake that we believe—and research shows—causes much more congestive and chronic diseases. With the New Basic Four, we are focusing on more vegetarian-based meals, along with some reasonable amounts of proteins and fats. This leads to a generally more nutritious diet, which we all need.

A diet following this plan might include fruits and whole grains for breakfast, often with some nuts and seeds added, wherein raw and organic are the best choices. Lunch and dinner can focus on vegetables with some added protein and/or starch, such as rice and vegetables with tofu or chicken, or a big green salad with some tuna or salmon, as a couple nourishing examples.

Important Phytonutrients

The study of "plant nutrients," or phytonutrients, has become an important area of study for researchers. For example, we know that phytonutrients feed your cells and tissues and can serve as antioxidants. These include fresh chlorophyll; carotenoids like beta-carotene; flavonoids and flavones such as quercetin and hesperidin; tannins/polyphenols; alkaloids and glycosolides; and sulfur compounds. It is these phytonutrients that basically provide the color, smell, and taste of fruits and vegetables. Although not proven yet, it is extremely likely that we need many of these phytonutrients for bodily functions and overall health. You can review more about this topic beginning on page 295 of Elson's book *Staying Healthy with Nutrition* (2006).

Each fresh fruit and vegetable has very specific phytonutrients, and each one has different, yet specific, supportive or protective action in the cells and tissues. We are continually learning about the many functions that these new nutrients play in our body. For example, we know most about the carotenoids and the antioxidant protection they provide. These orange, red, and yellow pigments are found in such foods as peppers, pumpkins, cantaloupe, cherries, papaya, mango, cabbage, and carrots. The most known, beta-carotene, is quite high in carrots (and drinking too much carrot juice can cause your skin to be tinted by this orange pigment). The beta-carotene converts in the body to the vitally necessary vitamin A that supports your eyesight, skin health, and immune system.

Flavonoids and flavones are found in almost every fresh food from Nature. They have anti-inflammatory, anti-allergy, antioxidant, and cancer-preventive actions. Bioflavonoids are often included in nutritional supplements, especially in vitamin C products. Quercetin, lutein, and hesperidin are the most commonly known, and these are naturally extracted from the white pulp that surrounds citrus fruit. Elson uses quercetin quite often in his practice in a program to reduce allergic reactions to foods and the environment. In appropriate amounts, it has a good anti-allergy, antihistamine effect. Each natural food—from fruits and vegetables, to nuts and seeds, to grains and beans—has specific phytonutrients that relate to their colors, flavors, and functions in the body.

Vegetables: Our Most Important Food Category

At least half of your lunch and dinner plate should consist of vegetables, which are generally low in calories, high in nutrients (vitamins, minerals, and especially phytonutrients), high in dietary fiber (which helps with waste elimination and prevents diseases of the intestines), and natural enzymes (which help you digest your foods).

Raw or Cooked?

It comes down to one simple fact: The fresher the vegetable, the more nutrition and enzymes it generally contains. Although many of the nutrients will remain in your vegetables even when you cook them, you can lose some of the vitamins, especially the water-soluble vitamins B and C, when you cook the vegetables. Cooking also breaks down some of the fragile enzymes. (Making soups with veggies may be an exception here, since most of the nutrients stay in the soup.) The minerals and fat-soluble vitamins (there are only a small amount in most veggies) will have more stability during cooking. Thus, in general, eating vegetables in their raw state offers the most *potential* nutrition.

We write "potential nutrition" because many people do not chew their food well enough to break them down and digest them sufficiently. Not chewing vegetables properly can actually prevent you from benefiting from their full nutrients. We suggest that you cook vegetables lightly to soften them a bit—as well as to maintain some of their freshness, texture, and flavor. This is especially important for the elderly or people with sensitive teeth.

Ideally, as you embrace a 50 percent vegetable diet, you want some raw and some cooked veggies. We'll show you how to do this with cooked vegetable mixtures and veggie purées, which have the added benefit of already being broken down to digestible size! Eating fresh greens in a salad is a daily part of a good diet. The organic mixed greens and lettuces, beyond the Iceberg Age, offer great nutrition and low calories, and, without tons of salad dressings, they are an important part of a weight reduction and maintenance program.

Restoring the Acid/Alkaline Balance

The acid/alkaline balance in your diet is also quite important. In fact, this relates to Elson's belief that there is one primary disease: cellular malfunction. The first of two causes is the *lack of necessary nutrients* that your cells need to do their thousands of functions every moment of every day of your life. Thus, you need foods that supply all the vitamins, minerals, amino acids, fatty acids, and phytonutrients.

The second cause is *toxins*—the chemicals that we get from food, air, and water, plus metals like lead and mercury, all of which may interfere with enzyme and cell function. People suffering from diseases and disease-like symptoms typically have these deficiency and toxicity issues. It's the overconsumption of acid-forming foods that leads to excess mucus and toxicity, and then inflammation and degeneration of the body tissues. This causes aging. Even the common cardiovascular diseases are now known to be caused by inflammation.

Let's look at this acid/alkaline issue a bit more. When foods are broken down in the body, they leave a residue, or ash, that has an acid or alkaline pH. The term pH stands for pressure of hydrogen, and it ranges from 0 to 14, neutral water being a pH of 7.0. A pH above that is alkaline and below that is acid. Your body tissues and blood are maintained at the alkaline pH of 7.41, and you have many mechanisms that keep that close. It is these many buffering actions with the kidneys, tissues, and even bones that alter the body's health and cause many problems. You buffer or store these extra acids in your tissues, which can slowly inflame, damage, and age them. Most people in the Western world consume too many acid-forming foods—flour and sugar products, animal meats and cheeses, sodas and baked goods—and prescription drugs and are exposed to too many chemicals. Fruits and vegetables are primarily alkaline-forming, and that's why we want you to say, "More vegetables, please!"

Environmental Reasons for Eating MVP

Avoiding chemicals is another important factor in protecting your health, and the health of our precious life-giving and food-providing dear Mother Earth. Can you tell Patty and Elson are friends of the environment? What each of us does to Earth, we do to our own bodies, as we eventually are exposed to the same substances, such as the mercury in the ocean and the chemicals in our food and water sources.

Ideally, local produce and organically grown foods are your best choices for avoiding introduced chemicals, yet there is some current thinking that locally grown food is even more important than organic food grown elsewhere. We think that whenever you can purchase either (or both!) you will be allowing yourself the freshest, healthiest option possible. We are fans of living healthfully with the seasons and supporting the local environment. The cost of shipping foods around the world is great both in adding cost to our foods and pollution to the air, since many growers choose to chemically treat the foods even more when they are shipped long distances. For these reasons, you might consider growing some (or all!) vegetables in your own garden.

Also, poor soil quality may not provide the best nutrients to our foods; thus, a carrot from one place may not provide the same nutrition as a carrot from another. So make sure your organic farm is using quality products.

Why Organic?

When you select organic foods, you are choosing more-nutritious foods, saying no to chemicals in you and your families' bodies, and supporting sustainable agricultural practices, which is environmentally imperative.

Top 10 Reasons to Buy Organic

Here are 10 reasons to choose organic food according to the California Certified Organic Farmers (CCOF):

1. PROTECT FUTURE GENERATIONS

"We have not inherited the Earth from our fathers, we are borrowing it from our children." —Chief Seattle

The average child receives four times more exposure than an adult to at least eight widely used cancer-causing pesticides in food. Food choices you make now will impact your child's future health.

2. PREVENT SOIL EROSION

The Soil Conservation Service estimates more than three billion tons of topsoil is eroded from U.S. croplands each year. That means soil erodes seven times faster than it's built up naturally. Soil is the foundation of the food chain in organic farming. However, in conventional farming, the soil is used more as a medium for holding plants in a vertical position so that they can be chemically fertilized. As a result, American farms are suffering from the worst soil erosion in history.

3. PROTECT WATER QUALITY

Water makes up two-thirds of our body mass and covers three-fourths of the planet. The Environmental Protection Agency (EPA) estimates pesticides—some cancer causing—contaminate the groundwater in thirty-eight states, polluting the primary source of drinking water for more than half the country's population.

4. SAVE ENERGY

American farms have changed drastically in the last three generations, from family-based small businesses dependent on human energy to large-scale factory farms. Modern farming uses more petroleum than any other single industry, consuming 12 percent of the country's totally energy supply. More energy is now used to produce synthetic fertilizers than to till, cultivate, and harvest all the crops in the United States. Organic farming is still based on labor-intensive practices such as hand-weeding, green manure, and crop covers instead of synthetic fertilizers to support soil.

5. KEEP CHEMICALS OFF YOUR PLATE

Many pesticides approved for use by the EPA were registered long before extensive research linking these chemicals to cancer and other diseases had been established. Now the EPA considers 60 percent of all herbicides, 90 percent of all fungicides, and 30 percent of all insecticides carcinogenic. A 1987 National Academy of Sciences report estimated that pesticides might cause an extra four million cancer cases among Americans. The bottom line is that pesticides are poisons designed to kill living organisms and can also harm humans. In addition to cancer, pesticides are implicated in birth defects, nerve damage, and genetic mutations.

6. PROTECT FARM WORKERS

A National Cancer Institute study found that farmers exposed to herbicides had six times more risk than nonfarmers of contracting cancer. In California, reported pesticide poisonings among farm workers have risen an average of 14 percent a year since 1973 and doubled between 1975 and 1985. Field workers suffer the highest rates of occupational illness in the state. Farm worker health is also a serious problem in developing nations, where pesticide use can be poorly regulated. An estimated one million people are poisoned annually by pesticides.

7. HELP SMALL FARMERS

Although more and more large-scale farms are making the conversion to organic practices, most organic farms are small, independently owned family farms of fewer than one hundred acres. It's estimated that the United States has lost more than 650,000 family farms in the past decade. Organic farming is one of the few survival tactics left for family farms.

8. SUPPORT A TRUE ECONOMY

Although organic foods might seem more expensive than conventional foods, conventional food prices don't reflect hidden costs borne by taxpayers, including nearly $74 billion annually in federal subsidies. Other hidden costs include pesticide regulation and testing, hazardous waste disposal and cleanup, and environmental damage. For instance, if you add in the environmental and social costs of irrigation to a head of lettuce, its price would range between $2 and $3.

9. PROMOTE BIODIVERSITY

Mono-cropping is the practice of planting large plots of land with the same crop year after year. While this approach tripled farm production between 1950 and 1970, the lack of natural diversity of plant life has left the soil lacking in natural minerals and nutrients. To replace the nutrients, chemical fertilizers are used, often in increasing amounts. Single crops are also much more susceptible to pests, making farmers more reliant on pesticides. Despite a tenfold increase in the use of pesticides between 1947 and 1974, crop losses due to insects have doubled—partly because some insects have become genetically resistant to certain pesticides.

10. TASTE, AS IN BETTER FLAVOR

There's a good reason why many chefs use organic foods in their recipes—they taste better. Organic farming starts with the nourishment of the soil, which eventually leads to the nourishment of the plant and, ultimately, our palates.

For more information about organic food and farming, and for the sources of the various studies mentioned, contact California Certified Organic Farmers at www.ccof.org.

If you are not able to purchase everything organically grown, at least consider those items that you consume every day. Also, invest in foods whose parts you are eating might have been directly sprayed, such as leafy greens; a food that can be peeled, like an orange, could be overlooked. Need more guidance? According to the Environmental Working Group (www.ewg.org), a watch group that measures produce crops and shipment for pesticide and other chemical residues, these are the top 10 most heavily sprayed foods, in alphabetical order:

Apples
Bell peppers
Celery
Cherries
Grapes
Nectarines
Peaches
Pears
Raspberries
Strawberries

In other words, this list represents the foods that you'll most often want to buy organic. And ideally, you should add to this list anything that you or your children consume on a daily basis, such as bananas or rice or baby food.

It is also a good idea to purchase milk, egg, and meat products organically grown or raised. All these foods may contain additives and various growth hormones. Also, some of the most concerning chemicals are stored in the fats of the food, and thus dairy products and especially butter (all fat) are good to buy organically produced.

Organically grown foods are definitely becoming more available and more cost competitive. When you choose local and organic food, the food hasn't traveled across the country (or the world for that matter) and therefore is more nutritious and certainly tastes better. It typically is not treated as much to protect it from damage, mold, or insect infestation. You are also supporting your local farmers and local economy. Many farmers offer Community Supported Agriculture (CSA) programs. This is a system whereby you receive food directly from the farmers who produce it. If you are a member of CSA, you will either pick up or have delivered a weekly box of produce that was picked fresh that day for you right off the farm. You receive what is seasonal, taking the guesswork out of what is available in your area.

Home Cooking!

Home is where the heart is, or, more appropriately, home is where the kitchen is. We all know that families and friends always seem to gather in the kitchen. It's comforting for most of us; the simple act of enjoying a meal at the table is an important aspect to the quality of our lives. It's the time to talk about the day's events and simply catch up. For children, the family meal is extremely important. There are studies that show that children who eat with their families, whether it be one parent or a large family, perform better in school, are more likely to attend college, and are less likely to do drugs. Even if your day has been very busy and you have purchased ready-made food, dine at the table. Let's dine, not simply eat.

Keep in mind that children learn behavior early in their lives, and these patterns become deeply laid for later years. So, set a good example! Teach your children to set the table, wait for the cook to sit down before eating, place their napkins in their laps, and not gulp down their food. These are all lessons in good manners—civility in the dining room, if you will. Take a moment before you eat to be thankful for the food in front of you. It's good for your soul and for your digestion! So how do you create meals that will bring your family together and give your children the foundation for a lifetime of healthy eating? It all begins with health education and making good choices in your foods.

Patty James, who is a great chef and teacher, will lead the way in showing you how to add those many-colored vegetables into your meals. We will make it simple and fun and, we assure you, quite tasty, such that no more will you hear, "Yuck, vegetables!" but the new request from our children, family, and friends: "More Vegetables, Please!"

Chapter 2

Vegetables: What Are They and How Should We Use Them?

Vegetables come in all colors, shapes, sizes, textures, and flavors. In this chapter, we will explore the wide variety of veggies from our productive Mother Earth. We will first go through their different classes, what each group provides, and what specific vegetables lie within each classification. Then we will discuss each in the alphabetical list below. Clearly, the vegetable queendom offers our widest variety and choices in food, yet they seem to be a second-class object to most people living in the modern world. We want to change that thinking for the health benefits of all. Since many nutritional authorities consider vegetables to be our most important category for good health, and the authors of this book agree, then it makes sense to know all we can about these important foods and learn how to prepare them so they are palatable, even loved, by most people. That's our goal. Are you with us?

Why You Should Love Vegetables

We mentioned the following points in chapter 1, but it never hurts to repeat a summary of the benefits of eating more veggies:

- Vegetables contain high amounts of water and thus support hydration.
- Vegetables contain good amounts of many vitamins and minerals and are thus very nutritious foods that are needed by our body for proper function.
- Many vegetables contain chlorophyll—made from light energy, or the sun's rays—which is a refreshing, vitalizing, and detoxifying plant substance.
- Vegetables contain many known and unknown phytonutrients that provide much support for the proper function and protection of the cells in our body.
- Vegetables contain fiber, which supports good health and proper bowel function.
- Most vegetables can be eaten raw for best nutrition, or they can be steamed, baked, roasted, or fried to bring out other flavors.
- Most vegetables can be juiced for an invigorating and nutritious beverage or meal.

Vegetable Categories

Every vegetable has a certain genus and species, just as we humans are Homo sapiens, and each also has a family, just as we do. Most of the categories we describe here are part of that classification. However, many are more general and categorize the vegetables into related groups, such as the Leafy Greens. The following review offers a summary and similar classification as Dr. Haas presents in his nutrition text, *Staying Healthy with Nutrition*. Mostly we are looking at how they are presented to us, rather than their genetic classification.

Let us make a couple comments about two families of vegetables: the nightshades and the cruciferous vegetables. The nightshade family, sometimes referred to as the "deadly nightshades," is not really that deadly. Some parts of some of the plants can be poisonous, yet their name comes from the idea that they irritate people's joints, especially those prone to arthritis. This doesn't seem to be the case. Most everyone eats nightshade plants regularly, as they are the most common vegetables consumed. These include potatoes,

Vegetable Categories* At a Glance

Leafy Greens
- Cabbage, chards, collards, kale, lettuce, spinach, watercress

Vegetable Flowers
- Artichokes, broccoli, Brussels sprouts, cauliflower

Flowering Vegetables
- Cucumbers, eggplant, peppers, pumpkins, squashes, tomatoes

Stem and Stalk Vegetables
- Asparagus, celery, leeks, rhubarb

Roots and Tubers
- Beets, carrots, garlic, onions, parsnips, potatoes, radishes, rutabaga, sweet potatoes, turnip, yams

Ocean Vegetables: Seaweed
- Agar-agar, arame, dulse, hijiki, kelp, kombu, nori, purple laver, wakame

Fungi: Mushrooms
- Button, chanterelle, maitake, morels, oyster, reishi, shiitake

Legumes: Peas and Beans
- Azuki (also spelled "adzuki" or "aduki"), black, green, kidney, lentil, lima, mung, navy, red, snap pea, sweet pea, wax

Sprouts: Seeds, Legumes, and Nuts
- Alfalfa, clover, and radish; black, lentil, and mung beans; almond and sunflower

*Categorized mainly by the part of the plant used.

tomatoes, bell peppers, eggplant, and nicotine (yes, cigarettes are in the nightshade family, and maybe that's why they got the deadly handle; the rest are not really deadly).

Truly, any foods that we overconsume can lead to reaction and inflammation. That's why doing elimination diets can help us decipher what causes problems and what foods are good for us. So if you have a negative reaction after eating some or a lot of nightshade foods, it may be the quantity, and not the vegetable itself, that is the problem.

Cruciferous vegetables have a much better reputation than nightshades. These include broccoli, cauliflower, cabbage, and Brussels sprouts. They are thought to have anticancer effects, antioxidant nutrients, good fiber, and lots of nutrients. There's nothing wrong with all of that. So, ideally eat some of these "cruciferi" every day. Raw cabbage in salads, lightly steamed broccoli and cauliflower, and even those dreaded sprouts from Brussels. Vegetable stir-fries are great, and even roasting any of these in the oven can work. Let's have more fun with all of these colorful veggies!

Leafy Greens

There a great variety of leafy greens grown all over the world. They easily grow during the spring, summer, and autumn in your locale and can be grown in the garden, in pots or boxes on your deck, or in greenhouses. They are definitely the most important veggies to consume because they provide such great nutrition, fiber, and purifying (chlorophyll-rich) foods. They are known for their folic acid (a B-vitamin), their carotenoid antioxidant pigments, some vitamin C, and many minerals, especially the vital magnesium, which is the core molecule of chlorophyll, which is the "blood" of the plant and related to human hemoglobin (wherein iron is the core molecule).

So, eat those greens! There are many different lettuces that can be consumed raw in salads; we recommend green salads daily. Also, lightly steamed greens—like spinach, chard, kale, and collards—are great on their own; with some extra-virgin olive oil, garlic, and other herbs; or added to stir-fried or steamed veggies just before the cooking time is up, since these leafy greens need very little cooking to soften and bring out the flavors. Cabbage is a cruciferous veggie, however it goes so well with these greens that we include it here, and it's great steamed in mixed-veggie juices or chopped raw into a salad.

Vegetable Flowers

This category includes the plants whose parts we eat will actually become a flower. Examples of these are artichokes, broccoli, Brussels sprouts, and cauliflower; the latter three are in the cruciferous family mentioned above. Well, maybe cabbage is a flower in the making, too. All of these are very nourishing veggies with fiber and vitamins A and C, folic acid, and minerals absorbed from the soil. Also, many people enjoy eating flowers. They can add quite a tasty and unusual flavor to a salad. Common flowers eaten include nasturtium and borage, wild mustard and radish, chives from onion plants, chrysanthemum and marigolds, and many more.

Flowering Vegetables

This class is one that causes some confusion, since many of these vegetables are really the "fruits" of the plant. As with many fruit trees, nuts, and vegetables, the plants in this category produce a flower first, and then that flower base grows into the "fruit." For example, there are flowering trees that produce apples and cherries, peaches and pears... yet flowering plants also produce "vegetables" like tomatoes and peppers, zucchini, and eggplant. Most of these flowering vegetables are from small bushes (peppers and eggplant) or vines (tomatoes, cucumbers, and sweet peas), and not from trees (like the apple). Many of these plants have mid- to late summer (peppers and tomatoes) and autumn harvests (eggplant and squashes).

Each one in this category varies in its water content and nutritional value. Cucumbers and tomatoes are mostly water, peppers more in between, and pumpkins and other squashes along with eggplant are a bit denser or "meatier." The seeds of many of these plants often have additional nutrients, such as vitamin E and essential oils. Cucumbers and tomatoes can be eaten raw, whereas the squash vegetables are great lightly baked or roasted.

Stem and Stalk Vegetables

This group includes asparagus, celery, leeks, green onion stalks (chives), and rhubarb. These are often more focused seasonally, with asparagus coming in the spring, and then eaten raw with dips or lightly steamed. Rhubarb must be cooked and is quite bitter. Leeks can be used in soups or cooked veggie dishes, while chives and green onions can be chopped and added raw to salads, added fresh to soups, or cooked in dishes. Celery is a watery vegetable that is great to chomp as a snack, especially for those looking to stay trim. Kids will enjoy them in their lunches, especially with peanut or almond butter spread into the celery stalk. Overall, this group has many vitamins and minerals as well as fiber.

Roots and Tubers

Roots and tubers are likely the most commonly consumed veggie world-wide, with potatoes leading the way. Roots and tubers grow underground: Carrots and beets are common roots, while potatoes are a common tuber, which is a projection off the root, maintaining its ability to keep producing when the edible part is extracted from the soil. These plants tend to be the starchiest of the vegetable kingdom, with a high sugar content yet with good fiber. Beets are one of the "sugar" plants, with beet-sugar sweetener coming from them.

Garlic and onions are the less starchy in this group and more medicinal and spicier, with lots of nutrients and not many calories. Radishes are also low in calories and a good cleansing food; they could be eaten much more often in our American diet. Potatoes have good amounts of many nutrients, with minerals like potassium and magnesium, while yams and sweet potatoes have more beta-carotene and a sweeter flavor.

Ocean Vegetables: Seaweed

Sea vegetables are an untapped source of nutrition for most people. Ocean water is like our blood, with loads of minerals, including salt and important iodine for healthy thyroid function. Seaweed is more typically used in Oriental cooking, yet Westerners are embracing this food group more in their diets. Soaking seaweed and rinsing it and then adding it to veggie dishes is one way to incorporate arame and hijiki; toasting nori and eating it crispy and crunchy is great, or using big sheets of it to wrap rice and other veggies, like scallions and avocado, offers a nutritious and tasty meal.

Fungi: Mushrooms

The fungi food group is a gourmet class of the vegetable beyond the white common button mushrooms people use in salads or sautéed with vegetables. We use them often, as they have some protein yet very few calories; they are considered to be the "meat" of the vegetable world with their good protein content. Mushrooms, like tofu, pick up the flavors of the ingredients in the dishes to which they're added. More-exotic mushrooms include chanterelles, boletus, and morels. The shiitake has become more popular as a very tasty and nutritious mushroom. French chefs use many varieties, as do Oriental cooks.

Legumes: Beans and Peas

Beans and peas are in the vegetable arena yet are more often classified with the seeds of the plant. Contained in the pods of the plant, they are typically the potential future plant. They are starchy and have some protein, and some have good fatty acids, as does the peanut, which is a legume and therefore misnamed. (Well, maybe it is a cross between a pea and a nut, get it?)

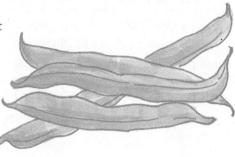

In general, legumes are an important part of a vegetarian diet and a useful food group for those of us wanting to reduce our meat consumption. Soaking beans and cooking them is the common way they are prepared. They often cause gas in people's digestive tracts, but this can be reduced during the soaking process. It is also minimized when beans are sprouted, and this is the most nutritious way to consume them.

Sprouts: Seeds, Legumes, and Nuts

Soak any peas, beans, raw seeds, or nuts and they will begin to grow tails, which is the beginning of a new plant. During the following one to three days, they utilize the starch to grow and have improved protein and nutritional content.

When you sprout seeds—as well as beans, nuts, and grains—you are beginning the growth of a new plant. These power-packed foods contain the future of their generation and can generate future health for us. As sprouts are a living food, they are an incredible source of enzymes that are needed for digestion and assimilation of the proteins, carbohydrates, and fats contained in them. The digestion and assimilation of vitamins, minerals, and trace elements are also partly dependent on enzyme activity. The greatest enzyme activity in sprouts is between germination and seven days. See the sidebar Sprouts: An Instant Garden in Your Home!, page 23.

Sprouts: An Instant Garden in Your Home!

Sprouting is simple. All you need is a glass jar and a mesh lid or piece of cheesecloth and a rubber band. Place your seeds or beans in the jar, generally a quart size, cover with pure nonchlorinated water to double or triple the height of the seeds, and soak for eight to ten hours or overnight. Place a fine-mesh lid on the jar, or use a piece of cheesecloth (something that will allow the water to drain, but not the seeds or beans) secured with a rubber band, and drain out the water. Keep the jar out of direct sunlight and rinse at least twice a day. The sprouts will increase several times over in volume. If you have children, this can be their fun "gardening" task.

We like to eat most sprouts within the first two to three days, although sprouted greens like sunflower sprouts or the new "micro" greens may take a couple days longer. Some of these green sprouts are grown in trays of soil that are 1-2 inches deep. Legumes and nuts do better in a jar. Dr. Haas's favorite colorful sprout mix is a combination of red lentils, mung beans (green), garbanzo beans (beige), and red azuki or black beans. These are all edible once they sprout little tails around day two.

Add the green sprouts to sandwiches and wraps, and the legume sprouts to salads and stir-fries. Add sprouts to your favorite sandwich spread or chopped in deviled eggs. Lentil sprouts are a wonderful addition to rice dishes, while onion or radish sprouts are great in coleslaw or potato salad. Try puréeing your favorite sprouts and topping your vegetables with the purée (try our Sprouted Garbanzo Hummus, page 85). Alfalfa sprouts are a nice addition to an omelet (or with scrambled eggs—see our Eggs and Sprouts Burrito, page 159), and many sprouts are perfect in baked beans. Experiment!

We suggest beginning with 2 to 3 tablespoons of seeds to see how you and your family like the various flavors and increase as desired in your future experiments. Keep them in the refrigerator after they have sprouted. Here is a chart with sprouting times for various seeds and beans:

Alfalfa	3–4 days
Amaranth (do not soak)	2–4 days
Buckwheat	1–3 days
Clover	3–4 days
Garbanzo	3–4 days
Lentil	2–4 days
Mung	2–4 days
Radish	3–5 days
Rye	2–3 days
Soybean	3–6 days
Sunflower	3–5 days
Wheat berry	2–3 days

Vegetables in This Book

The following alphabetical list includes the vegetables we utilize in this book with a brief discussion of what they are and some ideas about their uses and nutrient content. Take the time to really learn about your vegetable friends and how to use them to nourish the human body and soul.

Artichokes

One of the "vegetable flowers," artichokes are in the thistle family and offer dietary fiber, vitamins A and C, calcium, magnesium, phosphorus, and even some iron. Simply trim the stickers on the end of the leaves with scissors and steam for 30–40 minutes, depending on the size of the artichoke. Enjoy the meaty ends of the leaves, and, when you get down to the center, scrape off the fibrous "hairs" and enjoy! You can use all kinds of dips for the artichoke, the classics being butter and lemon and salt, or extra-virgin olive oil and soy sauce. Really any dip or dressing will work.

Arugula

The peppery leaves of arugula add a wonderful zest to your salads alone or combined with other leafy greens. Arugula is a good source of vitamin C, folate, and calcium. It's best to choose young tender leaves. You may also add arugula to many cooked dishes, and it is particularly good with beans and onions.

Asparagus

The bastion of spring! Asparagus is a good source of vitamins C and A, sulfur, folic acid, and potassium. The tender stems may be eaten raw or lightly steamed, grilled, or sautéed. You may choose to place the very lightly steamed and cooled asparagus atop a beautiful salad of tender spring greens or simply arrange this delicious vegetable attractively on your plate. Kids like finger goods, so let them pick up the tender stalks. And, like artichokes, many dips are a delicious companion.

Avocados

Although the avocado is actually a fruit, or really more like a nut nutritionally, with its higher fat and good essential fatty acids, we still place it in the vegetable category. Avocados are high in calories, but also high in potassium, magnesium, iron, and manganese. Many think of guacamole when they think of avocados, but, of course, they are wonderful sliced into salads, spread on wraps and sandwiches, or stuffed with seafood (see our versatile Avocado Dressing, page 109).

Beets

Beets can be shredded raw and mixed into salads as the "bloody" vegetable, or they can be roasted, making them sweet and juicy. Simply place the washed beets on a cookie sheet lined with parchment paper (which helps you clean up the sticky mess later) and roast until the skin collapses under your touch when you lightly squeeze them. Be sure to let them cool before you peel them, as they will be very hot because of the natural sugar content. Our favorite way to enjoy beets, however, is raw. Simply peel the beets and grate them on top of your already-dressed salad, unless you don't mind a pink salad! There are also golden beets and striped beets, so let your kids pick out a rainbow of beets. You may also steam or boil beets, or make them into a soup called borscht (see our Borscht with Sautéed Carrots recipe, page 130). Beets contain calcium, iron, magnesium, and vitamin C. The greens from the beets are high in vitamin A, iron, and calcium.

Broccoli

These "little trees" can be really fun for a child to hold and eat. Broccoli can be eaten raw, steamed, or even sautéed, but please do not overcook! You can add raw broccoli to salads and soups, and you can even lightly steam and purée them like you would for pesto for added nutrients to pasta. A little lemon and gomasio is nice on broccoli. Many kids will eat lightly steamed broccoli warm with a bit of melted butter and salt. Broccoli is a cruciferous vegetable that is thought to have cancer-fighting properties; it's high in vitamins A and C and folic acid. Be sure that the head of broccoli is deep green and that the flower buds that make up the head are tight together and not at all yellow.

Brussels Sprouts

Although many adults and children say "Yech" to these baby cabbage lookalikes, these little cancer-fighting gems are high in vitamins A and C, folic acid, and fiber. As with broccoli and most vegetables, overcooking truly makes them almost inedible. Trim the stems, then wash and steam them until they are soft and juicy. At this point, you can eat them just like they are or perhaps with a little sea salt and pepper; or let them cool and top with your favorite dipping sauce, or sauté them in a bit of extra-virgin olive oil with red onions and garlic. So good! You can also try to slice them thinly after they are steamed and add them to pasta sauce or even try them sprinkled on pizza. Or you can slice them in half, add to other roasting vegetables like onion, mushroom, zucchini, and bell peppers, mix with extra-virgin olive oil and seasonings, then bake 30–40 minutes at 325°F.

Cabbage

Cabbage is rich in chlorophyll, folic acid, and vitamin C. Cabbage can be eaten as coleslaw or consumed raw and mixed into a lettuce salad. It really tastes good this way and makes the salad seem fresh and crunchy. Fermented cabbages such as raw sauerkraut or spicy Korean kimchi, like other fermented foods, are high in nutrition because of the action of "good" bacteria during the fermentation process. You can simply steam cabbage wedges and drizzle them with a little butter or extra-virgin olive oil, or add the cabbage to a classic New England boiled dinner of corned beef (no nitrites please!) with lots of other vegetables. Do try our cabbage salad recipes: Spicy-Sweet Lime Slaw (page 100) and Chinese Chicken Salad (page 112).

Carrots

Children will often eat raw carrots before they will eat any other raw vegetables. You may also include them in roasted vegetables or steam them. Don't forget about carrot juice! One 8-ounce glass of carrot juice contains almost five times the RDA for vitamin A (as the beta-carotene form). Carrots are exceptionally high in the carotene pigments and also contain folic acid, vitamin C, and some selenium (if it's in the soil). Shredding carrots into salads and sauces adds a colorful veggie and provides a sweeter flavor that kids will embrace.

Cauliflower

Avoid purchasing cauliflower with brown areas on the head, as the head is not fresh anymore. Cauliflower is wonderful raw in salads or used on a fresh vegetable platter with your favorite dip. Let your kids arrange cauliflower florets (the flower bud of the plant, not including the stalk) with slices of red pepper, broccoli florets (raw or lightly steamed and cooled), asparagus tips, or whatever vegetables you have on a platter with your favorite dip in the center of the plate.

It's fun using many different colored vegetables and it helps kids understand the artistry of food. Cauliflower contains vitamins C and B6 and folic acid, as well as dietary fiber. Of course, it can be used in soups or in any mixed vegetable dishes.

Celery

Celery is high in vitamins A and C, potassium, and fiber but also relatively high in sodium, which is uncommon in vegetables. Most folks eat raw celery plain or stuffed with peanut or almond butter, hummus, or whatever else you or your family can think of. Celery is added to many soups, stuffing at Thanksgiving, stews and marinara sauce, and many other dishes. Remember that there is nothing wrong with eating celery leaves! Eating a few stalks of celery is a good idea during any program for weight reduction and/or maintenance.

Chard and Collard Greens

Swiss chard is a low-calorie, high-fiber leafy green vegetable that is almost one-third protein and is high in vitamin C. Collard greens are a rich source of vitamins A and C and folic acid. Both chard and collards can be sautéed and served with a little butter, sea salt, and pepper. Kids love to roll up food in a leaf, so lightly steam the leaves and let your children roll up their greens with grated veggies, guacamole, rice, beans, and just about anything they can think of! Roll up like a burrito and there you have it. Chard can also be used raw and sliced thinly as in The Best Kale Salad Ever recipe, page 99.

Chicories, such as Endive

The endive is part of the chicory family that includes radicchio, frisée, Belgian endive, and escarole. Nutrients of this family include folic acid, vitamin E, magnesium, and phosphorous. You can use the endive leaves as a "dipper" for your favorite dip, such as guacamole, or to scoop up some shrimp salad. Endive has a natural peppery taste and is quite refreshing in salads. The often more-bitter radicchio can be braised and added sliced in little ribbons to soups or to a vegetable sauté that might include white beans, onions, and other veggies.

Corn

Almost everyone loves corn. Technically corn is a grain that can be ground into flour, though most of us purchase our dried corn in the form of cornmeal and polenta. Polenta mixed with beans is a complete protein. Fresh corn can be boiled, steamed, grilled, or roasted, and fresh corn we refer to as a vegetable. It can also be eaten raw right off the corn stalk. Yum! Corn is high in fiber and has some vitamin C and folic acid; it's particularly high in vitamin B1, thiamine. Be sure to send the kids outside to husk the corn off the cob. It's simply a right of passage!

Cucumbers

Cucumbers offer some vitamin E (it's in the seeds) and have some vitamins A and C, as well as potassium. Cucumbers are generally eaten raw but can be cooked or fermented into pickles. They are also used medically for burns or for irritated tissues—we've all seen cucumbers over the eyes of spa attendees to cool their eyes. Your kids might get a charge out of that. A slice of cucumber in a glass of water is a very refreshing summer drink. Though cucumbers don't have to be peeled, the thicker-skinned varieties usually are, since the skin can be bitter. Also, watch out for waxed or nonorganic cucumbers; for those we suggest peeling. If you have your child peel the cucumbers, please remember to have them peel away from their body; as Patty has discovered in her years of teaching children that peelers are the source of many more cuts than knives. It is also very important for the parent to not be nervous (just careful), because your child may pick up on the nervous energy and might not try.

Dandelion Greens

Yes, they are considered by many to be weeds in your lawn, yet dandelion greens are very nutritious. The greens are low in calories, high in dietary fiber, calcium, vitamins C and A, and iron. Be sure your lawn (or your neighbor's lawn) is chemical free. Serve them raw in your salad or sauté with some onions and garlic. And, of course, you can buy these spring greens in your local store.

Eggplants

There are many varieties of tasty eggplants, which are part of the nightshade family along with tomatoes and potatoes. As eggplants act like a sponge when sautéing in oil, the slices are best baked or grilled so as to avoid consuming too much absorbed fat. They are wonderfully tasty when cooked into a Thai dish with coconut milk, curry paste, and other vegetables. Eggplants contain some niacin and potassium as well as small amounts of calcium and vitamins A and C. You can make dips from baked eggplant (see our Baba Ghanoush recipe, page 89) and add little bits to your pizza sauce and marinara sauce. When purchasing eggplant, make sure the skin is tight and shiny.

Fennel

Fennel is a feathery and fragrant plant that contains vitamin C, calcium, and potassium. When we speak of fennel in this book, we are referring to the bulbous fennel oftentimes referred to as sweet fennel. The leaves and seeds of the fennel plant are used in teas and herbal therapies. Fennel can be thinly sliced and added raw to a salad (you might toss the fennel with a bit of fresh lemon juice to prevent it from browning) or sautéed in a bit of olive oil and added to pizza. Fennel goes well with various fish, particularly salmon. Its slight licorice taste is something people generally really like or simply don't. The feathery leaves of the plant make lovely garnishes, so don't toss them into the trash. Cut the bulb about an inch from where the leaves begin and then slice.

Garlic

There are entire cookbooks devoted to cooking with garlic. We sometimes wonder how not to cook with garlic! Garlic contains antiviral and antifungal properties and has been known as "the poor man's antibiotic." Thus, it bridges the herbal and culinary worlds. You can use garlic raw minced in salad dressings, sauté the little cloves and add to a myriad of foods, or warp the entire head of garlic in parchment paper and roast for about 45 minutes for a milder flavor wonderful as a spread. Also, make your own garlic olive oil to use in cooking or salad dressings. Just chop up some cloves and place in a bottle of olive oil. Placed in nice bottles with olive oil and other herbs, such as tarragon or rosemary, they make nice holiday gifts.

Green Beans

There aren't many people who don't like green beans. Kids can snap them (a sure sign of freshness) and help prepare them, then hold them like finger foods. Steaming green beans (or yellow beans or any of the other colors available these days) is the simplest and one of the best ways to cook green beans. They should not be allowed to get soft and mushy. Along with sweet peas, they are very easy to grow in the family garden. Green beans can be added to many other vegetables for a nice medley; onions, tomatoes, mushrooms, and carrots are a few good choices. You can also steam then cool them and add fresh tomatoes, red onion slices, fresh parsley, and a bit of your favorite salad dressing for a delicious and satisfying summer salad. At Thanksgiving, you may use one of our sauce recipes, such as Basic Béchamel (page 66) or Cashew Béchamel (page 67) with a bit of cheddar cheese sprinkled in the sauce to doll them up if you like. Please avoid canned soup and dehydrated onions!

Kale

Green, leafy kale is one of the most nutritious vegetables you can eat, and it's so delicious! Do try The Best Kale Salad Ever recipe (page 99). If children are allowed to eat chiffonade kale leaves, they *will* eat it! Another wonderful way to eat kale is to steam it, drain it, and then sauté it lightly in extra-virgin olive oil with garlic and shiitake mushrooms. You can also add white beans and tomatoes if you like. You can add chopped kale to almost anything you can think of: sauces, soups, egg scrambles, curries, stews, and so much more. Do try to eat kale frequently. Kale is chock-full of folic acid, B-vitamins, vitamin A, calcium, iron, and antioxidants.

Kohlrabi

This odd-looking vegetable is not one of the most popular vegetables, yet it could be, as it's very versatile. It has a slightly spicy and unusual taste, especially in the raw form. It is rich in vitamin C and potassium. Kohlrabi can be grated raw to make a slaw or thinly sliced and added to salads. We mix it with equal parts grated apples and toss with a favorite dressing or simply a bit of lemon juice, walnut oil, sea salt, pepper, and fresh mint—yum! You can also steam kohlrabi and toss it with olive oil, butter, or ghee and season it with salt and pepper. Or it can be cooked like potatoes and added to soups and stews. Next time you make potato soup, use half potatoes and half kohlrabi and add a bit of curry powder, topping the soup with fresh chives. You may also bring a large pot of water to a boil and add kohlrabi, simmering until done, about 15 minutes. Plunge into cold water and set aside to drain. Cut off the tops and hollow out the bulb using a spoon or melon baller. Stuff with your favorite stuffing (don't forget to add the scooped-out kohlrabi!) and reheat in the oven. Delicious!

Kohlrabi can range in color from light green to reddish-purple. When purchasing kohlrabi, be sure the bulbs are not too big—about the size of a tennis ball is perfect (otherwise they can be dry and pithy). Store them in the refrigerator, unwashed, for about one week.

Leeks

Leeks are in the onion family and look like big green onions. They are fiber rich and contain potassium, folic acid, iron, and calcium. Leeks need to be carefully washed, as dirt can hide inside. One of the easiest and most efficient ways to wash leeks is to rinse the outside of the leek, slice off most of the fibrous green stalks, and slice the tender white part. Place the white edible part in a bowl of cold water and the leeks will float, but the dirt will sink to the bottom of the bowl. Use a strainer to lift out the leeks but not the dirt. Repeat if necessary. Kids like to do this step. The herb thyme is particularly good with leeks and white beans or potatoes. You may use leeks as you would any type of onions, only they offer a milder flavor.

Lettuce

There are so many varieties of lettuce: red, romaine, green, iceberg, and butter, to name a few. Iceberg lettuce is less nutritious than its greener, leafier counterparts. Lettuce contains chlorophyll (the darker the leaves, the higher the chlorophyll), vitamin A, and folic acid. Salads are a wonderful way to add more vegetables, please (MVP) to your every-day diet. Almost any vegetable on this list can be added to a green salad. Be sure to alter the vegetables and greens in your salads, and, of course, go light on the dressing.

Lima Beans

Young and tender lima beans are such a taste treat. If they are overripe they will be fibrous and mealy. Fresh lima beans only take a few minutes to boil. Dried lima beans need to be soaked first in cold water for about 8 hours and then simmered until done, but not too soft, about 1½ hours. You can also buy them frozen, which is probably the most common way people consume them. Add carrots, corn, and onion to make succotash or add them to sauces, soups, and stews. They are full of folic acid and iron.

Mushrooms

There are literally thousands of mushrooms varieties, and many are edible, however, we suggest you purchase your mushrooms at the grocery store, as some mushrooms are quite poisonous. There are the common button mushrooms, cremini, and portobellos. Shiitake, chanterelles, and oysters are more nutritious mushrooms containing protein, iron, niacin, and selenium. Mushrooms can be sautéed and added to a wide variety of sauces, soups, and stews as well as to polenta, rice, and bean dishes. And many mush-rooms are used medicinally for immune support, such as shiitake and maitake. Remember that mushrooms are not bioavailable unless they are cooked (except for the common button mushroom, which should be thoroughly washed before consuming raw, such as in salads) and that many mushrooms are grown on manure and therefore must be sprayed with chemicals to alleviate flies. Shiitake mushrooms, as one exception, are grown on wood, not manure, so fly prevention is not necessary.

Okra

Okra is a good source of vitamin C, vitamin B6, and fiber. It is an essential ingredient of gumbo, the famous Southern dish (and is featured in our Southern-inspired dish, Vegetarian Jambalaya with Smoked Tempeh on page 142). Boiled, it becomes a bit slimy, which many people do not like, but sautéed in a bit of extra-virgin olive oil or butter, it is quite tasty. (An acid such as vinegar or lemon helps reduce the "sliminess.") In the South okra is often served coated in cornmeal and fried. You can coat it with cornmeal and bake in the oven for a more nutritious preparation technique.

Onions

Onions are not high in any one nutrient, but they do have a mix of various nutrients, such as calcium, iron, folic acid, and vitamins A, E, and C. Like most vegetables, they will contain the minerals that are present in the soil. The onion family contains leeks, chives, scallions (often known as green onions); the three most common varieties are yellow, red, and white onions. You may use thinly sliced onions raw in salads (red onions are the common choice for salads) or sauté them in a little butter or extra-virgin olive oil and add them to veggies, sauces, on top of pizzas, and in sandwiches or wraps.

Parsnips

Parsnips are starchy vegetables that contain B-vitamins as well as a small amount of vitamins A and C and potassium. They should be washed and scrubbed but don't really need to be peeled. They can be added to roasted vegetables, soups, and stews. Also, try using a mixture of half parsnips and half potatoes the next time you make mashed potatoes for a yummy side dish.

Peas

Peas are actually legumes and are a good source of protein (amino acids) with no cholesterol. They are also rich in fiber and are a good source of vitamin C and thiamine. The pea family includes the standard green pea, snap, snow, and sugar peas. Fresh peas are a wonderful treat, though frozen peas are an acceptable alternative. Peas can be briefly boiled or steamed; snow peas can be added to stir-fries and other spring vegetable combinations. You can even make a version of guacamole using peas instead of avocadoes and spread it on sandwiches.

Peppers

There are so many types of peppers and chiles, such as green bell, red bell, jalapeño, Anaheim, and cayenne (a dried pepper), just to name a few. Peppers are high in vitamin C, carotenes (vitamin A), folic acid, and potassium. Peppers can be stuffed with other vegetables and rice, added to marinara sauce, or roasted and added to pizza toppings or your favorite enchilada recipe. Peppers are wonderful sautéed with onions, fresh tomatoes, and minced fresh garlic. The possibilities for using peppers in meals are endless!

Potatoes

Potatoes as French fries are the vegetable of choice for most Americans. In that form however, they are not a very healthy candidate; yet, baked, boiled, roasted, or sautéed, or when added to soups and vegetable dishes, they can be a good option since potatoes are naturally low in fat and contain vitamins C and B, potassium, magnesium, manganese, iron, and zinc. Almost all kids (and adults as well) love potatoes, which can be stuffed with steamed seasonal veggies and topped with grated carrots, beans, onions, and more. Walk through your grocery isles and let your children help decide what colorful veggies to top their potatoes with. This is a healthful advantage since potatoes by themselves are more caloric and starchy and are best used in moderation.

Radishes

These little roots are spicy and are wonderful sliced thinly and added to salads. They can also be braised in a little vegetable stock or added to roasted vegetables, soups, and stews. When cooked they take on the flavor of their cousin, the turnip. Radishes contain some vitamin C and folic acid.

Rhubarb

The leaves are poisonous on the rhubarb plant, so be sure to only eat the stalks, which need to be cooked, even though the vitamin C content is lost this way. Rhubarb is high in fiber and also contains some calcium and other minerals. Rhubarb is almost always paired with fruit because it's so tangy (see our Rhubarb Compote recipe, page 217). Most think of strawberry rhubarb pie, however the tanginess of rhubarb can be a nice pairing to poultry and salmon dishes.

Seaweed

Sea vegetables are some of the most nutritious foods available and are very high in iodine, calcium, potassium, and iron, and some varieties are high in protein. Seaweed is a mineral food, we dare say even a miracle food, that's how loaded it is in important nutrients.

We could write a book on the many varieties of seaweed and how to use them, but we'll just mention a few here. Nori is the seaweed used to wrap sushi but can also be sliced thinly in its dried form and added at the last minute (or it will become soggy) to the top of a green salad for a salty finish and added nutrients. Arame can be made into a salad (see page 103) or left dried and added to raw almonds for added flavor and nutrients. Agar-agar is often used to replace cornstarch as a thickener. Hijiki is very good added to rice dishes. Kombu is used in the soaking water for dried beans to make them more digestible so as to avoid the uncomfortable gas that some people experience when they eat beans. You can also add a piece of kombu to your stock recipes (take it out later) for a little salt flavor and added nutrients.

Shallots

Shallots are in the onion family and share the same nutrients but offer a milder flavor. Mince some shallots and add them to your next salad dressing or to your steamed green beans or peas. Thyme is a wonderful herb with sautéed or roasted shallots. Shallots are a wonderful addition to your béchamel sauce or a mild soup recipe.

Spinach

Popeye was right, spinach does make you strong, but please don't eat the canned variety! Spinach is one of the higher iron-containing vegetables; it also has vitamin A, folic acid, and some protein. Add fresh spinach leaves to your next egg dish for breakfast, to your green salad, to soups, to your favorite hummus recipe, and even a little handful to your smoothie (no one will know!). Spinach is great in sandwiches and wraps.

Summer Squash and Zucchini

There are so many uses for summer squash
and zucchini. Be sure to try our Wheat-Free
Zucchini Pizza recipe (see page 169); grate them into
cake, brownie, and muffin recipes; steam them lightly;
or stuff the larger ones with rice and other veggies or ground
turkey and beans. Add sautéed squash to your next omelet.
Throw them in soups and stews. These vegetables are high in
fiber, vitamins A and C, and potassium. Have your children grate
(carefully) zucchini and add it to their next wrap or sandwich.

Sweet Potatoes and Yams

Most people think of the holidays when we speak of yams or sweet potatoes; they're
often candied, which is puzzling, since they are naturally sweet. Yams and sweet potatoes
can simply be baked as you would a potato or they can be mashed, also like mashed potatoes. You can even rub them with a bit of extra-virgin olive oil
and grill them for a tasty treat. Slice the yams or sweet
potatoes like a French fry and have your children
place them on an oil-rubbed baking sheet and
enjoy yam fries. Yum! Yams and sweet potatoes
are high in beta-carotene, B-vitamins, vitamin
C, and potassium.

Tomatillos

Most often tomatillos are used as an addition to Mexican
dishes and salsas, such as green enchilada sauce, but they can
also be sliced thinly and added to salads or roasted. Tomatillos
come naturally wrapped in a papery husk, which needs to be
removed. They should then be washed, as they feel sticky.
Tomatillos contain vitamin C, potassium, and phosphorous.

Tomatoes

Yes, we know, it's a fruit of the vine. But most think of tomatoes as a vegetable, as does
the U.S. government. Many flowering vegetables, like zucchini and eggplant, are actually
fruits as well. There is nothing quite as good as a sun-ripened tomato out of the garden—
the epitome of summer! Tomatoes are made into sauces for
pasta and pizza, used in ketchup as a condiment, made into
juice, and more. You can stuff them whole and bake them,
add them to vegetable dishes, slice them for a sandwich, or
eat them in gazpacho (see page 131). Tomatoes are high in
vitamins C and A and potassium.

Turnips

Turnips are at their peak of freshness in early spring, so be sure to try them then if you have never had a turnip before. A root vegetable, turnips contain vitamin C, calcium, and potassium. Most often turnips are added to roasted vegetables, stews, and hearty soups.

Watercress

Watercress is a member of the tangy mustard family and grows at its peak in early spring. It is rich in vitamin C, potassium, iron, and magnesium. Most often watercress is added sparingly to green salads, but of course many think of the classic cucumber and watercress sandwich. You may also add some to your next potato soup for a little zip!

Winter Squashes (hard)

Winter squashes are very high in vitamins A and C and potassium. They can be halved and stuffed, added to hearty winter soups and stews, or steamed and eaten with a little butter or extra-virgin olive oil and fresh herbs. You can slice butternut squash thinly and add the slices to sandwiches, or try our recipe for Butternut Squash Upside-Down Cake (page 212). Almost everyone likes the naturally sweet winter squashes, such as acorn, Hubbard, or butternut. Have your children help make the stuffing for your winter squash (let them experiment) and allow them to stuff the squash. Kids will almost always try a dish that they have ownership in!

SEASONINGS FOR VEGETABLES

The following list offers seasoning suggestions for various vegetables. Fresh seasonings, whether it's various herbs or garlic or onions, are preferable to dried. That being said, we can assume that fennel seeds, as an example, are dried as are many other herbs purchased in stores. The basic ratio is that 1 tablespoon of fresh herbs is equal to 1 teaspoon of dried. Dried herbs have more intense flavor as a rule, unless they are from 1978. Store your dried herbs away from light and heat, but do use fresh when possible.

Note that for each recipe we have written whether the herbs used should be fresh or dried. In addition, it's assumed that all fresh herbs are washed and dried before using.

The seasonings recommended for each vegetable have been selected because their flavors pair well. Experiment with different herb groupings to find the tastes that appeal to you and your family.

Although salt and pepper aren't listed below, it's safe to say that either may be sprinkled on to taste. Use sea salt, and use it sparingly to avoid consuming too much sodium. Many people season with black and white pepper from the peppercorn, some as commonly as they use salt. We would like to suggest that you consider using cayenne (red) pepper in your shaker and use it more regularly as a spicy addition to your foods, unless you just can't tolerate the spiciness. Black pepper can be a bit irritating to the intestinal track while cayenne is an herbal natural stimulant, a warming herb, and a substance that helps cleanse the blood; like the chile pepper, it may have anti-cancer benefits. Keep in mind, however, that switching to cayenne pepper will undoubtedly alter the flavor of your meals, so proceed with baby steps.

ARTICHOKES: summer savory, garlic, lemon, parsley, mint, basil

ASPARAGUS: summer savory, thyme, dill, mint, orange or lemon, rosemary, shallots

BEETS: bay leaves, chervil, cloves, coriander seed, dill seed, fennel seed, thyme, lemon, Dijon mustard, onions, curry

BROCCOLI: oregano, garlic, onion, lemon, mint

BRUSSELS SPROUTS: marjoram, red onion, shallots, garlic

CABBAGE: caraway seed, cumin seed, dill seed, green dill, oregano, curry, lemon, parsley

CARROTS: anise seed, bay leaves, caraway seed, marjoram, mint, parsley, sage, garlic

CAULIFLOWER: dill seed, rosemary, tarragon, ginger, curry, cumin, cinnamon, nutmeg

CELERY: fennel seed, green dill, rosemary, thyme, tarragon

CELERY ROOT: tarragon, parsley, fennel seed

CORN: garlic, chiles, lemon, cilantro, parsley, onions, paprika, oregano, lemon

CUCUMBERS: green dill, garlic, mint, parsley, rosemary, green onions, basil, lemon

EGGPLANTS: basil, chervil, rosemary, sage, thyme, cumin, lemon

FENNEL: lemon, parsley, garlic, onions, figs (yes, figs)

GREEN BEANS: basil, dill seed, green dill, mustard seed, rosemary, summer savory, thyme, parsley

JERUSALEM ARTICHOKES: mint, lemon, parsley, cumin

KALE, CHARD, COLLARDS, AND OTHER LEAFY GREENS: garlic, onion, curry, parsley, lemon, ginger

LIMA BEANS: sage, summer savory, thyme

MUSHROOMS: lemon, oregano, rosemary, tarragon, bay leaves, garlic, parsley, cumin

ONIONS (INCLUDING RED, YELLOW, AND WHITE), SHALLOTS, AND LEEKS: basil, marjoram, oregano, sage, thyme, garlic, chives, parsley, tarragon, Dijon mustard

PARSNIPS: green dill, garlic, onion, thyme

PEAS: basil, chervil, fennel seed, marjoram, mint, rose, green onion

PEPPERS: garlic, onion, cumin, parsley, basil, rosemary, thyme

POTATOES: bay leaves, caraway seed, chervil, coriander, green dill, parsley, poppy seed, nutmeg

PUMPKINS: allspice, fennel seed, nutmeg, sage, thyme, garlic

RADISHES: lemon, chives, mint

SPINACH: chervil, lemon, mace, marjoram, mint, rosemary, tarragon

SQUASHES: allspice, saffron, garlic, onion, curry, cinnamon, basil, parsley, cilantro, ginger, chiles

SWEET POTATOES AND YAMS: allspice, cinnamon, cloves, garlic, onion, cumin

TOMATOES: basil, bay leaves, celery seed, chervil, oregano, parsley, sage, tarragon, thyme, cilantro, garlic

TURNIPS: caraway seed, garlic, parsley, onions, basil, parsley

ZUCCHINI: basil, marjoram, mint, oregano, rosemary, saffron, thyme, garlic, onion

Chapter 3

Bringing More Vegetables into Your Meals: The Basics

For all the reasons that we explained in chapter 1, you and your children need to eat more vegetables, please (MVP). How do you start? Let's first look at the basics of how to bring vegetables into our individual and family meals.

To begin with, you need to determine where the best availability of vegetables is. Since we believe that it is quite important to eat a wide variety of local, seasonal, organic vegetables, we suggest you start by establishing your own garden and checking out your local farmers market. When you eat a lot of different types (and colors!) of foods, you are more likely to obtain a wider variety of nutrients. If you have a spinach salad today, have a mixed-greens salad tomorrow, and so on. Try to incorporate a four-day rotation of most foods and drinks. If you have oatmeal for breakfast today, try an egg or tofu scramble tomorrow (with added veggies of course), perhaps an oat bran muffin on day three, and on day four, try a fruit smoothie, perhaps with some whey powder or other protein powder.

Most of our recipes will offer seasonal variations (see Seasonal Eating, page 43) and nutrition tips as well as menu suggestions. You will be learning about nutrition as you prepare these delicious recipes. Be sure to involve your children in this learning process; one of the most important things you can teach your child is about real foods and their preparation, including shopping for, cleaning, and preparing them. They will thank you for their good health and cooking skills and will be able to feed themselves and others throughout their lives.

Remember that it's poorly balanced meal choices that are the cause of numerous health problems. Fast food and other modern "comfort" dishes are loaded with fats, sugars, salt, and calories. Vegetables are low in all of those categories and are packed with more nutrition than most other foods. Veggies are more nutrient dense and have a higher nutrient-to-calorie ratio. Plus, the higher water and fiber content makes them ideal for intestinal function. So start trading those prepared fast food burgers for some veggie-packed turkey meatloaf.

Now, let's begin to look at the focus of this book. How do you bring MVP into your diet? We will show you, step by step. We will discuss simple but effective transitions to your daily routine; review tasty meat "alternatives"; encourage you to eat with the seasons; offer tips on getting kids to help with meals; suggest menus; and we'll even show you how easy it is to add MVP to common modern meals—like macaroni and cheese—without sacrificing taste. You can do it!

Simple Transitions

When you first begin any new routine, many people find that small transitions are more doable than cold-turkey changes. If you are shifting from a meat-based diet to the MVP way of eating, then your dietary fiber intake will, healthfully, greatly increase. For some, a rapid increase in dietary fiber intake can cause gas and bloating. It is recommended that you limit your increase of dietary fiber intake to a few grams per week or until your body adjusts. As we have previously discussed, we are all biochemically different, so you might not notice any difference at all with greatly increased fiber intake, but if you do, then cut back slightly while your body adjusts. Remember, with increased fiber intake comes the necessity to consume an increased amount of water.

Here are some tips to making MVP an easy transition:

- Half of your plate should be vegetables, and most of them should be non-starchy veggies.

- Try a Meatless Monday.

- Consume smaller portions of meat while increasing veggies.

- Make Wednesdays your beans and legumes day. As one example, purée any white beans and add them to your spaghetti sauce.

- Make raw veggies your snack. Try one of our great dip recipes (like our delicious and versatile Hummus, page 85). Many children like ranch dressing, so take a small amount of organic ranch dressing, add some hummus to it, and perhaps some finely diced red pepper. This lowers the fat content and adds MVP.

- Shredded veggies can be added to egg dishes, salads, and, well, almost anything.

- Try "composing" your meal. Make the center of your plate a beautiful vegetable dish or, better yet, place some steamed broccoli in the center with a lemon wedge next to it, then add grains or a small amount of meat protein around the broccoli, making the veggie the star of your setting.

- Preparation is key in obtaining and maintaining good health. Perhaps on Sunday wash some carrots and celery, cut them, and place them in containers for use throughout the week. Cook up some additional foods to have as part of your meals the next couple days. Vegetables are most nutritious when washed and used right away, but that is not always possible, so forethought and preparation is often necessary to eat a healthy diet. We also realize that with everyone's busy lives, prewashed vegetables, already-grated carrots, or canned beans might be necessary conveniences. And that's okay sometimes. Just remember that fresh food only has good nutritional value if you actually eat it!

More Vegetable Support

Let's say you think you want chicken tonight, but just had it last night. What do you do? You know you need protein but have had meat protein three times already this week. Now what? Here are some ideas for vegetable protein substitutions to meats:

- **Veggie burgers:** Many veggie burgers are bean-based with lots of seasonal vegetables shredded inside. Serve with lettuce, avocado, tomatoes, and sliced onion for veggie heaven! (See our Vegan Patties recipe, page 151.)

- **Meatloaf:** Just like the veggie burger, you can make a veggie "meatloaf" with nuts, grains, beans, and lots of veggies. Or make a "regular" meatloaf with vegetables included and serve with steamed seasonal veggies or a nice big salad. (See our Turkey Meatloaf recipe, page 167.)

- **Tempeh:** These fermented soybeans are simply wonderful, in flavor and nourishment, and typically come in a compressed block. You slice then steam it for about 10 minutes, then either bake, sauté, or stir-fry for a hearty, "meaty" chewiness that many people like.

- **Tofu:** This is another form of soybeans (the curd of the soy, much like cheese is the curd of cow's milk) that is naturally low in fat and high in protein. You can cube it to include in soups or slice it and bake or sauté or stuff it! (See the Sesame-Crusted Tofu Stuffed with Vegetables recipe, page 141.)

Vegetarianism

If you have been toying with the idea of becoming a vegetarian and have thus far been a fairly significant meat-eater, you need to slowly make the shift to see if it works for you. Remember to listen to your body, as it gives you clues as to what it needs; a vegetarian diet may or may not work for you.

It can be difficult to change a dietary pattern, even if it is unhealthy, from our old, programmed habits. We recommend taking a seasonal approach, as each season has its habits and traditional foods, meals, and meats. Keep in mind that obtaining certain nutrients that we get from meats can be more of a challenge in a vegetarian diet. Here are some considerations:

- **Protein:** Ovo-vegetarians and lacto-vegetarians can get protein from eggs and cheese, but for those who choose to avoid eggs and cheese, soy products like tofu; nuts and seeds; and legumes such as lentils, dried beans, or peas are excellent protein choices. Remember, constantly eating quesadillas, pizza, or any bread-and-cheese combination that contains no vegetables make you a junk-food vegetarian!

- **Calcium:** Dark vegetables like broccoli, spinach, and collard greens contain ample calcium (and some iron and zinc). Drink calcium-enriched soymilk or juices and eat tofu to up your intake.

- **Vitamin B-12:** Lacto-ovo-vegetarians and lacto-vegetarians can get B-12 from milk, eggs, or cheese. B-12 is of particular concern for vegans who consume no foods from animals, but luckily it can be found some in sea vegetables, fortified soy products, enriched cereals, or supplements.
- **Iron:** Foods high in vitamin C will help your body absorb iron, therefore eat iron-rich foods such as spinach and other greens, raisins or prunes, whole grains, and some fruits, like oranges and strawberries. Iron is more important for women, especially during child-bearing years and during their monthly cycle as a blood builder.
- **Zinc:** Whole grains, wheat germ, soy products, nuts, and seeds are all high in zinc. Pumpkin seeds are particularly good. Zinc may be a bit more important for men.

Many of the recipes in this book give nutrition information under the heading Health Note, educating you as to which ingredients are high in what nutrients. Be sure to read all the notes so that you can be your own nutritionist. Share your new information with your family over dinner.

Now, let's look at the importance of seasonal eating with a few ideas of how to adapt them seasonally.

Seasonal Eating

 Seasonal eating compels us to be attuned to Nature and what our dear Mother Earth provides us to eat in the locale in which we live. Thus, this varies for people around the world, although the aspect of seasons has a consistent theme. Spring brings in the greens, and plants begin to mature and are harvested over the summer and autumn. In the colder snow-covered northern regions, the foods consumed during the winter months are traditionally those that have good storage qualities, since they would need to hold up during less-fruitful times. However, in many areas, there are some fresh foods that are available year-round.

This practice of seasonal eating has been around for millennia, yet with modern-day grocery stores and food availability, many of us have missed out on its basic aspects. Dr. Haas repopularized this notion right at the beginning of the back-to-nature movement in the mid- to late 1970s and early 1980s with his book *Staying Healthy with the Seasons*. The practice brings out the Oriental concepts of the elements and seasonal medicine. The basic idea is that the foods that are available to us in our locale throughout the year help to balance us and protect us from the external climates. Thus, in the spring, when our body needs to cleanse and lighten, we have the fresh greens with chlorophyll to purify our body. During the warm months of summer, juicy and cooling fruits and vegetables are available, such as peaches and melons, tomatoes and cucumbers. And then as the days shorten and it becomes cooler, we harvest and use the foods that need more heat to cook and prepare them, which include grains and legumes, hard squashes, and nuts and seeds. These oilier foods also help us build our bodies to protect us from the colder winters.

Use this brief summary to guide your shopping and menu selection:

Spring: Focus on tender, leafy vegetables that represent the fresh new growth of this season. These foods include Swiss chard, arugula (makes great pesto), romaine lettuce, spinach, fresh parsley, nettles, and the very symbol of springtime, asparagus (admittedly more stalky than leafy), just to name a few.

Summer: Enjoy light, cooling foods that are higher in water content for the warmest season. These foods include zucchini and other summer squashes, corn, peppers, broccoli, eggplant, and so many more. Of course, many fresh fruits can be enjoyed this season, when our bodies can handle their cooling effects.

Autumn: More warming foods are appropriate, such as carrots and other root vegetables, yams, onions, and garlic. The harvest season in your area may still be in full-force, so you may still have many summer vegetables. Also, many more fresh fruits are harvested here, such as apples and pears, and then persimmons and pomegranates.

Winter: Foods that take longer to grow are generally more warming than foods that grow quickly. Root vegetables, including carrots, potatoes, yams, onions, and garlic, as well as the winter squashes, are good choices.

Kids in the Kitchen

Eating with the family and sharing food and stories with our loved ones around the table is something that we might all embrace. Throughout the world, we should never give up this circle of love and connection. We are grateful that *More Vegetables, Please!* provides support for that process. Engaging our youngsters not only around the table, but in writing shopping lists, helping at the grocery store, putting foods away, helping to prepare and even serve meals, and, maybe most important, helping clean up and even doing some dishes will help lay the groundwork for a healthy lifestyle.

To begin with, if kids are allowed to help make the meal, they are more likely to eat it! For example, kids will eat about anything that they can make into a chiffonade, even raw kale salad! They are so proud when you enjoy their creations. You will begin a life-long habit and love of kitchen creativity and connection to healthy, delicious food when you cook with your children. And an added bonus, it's a terrific way to spend quality time.

This is a wonderful opportunity for your children to learn where their food comes from as well. Have them help plan the week's meals. Take them shopping with you to your local farmers market or farm, if at all possible, besides your neighborhood supermarket. Everyone has more respect for food when they understand the source of their food. When a child can pull a carrot up from the soft dirt, this creates a respect for food and Mother Earth. Even if you live in an urban area, you can look at books and talk about where food comes from. Plus, you can still grow some food in boxes on your deck or in your backyard. Don't forget that everyone has room to grow sprouts! (See Sprouts: An Instant Garden in

Your Home!, page 23.) As parents, we set the example for our children and are responsible for their health. You will all benefit from time together in the kitchen making memories and meals!

Family Meal Tips

- First and foremost, read the Safety in the Kitchen sidebar on page 55, and teach your children these basic safety and sanitation concepts.

- Be sure to read through a recipe first and get out all necessary kitchen equipment. This is also a great way to help your kids learn life skills, such as math, as well as just good basic organization and preparation before beginning any project.

- It's nice to teach your kids to clean as they work. It is also safer, we feel, to have a tidy work surface.

- Don't hover. Patty has seen plenty of panicky parents making their children really nervous in the kitchen. There is a fine line between proper supervision and hovering. You will learn. If your children are old enough to use a knife, show them various cuts and explain that when they are cutting, their eyes are only on what they are doing. If they are too young to handle knives, then have them use a regular dinner knife to slice or "chop" soft foods such as avocados or perhaps bread. (Note: Sharp knives are actually much safer than dull knives, because you do not need to put as much pressure on the knife.)

- Be aware that there is a lot of dangerous equipment in a kitchen. In Patty's experience teaching many children, the list is, beginning with the greatest hazard: potato peeler, grater, knives, stovetop, and taking baked goods out of the oven.

- Also, floors can become slippery, so be aware. Teach the young ones to pay attention and clean up water spills or dropped foods that can make the floor even more slippery, like with avocado or fruit pieces (remember the banana peel!).

In this book, many recipes are accompanied by tips especially with kids in mind. You will read about suggestions like having your kids grease the pan, measure the milk, slice the tomatoes, cut the kale, and so forth. As your family's nutritionist, use this book to teach your children that carrots are good for their eyes, collard greens are good for their bones, and red peppers are full of vitamin C that helps to keep their immune system strong so they won't get sick as easily. In this way, education and kitchen fun will both happen at the same time!

Here are some other useful tips for the family and especially the young ones:

- If you "hide" vegetables all the time, you are setting your kids up with the idea that vegetables are something not to like. Be enthused yourself and, again, set a good example.

- Alternate your foods. Change your vegetable choices daily, weekly, and with the seasons.

- Give your kids choices also about what foods to include in the family meals; find out what they like. You'll ultimately make the decision, however, when you ask them to choose between two foods, for example, "Would you prefer broccoli or green beans today?"

- Try rolling up your child's salad in a wrap. Kids love wraps, and there are many healthy wrap choices, including corn or whole wheat tortillas that have been warmed.

- Finger foods are many children's favorite. Cut raw veggies into hand-size pieces. Have them help you make a dip to go with them.

- Remember that kids can take up to ten tries of eating a new food before they decide that they like it. Don't give up!

- Don't overcook your veggies. Nothing is worse than mushy broccoli or totally limp asparagus.

- Let your child create a rainbow of colors on their plate with red pepper slices, white cauliflower, green beans, or whatever they choose. It's fun and healthy.

- Kids love to dip, so learn to make some healthy dips, selecting from one of our many choices—yet another way to eat MVP!

Transform Your Breakfast, Lunch, and Dinner

Sometimes we all need a little inspiration to get our creative juices going...and then we get the hang of it and off we go! This can be especially true with our diets and changing the routine in the kitchen. In the case of vegetable additions to every meal of the day, we have devised some sample menus to help you get started, followed by the many recipes in chapters 4-10.

Breakfast

Our suggestions for adding MVP to the first meal of the day is a litter longer, since this is when most people have told us that they get "stuck:"

- Sautéed onions, red bell peppers, zucchinis, mushrooms—almost any seasonal veggie you can imagine—are wonderful in your scrambled eggs or omelet. You may use tofu instead of eggs if you prefer, or do a combination of mashed tofu with some eggs.

- Cook kale, garlic, and shiitake mushrooms in a little water, then crack eggs or place tofu cubes on the kale mixture. Cover and cook until done. Sprinkle with a little salt, paprika, or seasonings of your choice.

- Add some peas or a handful of spinach leaves to your next smoothie. You will hardly notice, but a little added veggies at a time add up to extra nutrition!

- Odd as it might sound, soup can be very satisfying in the morning. Lentil soups with some chopped veggies, such as carrots, onions, and greens are delicious and nutritious and a great blood sugar regulator. And they are quite warming during the colder months.

- Puréed winter squashes can be added to your pancake or waffle batter.

- Add shredded zucchinis to your muffin recipes.

Oatmeal, Oh My!

Next time you make oatmeal, add some cooked cubed (or puréed) pumpkin while it's cooking. Don't forget a little cinnamon. It's all sweet! Winter squash along with grated apples work really well in hot cereal. Sunflower seeds also add a bit of protein and oil, and taste great in oatmeal. Of course, raisins, sliced banana, and apples are tasty, too.

Lunch

We all know we should eat a healthy breakfast and plan for dinner, but what about lunch? Lunch is a great time of day to augment your diet with MVP. A nice big salad, leftover sautéed veggies in a wrap, a sandwich—always an easy choice—can be chock-full of veggies. Here are some ideas:

- Sandwiches and wraps can be a terrific way to add almost any veggie you can imagine to your eating routine. For an interesting sandwich spread, try puréed peas by themselves or mix in avocados or hummus. Spinach can also be puréed along with your favorite sandwich spread recipe, with our Hummus and Pesto recipes (pages 85 and 60), and even with plain mayonnaise or egg-free or tofu-based mayo and a little lemon juice for zip.

- A great big green salad with many other colored vegetables is an easy way to add MVP.

- Try a grilled cheese sandwich with sliced tomatoes, lightly sautéed zucchini slices, or grated carrots.

- Add diced red bell pepper, onion, celery, and shredded carrots into your tuna or chicken salad sandwich.

- Don't forget that veggie-added smoothie. That could be lunch today instead of breakfast.

Dinner

Dinner is the easiest meal in most people's mind to add MVP. This book is full of dishes that incorporate vegetables—and lots of them:

- Start your meal with some veggie slices as a healthful appetizer. With a little dip, the whole family will eat them up.

- As a side dish, veggies are simple and easy. Lightly steam them and you're set.

- Add veggies to almost any and every dish.

- Cook your own cannellini (white) beans or purchase them canned. Sauté red bell peppers with onions and tomatoes and add spinach leaves, then toss with beans, extra-virgin olive oil, and garlic. Yum!

- Bake potatoes and top with sautéed vegetables of almost any kind.

- Make chili with the standard onions, peppers, and tomatoes (of course), but also experiment with the addition of broccoli and your favorite greens. It's easy to add five or six veggies!

Common Meals with MVP

The meals that Americans and other Westerners most commonly eat are high in fats, sugars, salt, and calories. They also have a very low nutrient-to-calorie ratio, which is where we get the term "empty calories." We realize it's going to take more than our book to change these eating habits, but we can at the very least show you how to start to reform your habits by changing some of your recipes.

Here are three typical American dishes and our advice for adding more veggies into them:

Marinara Sauce for Spaghetti, Pizza, and More

Spaghetti sauce is one of the easiest ways to add more vegetables to your diet. It's also versatile: You can use the sauce on pasta, in eggplant Parmesan, on spaghetti squash, on pizza, and on any vegetable mix, to name a few. Whether you use jarred sauce or make your own from scratch, adding MVP adds nutrients and flavor. We think you should experiment with veggies to create your own signature sauce, but if you'd rather follow a recipe, try our Marinara Sauce on page 69. Here are some easy ways to incorporate veggies into marinara sauce:

- First, start with fresh tomatoes. Their best season is the summer, when they are ripe and juicy. Some people like to peel and seed the tomatoes; we don't do that, but you may if you like—it's just a bit more work. Simply chop the fresh tomatoes and measure them according to the recipe.

- For an interesting change, try washing the tomatoes, de-stemming them, and placing them on a pan with a bit of extra-virgin olive oil. Roast them for about 30 minutes in a 375°F oven (or longer at temperatures as low as 325–350°F) before continuing with your recipe. The flavor is deeper and richer in contrast to the bright and fresh flavors of the fresh tomatoes; both are equally good, just different. In terms of nutrient value, though, the fresher the better. When fresh tomatoes are no longer available, use a good brand of canned tomatoes (if you don't can tomatoes yourself).

- Purée vegetables like carrots, celery, broccoli, and zucchini and add them to your sauce. No one will know they're there!

- To add color and texture, grate zucchini (bountiful in summertime) or carrots. Cut spinach or kale into little ribbons by rolling the leaf up like a cigar (for lack of a better visual) and then slicing them very thinly. This cut is called a chiffonade and, as Patty always says, kids will eat anything if they can chiffonade it! You can also add diced onions or scallions, peeled eggplant, and red or green bell peppers.

- To sweeten your sauce, try what an elderly Italian woman Patty once knew would do: Place a whole carrot in your sauce while cooking to "add sweetness" and then remove it and eat it later. Patty's Mom would put slices of celery in her sauce, also a good choice.

Change the ingredients in your sauce seasonally. Shop at the farmers market or grocery store for fresh, local ingredients. Mother Nature often has a way of having vegetables that go nicely together available at the same time. During the summer, use garlic, fresh basil, parsley, oregano, and bay leaves; sometimes we just use thyme and a bit of salt and pepper. In winter, use onions and cubed butternut squash or pumpkin. Don't forget the root vegetables, such as parsnips and turnips, and our favorite, leafy greens. Leafy greens like kale, chard, collards, and spinach like to grow in cool weather, so if you have them available in your area, do add them to your sauce. In spring add dandelion and mustard greens (remember to chiffonade!), peas, green garlic, green onions or scallions, and asparagus.

Macaroni and Cheese

Who doesn't like macaroni and cheese, the ultimate comfort food? The problem is that much of macaroni and cheese, which comes in a box, is full of dyes, preservatives, and chemicals that your body knows is not "real" food. And truthfully, Dr. Haas finds that many people are reactive and have problems from the overconsumption of wheat and dairy products, which is, you guessed it, the basis of mac and cheese. Still, it's yummy to the tummy for most people and one of the lifelong comfort foods.

Homemade macaroni and cheese can be healthy or not, and we base that on how natural or processed the ingredients are. The "not" version contains macaroni noodles made from white, processed flour and a sauce that has too much cheese, cream, and food dyes. To make your mac and cheese more nutritious, use our recipe on page 155 or get creative on your own with our healthful tips:

- Use whole grain, brown rice, or vegetable noodles.

- Make your own cheese sauce, which is really quite simple, using organic cheese.

- In the spring, add steamed green peas, little pieces of asparagus, broccoli, spinach leaves, and parsley.

- In the summer, try steamed broccoli (in very small pieces), celery, zucchini, basil, and other fresh herbs. We also slice fresh tomatoes thinly and place them on the top of the macaroni and cheese, sprinkled with buttered breadcrumbs. Then place it in a broiler-proof pan under the broiler and broil until the breadcrumbs are golden brown. Even kids who say they don't like tomatoes like them this way.

- During autumn and winter, use cubes of winter squash and chopped leafy greens, such as spinach, chard, or kale. See how easy it is to add MVP?

Sandwiches

Sandwiches are a great way to add MVP to your diet. They are mobile and quick to make, and the options are endless. Let your imagination run free! In this book we offer nine different ideas for sandwiches in our Sandwiches Galore recipe (page 134). But if you want to get a jumpstart, here's how you do it:

- Use whole-grain or whole-wheat bread, rolls, or wraps.

- Get creative with spreads. Purée broccoli, roasted peppers, squash, garbanzo or black beans—just about any vegetable you want—and then spread onto your bread. You can also purée arugula into pesto. Or use a peanut sauce or guacamole (see pages 82 and 88) for a really unique flavor.

- Fill the sandwich or wrap with sprouts, lettuce, leftover sliced butternut squash, fresh or roasted tomatoes, grated carrots, sliced celery, roasted peppers, grilled onions, and on and on.

- Pack it up into your kid's (or your) lunch bag and you've got a healthy meal with MVP!

Shopping and Food Prep

Before you begin a recipe be sure to read it all the way through to make certain that you have the necessary ingredients. Almost all recipes mention some seasonal variations, so take note of these before you purchase your groceries or begin preparing the dish. If you need to make substitutions for a certain ingredient, refer to the Variations information included for many recipes. For example, if you really would love some whipped cream on that luscious pumpkin pie, but dairy makes you feel bloated and a little ill, then whip up some cashew cream, which is raw cashews blended with water, vanilla, and maple syrup to desired sweetness and to the consistency of whipped cream. If a recipe calls for a pan size you don't have, see if you have a pan that holds the same amount of batter or ingredients.

If you have children, make sure to include them in your shopping trip when you can. They are more likely to eat something new when they have been a part of the process. Farmers markets, if not your own garden, are wonderful places to purchase local, organic foods. Most grocery stores offer local, seasonal selections as well. If not, ask that they start. Peruse the produce area to find the freshest veggies and fruits that you can. Be sure to try something new just for fun.

Seasoning is the process of adding or improving the flavor of your food. Salt is the most common flavor enhancer, and most people overuse it. When you do use salt be sure to avoid the highly processed versions commonly found on grocery store shelves and use sea salt instead. Nowadays, there are special salts that contain many minerals, not just the overused sodium chloride, which can affect water retention and blood pressure. Seasonings include fresh and dried herbs, spices, condiments, and infused oils and vinegars.

Patty has herbs in the garden at her school, and during one class she was standing in front of sage, rosemary, and thyme with a group of ten- to twelve-year-olds. She asked them what foods came to their mind as they smelled these particular herbs. Their unanimous answer was "Thanksgiving!" What a fun way to learn how to use those herbs and to also be reminded of the power of our sense of smell in combination with our memories. Remember that many herbs are best when used seasonally or dried while in season. There are very few places where fresh basil is grown in December! (You can have a little plant growing on your kitchen shelf indoors.) Generally, if you want to make pesto in December, use spinach instead.

Basic Cooking Methods and Equipment

There are basic cooking methods and kitchen gear that recipes in this book, or most books for that matter, will call for. Let us briefly clarify them in alphabetical order:

Al dente: This means to cook something until it is tender but still firm. So for pasta or rice, al dente means it should not be entirely soft—it should be somewhat firm. For veggies this means they should be cooked so that they are still crispy, not wilted or flexible, and usually the cooking time is very short. "Chewiness" and "toothiness" are other words that are interchangeable.

Bake: To bake means to cook in a dry oven. Most often people think of baking breads, muffins, and so on. There are a few dishes that, just to confuse you, call for baking—but then have you place the cooking dish into a larger pan of water. Custards come to mind. Generally, however, there is no moisture.

Blanch or Parboil: When you blanch something you, in essence, soften it before going on to another step. With blanching, you plunge the food into a pot of boiling water (not too much food at once, because you need to keep the water boiling) for the short duration prescribed by your recipe. Then you either take it out and drain it, or plunge the food into ice-cold water. Often this is done to either set the color or to peel the skin, such as for peaches or tomatoes.

Boil: It's important to boil a lot of water or stock so that when you add the vegetables, they cook quickly. When almost done, drain immediately or the veggies will continue to cook.

Braise: This method of cooking is most commonly used for foods prepared in a small amount of water or stock. Meat or vegetable stews are the most common braised dishes. The dish is usually covered for most of the cooking and can be done on the stovetop or in the oven.

Broil: This is when food is heated on one side, generally 4–6 inches from the heating element, until browned. Some foods are cooked completely under the broiler and some are simply browned for a few moments or less. In contrast, typical baking heats the food from the bottom.

Chiffonade: The name of this slicing technique comes from a similar French word meaning "rag." But don't let that term trick you—it's really an elegant cut. Slice large-leafed greens into thin ribbons by stacking the leaves (or doing it one at a time), rolling them up like a cigar, and then slicing them very thinly.

Double Boiler: This is a pot that fits within a pot so that when you heat your ingredient—generally chocolate, eggs, or cream—the heat is greatly diffused and the food is protected from excess heat or burning. The water in the pan that is on the heating element maintains a simmer and not a boil. If you don't have a double boiler, simply use a stainless steel bowl and place in a pot. Improvise!

En Papillote: All Patty's kids know how to make Salmon en Papillote. "En papillote" simply means "in parchment." You wrap your ingredients in parchment paper, place it on a cookie sheet, and bake it. How simple is that? Once you master this simple technique, a myriad of variations will come to mind; start with the Salmon en Papillote recipe on page 161. (You can also wrap food in a banana leaf, corn husks, grape leaves, or even collard greens.)

Grill: Most people think primarily of barbecuing meats, yet grilled vegetables are just wonderful. Even though this happens mainly outdoors, there are indoor grill attachments to kitchen ranges as well. The grilling process adds a unique and enjoyable flavor to almost everything, and people will rave about vegetables on the grill. Dr. Haas offers these at most every party, with a combination of mushrooms, onions, garlic cloves, peppers, carrots, and zucchini. Special grilling baskets are now available and make this process quite easy, plus the vegetables can be cut into bite-size pieces before they are grilled.

Persillade: Typically used as a flavoring or garnish, persillade is generally equal parts fresh parsley and fresh garlic. It can be added to a dish while cooking or at the end for more zip! It is particularly good stirred into butternut squash the last 5 minutes of roasting or added to our Roasted Roots with Garlic side dish (page 191) after they come out of the oven in lieu of other seasonings.

Poach: This is a moist heat method whereby the water or other liquid that the food is poaching in maintains a temperature just under the boiling point. You can poach an egg in water or poach a piece of salmon in white wine.

Purée: This is when you finely blend your ingredient, usually vegetables or beans. Often soups are puréed, or you can purée beans (or even oatmeal) to use as a thickener of a soup or sauce. You can use a food processor, food mill, immersion blender, or potato masher to purée.

Reduction: A reduction is a sauce in which liquid, generally wine-based, is simmered on the stove, uncovered, until it reduces by one-third or one-half. You may also reduce almost any vegetable juice. This procedure is used to intensify a flavor. As an example, you can place carrot juice in a pan and simmer it, uncovered, so that the liquid evaporates and the flavor intensifies. We give examples of these "reductions" in chapter 4.

Roast: No moisture is added when you roast. The oven is almost always preheated to the required temperature. Roasting often causes the caramelization of food, a wonderful flavor enhancer. Vegetables and meats are often roasted. Dr. Haas loves to roast vegetables; he likes to chop them first, then add some oil, balsamic vinegar, Bragg Liquid Aminos (or salt, or soy sauce), and herbs, and then toss them before laying them in a pan to roast in the oven.

Sauté: This comes from the French word sauter, which means "to jump." Sautéing is done in a pan without a lid. When you sauté, the food needs to be thin or minced and is generally in a single layer, otherwise it will steam. First you heat the pan, then add a bit of oil, and then the vegetables. You need to stir occasionally, but not constantly, or your vegetables will not brown. If you are adding garlic, do so at the end or else your garlic can burn. Water sauté variation: To use less oil, you can sauté with some water and then add the oil toward the end for flavor, however, the vegetables will be less browned and more steamed.

Simmer: This means that the food is cooked at a gentle heat and not at a boil.

Steam: This is when food, primarily vegetables, is cooked over, not in, boiling water. Generally a steaming basket is used. When steaming, a lid is always used to trap the heat and moisture. Be sure to use the steaming water in your next soup or you can simply drink it, once it cools a bit. There are some nutrients that drip into this "pot liquor."

Suribachi: A *suribachi* is a mortar and pestle with ridges inside.

Safety in the Kitchen

Be sure to explain the importance of sanitation to your children—and teens, adult family members, and visitors for that matter—before beginning to cook. Share with them these important personal sanitation tips:

- Wash your hands in warm, soapy water both before you begin to prepare food and after any act that might contaminate foods, such as touching your eyes, hair, nose, or mouth, as well as eating, smoking, petting an animal, using the restroom, touching dirty surfaces, or handling raw meats.

- Don't handle food when you are sick.

- Cover burns, cuts, and sores with a tight bandage.

- Keep yourself clean! Clean your body, clothes, aprons, and so forth.

- Keep your hair tied back if it's long.

And teach them these safety measures regarding the food itself:

- Keep raw foods away from cooked foods.

- Keep food away from chemicals (hopefully you don't use many; there are plenty of natural products available).

- Wash all raw fruits and vegetables before preparation. Always rinse off your meats and fish before cooking.

- Maintain food at proper temperatures. Cold foods should be kept at 40°F. Hot food temperatures depends on what it is: Stuffed meat and reheated leftovers should be kept at 165°F; beef and other hot foods at 140°F; fish and poultry at 145°F; and cooked pork, hamburgers, and eggs at 155°F.

- Do not refreeze food after it has thawed.

- Store raw and thawing foods in a bowl on the bottom shelf of the refrigerator to avoid dripping and contamination. Do not thaw foods at room temperature unless you are prepared to cook it immediately.

We would like to include one other health tip, and that is to use your stovetop or oven—not a microwave—to cook and reheat. It might take a bit of adjustment, but you can do it. Suffice it to say that microwaved foods are altered foods.

Now that you and your children understand how to set up a kitchen, know some kitchen lingo, have the basics of bringing MVP into your diet, as well as utilizing substitutions and seasonings, let's get cooking with MVP Recipes begin in the next chapter. Enjoy all the new flavors and added nutrients, health, and vitality from incorporating more vegetables into your meals.

Chapter 4
Seasonings, Sauces, and Spreads

This chapter covers some cooking basics: special seasonings and spreads, béchamels and butters, reductions and relishes. If you can learn these recipes—and they are all fairly easy—then you can always whip up a special meal with the added flavor that these recipes provide.

These recipes won't yield an entire meal, but they can make a meal complete—and, at the very least, and some More Vegetables, Please (MVP) to your plate. They're meant to augment your vegetables, not be the main flavor, and using them will add complexity to your dishes that your taste buds will appreciate. If you have children, there are many simple recipes, such as the Gomasio (page 63) and Maître d' Hotel Butter (page 61), that are fun to make and will give them a sense of being real chefs—and they'll likely eat more vegetables when they've helped in the kitchen!

Basic Vegetable Reduction

Reduction sauces are generally wine-based. But you may also reduce almost any vegetable juice. Use the Seasonings for Vegetables list on page 36 if you would like to season the sauce after you reduce. Vegetable reductions are a wonderful way to add MVPs to your meals. Use your imagination and experiment!

Chopped onions to taste

Garlic to taste

Extra-virgin olive oil

Vegetable juice

Simmer some onions, garlic, and olive oil in a small saucepan for a few minutes. Add vegetable juice and simmer until reduced by half.

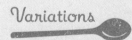

Variations

MUSHROOM BROTH (PAGE 118) CAN BE REDUCED FOR A RICH SAUCE; ADD SOME SHERRY AND SAGE—WONDERFUL.

Carrot Reduction

Bring some gusto to your plate—and your palate—by tossing this easy-to-prepare reduction with pasta and steamed veggies.

YIELDS ½ CUP

1 cup carrot juice

½ teaspoon curry powder

2 tablespoons rice wine vinegar

Sea salt to taste

Black pepper to taste

Simmer the carrot juice and reduce by half. Add the remaining ingredients, whisk together, and serve. Try adding a splash of balsamic vinegar sometime.

PER SERVING (2 TABLESPOONS): 26 CALORIES; TRACE FAT (4.0% CALORIES FROM FAT); 1G PROTEIN; 6G CARBOHYDRATE; 1G DIETARY FIBER; 0MG CHOLESTEROL; 17MG SODIUM.

Pesto

Pesto is Italian for "pounded." Often pesto is made from basil with the addition of garlic, pine nuts, Parmesan cheese, and olive oil. We think the addition of lemon juice brightens the color and flavor of this arugula-based pesto. Pasta and pesto (with lots of vegetables!) is the typical use for pesto, but you can spread it on sandwiches by itself or mixed with a little mayo or plain yogurt. Add to roasted veggies or stir into soups or salad dressings. Toss it onto steamed vegetables, brown rice or other grains, white beans, grilled meats, or fish.

YIELDS 1 CUP

1 cup arugula leaves

1 cup fresh Italian parsley

3 cloves garlic

¼ cup Romano cheese (optional)

1 teaspoon sea salt

½ teaspoon freshly ground black pepper

2 teaspoons freshly squeezed lemon juice

½ cup extra-virgin olive oil

Place all of the ingredients except the oil in blender or food processor and purée. Slowly add the oil. You may use a mortar and pestle if you prefer that to blending your fresh herbs.

PER SERVING (2 TABLESPOONS): 139 CALORIES; 15G FAT (92.3% CALORIES FROM FAT); 1G PROTEIN; 1G CARBOHYDRATE; TRACE DIETARY FIBER; 4MG CHOLESTEROL; 282MG SODIUM.

Eating Seasonally

PRACTICE EATING SEASONALLY BY ADDING ANY OF THE VEGETABLES BELOW, OR SUBSTITUTING THEM FOR THE MAIN INGREDIENT IN THIS RECIPE, DEPENDING ON THE TIME OF YEAR.

Spring: ALMOST ANY TENDER LEAFY GREENS

Summer: BASIL, ROASTED PEPPERS, PARSLEY, OTHER SUMMER GREENS

Autumn: BASIL, PARSLEY

Winter: SUN-DRIED TOMATOES, SPINACH LEAVES

Variations

THINK OUT OF THE BOX WITH PESTO. USE THE SEASONAL INGREDIENT SUGGESTIONS TO CHANGE THINGS UP, LIKE USING SUN-DRIED TOMATOES. YOU CAN MAKE PESTO WITH JUST ABOUT ANYTHING! ONCE PATTY WAS TALKING ON THE PHONE AND FORGOT THAT SHE HAD BROCCOLI IN THE STEAMER, AND SINCE SHE CAN'T STAND MUSHY VEGETABLES (WHO CAN?) SHE PURÉED THEM AND STIRRED THE "PESTO" INTO PASTA WITH OTHER VEGGIES. THE MISTAKE TURNED INTO ANOTHER WAY TO ADD MVP. (DON'T OVERCOOK VEGETABLES ON PURPOSE, BUT DO TRY NEW THINGS!)

Maître d' Hotel Butter

Use a little of this butter on steamed vegetables, mashed potatoes, fish, or chicken. You may add minced garlic if you like and even a dash of Tabasco. There are as many variations as there are cooks.

YIELDS 1 CUP

2 sticks unsalted butter, room temperature

2 teaspoons fresh lemon juice

2 teaspoons grated lemon zest

3 tablespoons finely chopped parsley or other fresh herbs

¼ cup finely minced shallots

Sea salt to taste

Freshly ground black pepper to taste

Beat the butter in a bowl until softened. Beat in the lemon juice a little at a time and then mix in the rest of the ingredients. You may roll this in parchment paper and store in the freezer.

PER SERVING (1 TABLESPOON): 208 CALORIES; 23G FAT (97.1% CALORIES FROM FAT); TRACE PROTEIN; 1G CARBOHYDRATE; TRACE DIETARY FIBER; 62MG CHOLESTEROL; 5MG SODIUM.

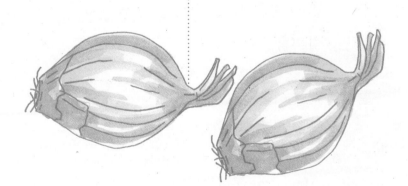

Bouquet Garni

French for "garnished bouquet," bouquet garni is a bundle of herbs tied together with kitchen string, placed into a soup, stew, or sauce, and removed before consuming. There are variations to bouquets garnis but most are as follows:

YIELDS 1 BOUQUET

One 3" celery stalk with leaves

3 sprigs parsley

1 bay leaf

2 sprigs thyme

To make the bouquet garni, place the celery stalk on a flat surface, followed by the parsley and then the herbs. Tie all pieces together with some kitchen string. Alternatively, the ingredients may be placed into cheesecloth or a tea strainer.

Gremolata

Use gremolata in sauces or tossed on veggies or beans. Or use it as a garnish (just a little!) on a hot bowl of soup.

YIELDS ABOUT 2 TABLESPOONS

2 tablespoons finely chopped parsley, stems removed

1 clove garlic, minced

½ teaspoon lemon zest

Place the finely chopped parsley in a small bowl and stir in the minced garlic and lemon zest. Cover and refrigerate or serve immediately.

PER SERVING (CALORIES ARE FOR WHOLE RECIPE; USE AS DESIRED): 7 CALORIES; TRACE FAT (3.6 CALORIES FROM FAT); TRACE PROTEIN; 1G CARBOHYDRATE; TRACE DIETARY FIBER; 0MG CHOLESTEROL; 2MG SODIUM.

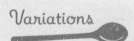

Variations

TO MAKE PERSILLADE, SIMPLY OMIT THE LEMON AND INCREASE THE GARLIC. PERSILLADE IS GENERALLY EQUAL PARTS PARSLEY AND GARLIC. IT CAN BE ADDED TO A DISH WHILE COOKING OR, FOR MORE INTENSITY, AT THE END.

Gomasio

Try this seasoning sprinkled on steamed broccoli that has been drizzled with a bit of lemon juice. It's also excellent sprinkled on seaweed salad.

YIELDS 4 TABLESPOONS

2 teaspoons coarse sea salt

5 teaspoons sesame seeds

Lightly dry-toast the salt and sesame seeds, stirring frequently until aromatic. Allow them to cool and grind them in a *suribachi* or a clean coffee grinder. Store in a lidded glass jar in a dark cupboard for 3 months, or longer in the fridge.

PER SERVING (¼ TEASPOON): 2 CALORIES; TRACE FAT (73.1% CALORIES FROM FAT); TRACE PROTEIN; TRACE CARBOHYDRATE; TRACE DIETARY FIBER; 0MG CHOLESTEROL; 104MG SODIUM.

Kids in the Kitchen

A SURIBACHI IS A MORTAR AND PESTLE WITH RIDGES INSIDE. KIDS LOVE TO GRIND THIS TOPPING AND WILL EAT MANY DIFFERENT FOODS IF THEY CAN SPRINKLE A LITTLE GOMASIO ON TOP.

Ghee

Ghee, also known as clarified butter, does not burn like butter because the milk solids settle to the bottom of the pan and the liquid that foams and floats to the top is also removed. It's often used in Indian cooking. You can mix together equal portions of olive oil and ghee; this mixture contains healthy monounsaturated fat and will still spread like butter. Keep in mind that ghee is 100 percent fat and should be used sparingly. Ghee does not need to be refrigerated and can be kept at room temperature for up to one month. We generally refrigerate it anyway.

1 pound of organic, unsalted butter

Extra-virgin olive oil (optional)

Melt butter over medium-low heat in a small saucepan. Skim the white foam off the top. Let simmer over low heat until the milk solids on the bottom have turned a light brown, about 15 minutes. Strain though a coffee filter or cheesecloth into a jar.

Pass the Purée, Please

There are many ways to prepare vegetables, and we'll cover them all in this book, from steaming to roasting to just plain eating them raw. But we think the method of puréeing deserves it's own special mention. Why? Because it is one of the best ways to "secretly" add MVP into your meals. Not that we think vegetables should be hidden. But if you are transitioning into a more veggie-centric diet, purées are a great start. And for kids, it's a terrific way to get those veggie nutrients into their diets, at least in the beginning.

Basically, "purée" means "blend really really well" until there are no lumps. Many sauces, dips, soups, and spreads are, essentially, purées. Think about the infinite number of purées your food processor or blender could yield with an equally limitless number of veggie and herb combinations!

You can purée cooked beans and vegetables and add them to just about any dish, from muffins to pizzas. Puréed cannelloni beans, minced garlic, a splash of olive oil, and sea salt and pepper make a delicious Mediterranean-inspired dip. Or head south of the border and dip jicama or pita chips into either puréed pinto beans or a puréed avocado salsa. Lightly steam your choice of veggies, add seasonings (check out the seasonings list on page 36), then purée and stir into pasta or place atop brown rice or another veggie. Use your imagination!

And don't forget the kids. Purées are a great way to teach children that cooking is fun, creative, and healthy.

Béchamel Variations

Béchamel is a sauce that everyone should know how to make. It is a basic white sauce that typically serves as the foundation for other sauces. The recipe is so versatile that you can make several substitutions for various results: use olive oil instead of butter, garbanzo flour instead of wheat flour, and almond or rice milk instead of cow's milk.

YIELDS 1 CUP

Basic Béchamel

2 tablespoons unsalted butter or extra-virgin olive oil

2 tablespoons flour

1 cup warm milk

¼ teaspoon sea salt

1 pinch freshly grated nutmeg (optional)

Heat butter or oil in small saucepan over medium heat. Stir in flour, mixing thoroughly as you go. Cook and stir for 1 to 2 minutes.

Slowly whisk in a small amount of milk to form a smooth paste. Continue until all the milk has been whisked in and the sauce is thick. Add salt and nutmeg, if you like, to taste.

PER SERVING: 103 CALORIES; 8G FAT (67.9% CALORIES FROM FAT); 2G PROTEIN; 6G CARBOHYDRATE; TRACE DIETARY FIBER; 24MG CHOLESTEROL; 148MG SODIUM.

Mornay Sauce

Add ½ cup grated cheese to 1 cup of hot Basic Béchamel; stir over low heat until cheese is melted. Season with a little dry or prepared mustard or Worcestershire sauce to taste.

Velouté Sauce

Substitute chicken, beef, fish, or vegetable broth for the milk in the Basic Béchamel recipe and prepare as directed.

Herb Sauce

Add 1 teaspoon chopped fresh herbs (or ½ teaspoon dried herbs) to 1 cup of hot Basic Béchamel. Cook 1–2 minutes longer to get more flavor from the herbs.

Mustard Sauce

Follow the Basic Béchamel recipe, except whisk together 1 teaspoon dry mustard with the flour, and prepare as directed. This sauce is especially good with fish and chicken dishes.

Cashew Béchamel

Cashews put a twist on the classic sauce. You can also make an excellent vegan version with vegetable or mineral broth. Soak ¼ cup whole, raw cashews in cold water for ½ hour to soften and then drain. Using a blender, blend 2 tablespoons spelt flour (or garbanzo or other flour), 1 cup chicken (or vegetable) broth, ¼ teaspoon sea salt, and 1 pinch cayenne pepper. Put mixture into a small, heavy-bottomed saucepan. Bring to a boil over high heat, stirring constantly. Remove from heat and add ¼ cup finely minced parsley and mix well. Serve.

PER SERVING (4 TABLESPOONS): 89 CALORIES; 5G FAT (47.8% CALORIES FROM FAT); 3G PROTEIN; 9G CARBOHYDRATE; 1G DIETARY FIBER; 1MG CHOLESTEROL; 528MG SODIUM.

Mushroom Gravy

This rich, wonderful sauce is terrific on pasta or drizzled onto vegetables. You may also decoratively splash a little onto your next bowl of butternut squash soup. Delicious!

YIELDS ABOUT 1½ CUPS

2 tablespoons unsalted butter or extra-virgin olive oil

½ pound shiitake mushrooms, thinly sliced with tough stems removed

1 medium onion, finely chopped

¼ cup thinly sliced celery

2 tablespoons flour

½ teaspoon sea salt

½ teaspoon black pepper

1 tablespoon sherry

1 teaspoon fresh thyme leaves

1 cup vegetable broth (page 117)

2 tablespoons minced fresh parsley, stems removed

Melt the butter in a skillet over medium heat, then add the mushrooms, onion, and celery and sauté, stirring frequently, until softened, about 8–10 minutes.

Sprinkle the flour, salt, and pepper over the mixture and cook for 2 minutes, stirring constantly. Stir in the sherry and thyme. Whisk in the broth and cook, stirring frequently until thickened, about 5 minutes. Add parsley and serve.

PER SERVING (4 TABLESPOONS): 195 CALORIES; 5G FAT (20.6% CALORIES FROM FAT); 5G PROTEIN; 37G CARBOHYDRATE; 5G DIETARY FIBER; 11MG CHOLESTEROL; 439MG SODIUM.

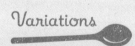

Variations

YOU MAY DELETE THE SHERRY AND ADD TAMARI, IF YOU LIKE. YOU MAY USE ANY TYPE OF MUSHROOMS FOR THIS GRAVY. WE HAVE ALSO LEFT OUT THE FLOUR AND ADDED PURÉED OATMEAL AS THE THICKENER WITH GOOD RESULTS. IF YOU ARE GLUTEN AND/OR OAT INTOLERANT, TRY USING GARBANZO FLOUR.

Health Note

SHIITAKE MUSHROOMS ARE HIGH IN IRON AND B-VITAMINS AND ARE GOOD FOR YOUR IMMUNE SYSTEM. THEY ARE ONLY BIOAVAILABLE WHEN THEY ARE COOKED.

Marinara Sauce

This is an easy way to add MVP to whatever lucky dish you pour it on, from pizza to eggplant Parmesan to sautéed vegetables. Use an equal amount of fresh tomatoes instead of canned when you have them ripe off the vine.

YIELDS 7 CUPS

2 tablespoons extra-virgin olive oil

½ medium onion, diced

4 cloves garlic, chopped

¼ cup grated carrots

¼ cup sliced celery

⅓ cup sliced zucchini

One 28-ounce can crushed tomatoes

1 teaspoon fresh thyme

2 tablespoons chopped fresh basil

2 tablespoons chopped parsley

3 medium Roma tomatoes, chopped

1½ teaspoons sea salt, or to taste

1 teaspoon black pepper

Heat the oil in a large saucepan over medium heat. Add onion, garlic, carrots, celery, and zucchini. Cook until al dente, about 5 minutes. Add the canned tomatoes and their juices, bring to a boil, then turn the heat down and simmer, covered, for about 10 minutes. Add the thyme, basil, parsley, tomatoes, salt, and pepper. Simmer for another 5 minutes.

PER SERVING (ABOUT 1 CUP): 111 CALORIES; 5G FAT (37.6% CALORIES FROM FAT); 3G PROTEIN; 16G CARBOHYDRATE; 4G DIETARY FIBER; 0MG CHOLESTEROL; 671MG SODIUM.

Eating Seasonally

PRACTICE EATING SEASONALLY BY ADDING ANY OF THE VEGETABLES BELOW, OR SUBSTITUTING THEM FOR THE MAIN INGREDIENTS IN THIS RECIPE, DEPENDING ON THE TIME OF YEAR.

Spring: PEAS, ASPARAGUS, GREEN GARLIC

Summer: FRESH TOMATOES, EGGPLANT, RED BELL PEPPERS, CORN

Autumn: FRESH TOMATOES, JERUSALEM ARTICHOKES

Winter: CUBED WINTER SQUASHES, PARSNIPS, TURNIPS

Variations

YOU MAY ADD SOME RED WINE TO THE SAUCE IF YOU LIKE, ABOUT ⅓ CUP, WHEN YOU ADD THE CANNED TOMATOES.

Kids in the Kitchen

HAVE YOUR OLDER CHILDREN GRATE THE CARROTS, BUT REMIND THEM TO WORK SLOWLY SO AS NOT TO GRATE THE TIPS OF THEIR FINGERS! LET YOUR CHILDREN ALSO HELP YOU ADD THE VEGGIES AND STIR THE SAUCE.

Traditional Aioli

Aioli can be chilled up to two days. The egg yolk in this recipe is not cooked, so make sure you have fresh eggs from healthfully raised hens. It's great on crab cakes and baked potatoes, as a salad dressing and sandwich spread, and served atop our Egg, Rice, and Veggie Bake dish (page 156). Since aioli is high in fat and calories, you won't want to get in the habit of making it an everyday condiment.

YIELDS 1 CUP

3 cloves peeled garlic

Pinch sea salt

1 egg yolk

2 teaspoons water or fresh lemon juice

1 cup extra-virgin olive oil

In a mortar and pestle or food processor, grind the garlic with the salt. In a small bowl, mix the egg yolk with the water or lemon juice. Add the garlic to the egg yolk or, if using a processor, add the yolk to the garlic. Slowly whisk in or pour in the olive oil.

PER SERVING (2⅔ TABLESPOONS): 330 CALORIES; 37G FAT (98.7% CALORIES FROM FAT); 1G PROTEIN; 1G CARBOHYDRATE; TRACE DIETARY FIBER; 35MG CHOLESTEROL; 2MG SODIUM.

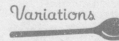

Variations

WE HAVE MADE AIOLI WITH THE ADDITION OF 1 TEASPOON PREPARED MUSTARD AND EVEN HALF OF A JALAPEÑO PEPPER.

Garlic Herb Aioli

This aioli will keep for up to one week since raw eggs are not used. Use it as a dip for veggies or as a salad dressing. Toss a little in with roasted veggies or add some to your potato salad. It's wonderful on sandwiches, too. And when you're ready for a change of pace, get creative and add roasted peppers, Dijon, or saffron to the recipe.

YIELDS 2 CUPS

12 ounces drained silken tofu

3 to 5 cloves garlic, minced, depending on your taste

2 tablespoons miso (any type is fine)

⅓ cup fresh lemon juice

1 tablespoon capers, drained

2 tablespoons chopped fresh parsley, stems removed

½ teaspoon dried dill

½ teaspoon dried oregano

½ teaspoon dried tarragon

1 tablespoon nutritional yeast

2 shakes cayenne pepper

½ teaspoon freshly ground black pepper

½ teaspoon sea salt

2 tablespoons water

Place all ingredients in a blender and purée. You might also use orange juice instead of lemon juice.

PER SERVING (ABOUT 3 TABLESPOONS): 42 CALORIES; 2G FAT (39.9% CALORIES FROM FAT); 4G PROTEIN; 4G CARBOHYDRATE; 1G DIETARY FIBER; 0MG CHOLESTEROL; 231MG SODIUM.

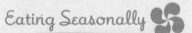

Eating Seasonally

THIS RECIPE CALLS FOR MOSTLY DRIED HERBS. BUT IN THE SUMMER (OR ANY SEASON IF YOU GROW SOME ON YOUR WINDOWSILL), USE FRESH HERBS. REMEMBER THAT 1 TABLESPOON OF FRESH HERBS IS EQUAL TO 1 TEASPOON OF DRIED.

Mustard Sauce

This is wonderful on grilled veggies, chicken, or turkey cutlets. We're sure you will find many uses for this easy sauce—in veggie wraps perhaps?

YIELDS 1 CUP

1 cup plain yogurt

2 tablespoons Dijon mustard

1 teaspoon brown rice vinegar

½ teaspoon honey

Combine ingredients in a bowl! You may heat this sauce if you like.

PER SERVING (2 TABLESPOONS): 40 CALORIES; TRACE FAT (9.5% CALORIES FROM FAT); 4G PROTEIN; 6G CARBOHYDRATE; TRACE DIETARY FIBER; 1MG CHOLESTEROL; 137MG SODIUM.

Roasted Red Pepper Sauce

You can divide this recipe in half if this is too much for your family. The sauce is wonderful on pasta, roasted veggies, salads, grilled meats—you name it.

YIELDS 1½ CUPS

3 whole red bell peppers

½ head garlic, cloves peeled

1½ teaspoons Dijon mustard

1 tablespoon tamari or other soy sauce

1½ teaspoons honey

½ teaspoon black pepper, or to taste

Preheat oven to 375°F. Place peppers and garlic on an oiled cookie sheet. Roast peppers and garlic in oven for 25–30 minutes. When done, place peppers in bowl, cover, and let steam. You may also place them in a paper bag. When cool, peel and seed peppers.

Place peppers, garlic, and remaining ingredients in food processor or blender and blend.

PER SERVING (4 TABLESPOONS): 25 CALORIES; TRACE FAT (5.5% CALORIES FROM FAT); 1G PROTEIN; 6G CARBOHYDRATE; 1G DIETARY FIBER; 0MG CHOLESTEROL; 185MG SODIUM.

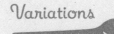

Variations

FOR ADDED FLAVOR, ADD LEMON JUICE AND ZEST. FOR SALAD DRESSING, ADD ½ CUP BALSAMIC VINEGAR AND 1 CUP EXTRA-VIRGIN OLIVE OIL (AND KEEP WHAT YOU DON'T USE IN THE FRIDGE). FOR A THINNER SAUCE, ADD ½ CUP WATER AND ½ CUP EXTRA-VIRGIN OLIVE OIL.

Ginger-Sesame Marinade

This is a very versatile marinade that you will use often once you discover how simple it is to prepare. It is wonderful on tempeh, which is an excellent protein source: Slice tempeh into ½" slices then steam for 15 minutes over, not in, water; drain and place in a bowl; pour the marinade over the tempeh and marinate for an hour; grill or sauté for 5 minutes on each side; then serve with a cabbage slaw and buckwheat noodles that you have cooked in miso-flavored water. It makes a nice lunch or casual dinner.

YIELDS ABOUT 1¼ CUPS

½ cup rice wine vinegar

¼ cup water

¼ cup yellow miso

¼ cup chopped green onions

2 tablespoons sugar (see Sweet as Sugar, page 209)

2 tablespoons peeled and minced fresh ginger

2 tablespoons low-sodium soy sauce

4 teaspoons extra-virgin olive oil

2 teaspoons dark sesame oil

Place all ingredients in a bowl and whisk until well blended. Store, covered, in a glass container or jar in the refrigerator for up to 1 week.

PER SERVING (2⅔ TABLESPOONS): 88 CALORIES; 5G FAT (50.8% CALORIES FROM FAT); 2G PROTEIN; 10G CARBOHYDRATE; 1G DIETARY FIBER; 0MG CHOLESTEROL; 762MG SODIUM.

Salsa

There are endless recipes for salsa. We have perfected this one. In the summer, there is nothing as refreshing and delicious as peeled and sliced jicama served with this salsa. Also try it with your favorite fish dish, on baked potatoes, or as a condiment on just about anything. This is especially good on an omelet.

YIELDS ABOUT 3 CUPS

1 jalapeño pepper, seeded and minced

1 to 2 large cloves garlic, finely chopped

1 red bell pepper, seeded and chopped

2 large tomatoes, finely chopped

1 cucumber, peeled and finely chopped

2 tablespoons extra-virgin olive oil

Juice of 1 lemon or lime

Sea salt to taste

Black pepper to taste

Cilantro or parsley, for garnish

In a bowl, combine all the ingredients well. Garnish with parsley or cilantro.

PER SERVING (¾ CUP): 93 CALORIES; 7G FAT (64.9% CALORIES FROM FAT); 1G PROTEIN; 7G CARBOHYDRATE; 2G DIETARY FIBER; 0MG CHOLESTEROL; 8MG SODIUM.

Tomatillo Relish

We have served this relish on steamed veggies, with carrot soup, as a garnish on tacos or burritos, and spooned onto the slices of half an avocado.

YIELDS 2 CUPS

1 pound tomatillos

1 fresh jalapeño, seeded

1½ cups lightly packed fresh cilantro

1½ cups lightly packed fresh parsley, stems removed

2 tablespoons extra-virgin olive oil

Sea salt to taste

Remove papery outer layer from tomatillos and rinse well. Place them in a single layer into a 10" x 15" baking pan and bake in a 400°F oven until slightly browned, about 25 minutes. Meanwhile wash and dry the fresh herbs.

Transfer tomatillos to a food processor and add jalapeño, cilantro, parsley, and oil. Pulse until mixture is coarsely chopped and slightly chunky. If you do not have a food processor, simply chop by hand. Add salt to taste.

PER SERVING (3 TABLESPOONS): 51 CALORIES; (69% FROM FAT); 3.9 G FAT (SAT 0.5G); 0.8G PROTEIN; 3.8G CARBOHYDRATE. 1.5G FIBER; 0.0G CHOLESTEROL; 5MG SODIUM;

Health Note 🖤

CILANTRO IS A NATURAL CHELATOR, WHICH MEANS IT ASSISTS IN THE REMOVAL OF POTENTIALLY TOXIC METALS (SUCH AS MERCURY) FROM THE BODY. "CHELATE" MEANS "CLAW," AND CHELATORS BIND WITH MINERALS TO HELP THEM MOVE AROUND THE BODY. FOR EXAMPLE, MINERAL CHELATES ALSO ALLOW FOR BETTER ABSORPTION, AND TYPICALLY THE CHELATED MINERALS ARE BOUND WITH AMINO ACID DERIVATIVES, SUCH AS CALCIUM ASPARTATE.

Cucumber Feta Salsa

This salsa is wonderful in the summer. There are several ways to serve it: Try spreading it onto a thick slice of a tomato. You can also heap 6 tablespoons of the salsa over grilled or broiled chicken breasts atop mesclun or spring lettuce mix and then garnish the dish with a lemon or lime wedge. Or spoon the salsa onto a sprouted grain tortilla with lettuce and garbanzo beans, or serve it in an endive leaf as an appetizer.

YIELDS ABOUT 3 CUPS

1 cup crumbled feta cheese

2 tablespoons lemon or lime juice

½ teaspoon freshly ground black pepper

1½ cups seeded and diced cucumber

1 cup diced red onion

3 tablespoons chopped fresh mint

3 tablespoons chopped fresh dill

Combine the feta, lemon juice, and pepper and mash with a fork until crumbly. Add the cucumber, onion, mint, and dill, stirring gently.

PER SERVING (¾ CUP): 129 CALORIES; 17G FAT (55% CALORIES FROM FAT); 7G PROTEIN; 9G CARBOHYDRATE; 2G DIETARY FIBER; 33MG CHOLESTEROL; 427MG SODIUM.

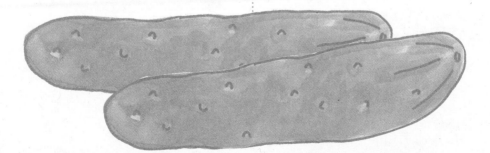

Chapter 5
Appetizers and Dips

What is an appetizer? We can all probably agree that it's something to tide us over while the main course is being prepared. In our families, appetizers are also fun things to nibble and a great opportunity to add more veggies to our diets. You can easily bring more vegetables, please (MVP) to your dips: Add spinach leaves to hummus, grated carrots to cheese dip, and shredded zucchini to your spinach dip. Be sure to use veggies instead of or in addition to chips and crackers.

There are many tried and true appetizers that everyone serves—cheese and crackers, crostini (little toasts with some kind of spread), bruschetta (toasts with chopped tomatoes, basil, garlic, and olive oil), and dips and veggies. They may be a bit overdone, but the reason they are so popular is that everyone likes them! We have included some of the basics and some new twists on old favorites. The sprouted hummus, as an example, takes some forethought, but it's fun sprouting seeds and enjoying the health benefits of sprouts. You might want to try preparing many different recipes at once and serve them for lunch or even dinner. Enjoy!

Chanterelle Crostini

A bit extravagant, but so good! This is Patty's mushroom version; generally the chanterelles are chicken livers.

SERVES 16

1 medium red onion, chopped

1 stalk celery, chopped

1 medium carrot, chopped

½ bunch Italian parsley, stems removed and chopped, plus more for garnish

3 tablespoons extra-virgin olive oil

4 cups coarsely chopped chanterelle mushrooms

1 cup white wine

3 tablespoons capers

3 whole anchovies (optional)

1 teaspoon sea salt (optional)

2 cups warm vegetable broth (page 117) or chicken broth (page 119)

1 loaf Italian baguette, sliced

Italian parsley, coarsely chopped for garnish, if desired

Heat the olive oil in a sauté pan over medium-high heat and then add the onion, celery, carrot, and parsley. Simmer 2–3 minutes. Stir in the mushrooms and simmer until soft, stirring occasionally. Add the wine and allow the liquid to reduce. Add the capers and anchovies to boost flavor and, if needed, add sea salt.

Remove the pan from the heat. Allow mushroom mixture to cool slightly. Remove from the pan and chop, but not too finely. You may use pulse on your food processor if you like.

Add mushroom mixture back into the pan and simmer for another 45 minutes, slowly adding the broth while it simmers.

Lightly toast good Italian bread. Spread with mushroom mixture. Coarsely chop some parsley to sprinkle on crostini, if desired.

PER SERVING: 94 CALORIES; 3G FAT (26.6% CALORIES FROM FAT); 2G PROTEIN; 15G CARBOHYDRATE; 2G DIETARY FIBER; 1MG CHOLESTEROL; 168MG SODIUM.

Variations

IN ITALY, THE TOASTED BREAD IS DIPPED INTO CHICKEN BROTH BEFORE SPREADING WITH THE CROSTINI MIXTURE. OF COURSE, ITALIANS USE CHICKEN LIVERS IN THIS RECIPE AS WELL. WE PREFER THE CHANTERELLES. IF CHANTERELLES ARE OUT OF YOUR BUDGET, SUBSTITUTE YOUR FAVORITE MUSHROOMS. TO MAKE IT VEGETARIAN, YOU MAY DELETE THE ANCHOVIES AND ADD 1 ADDITIONAL TABLESPOON OF CAPERS.

Dolmas with Feta and Cranberries

These serve double-duty as an appetizer or lunch and are good warm or cold. We like the dolmas drizzled with orange-infused olive oil (a little fresh orange juice in some olive oil) or simply sprinkled with fresh orange juice or grapefruit juice. For lunch, serve with a mixed-greens salad with lemon vinaigrette. Toss some (unsprayed) rose petals in the greens for a gorgeous presentation. We like these served at room temperature, but you may reheat if you like: Place dolmas in a steamer over—*not in*—boiling water for 5 minutes. Vegetable additions could be peas, corn, finely diced red bell pepper, and celery—or all of the above. And remember: Kids will eat almost anything if they get to roll it up!

SERVES 6

1 cup short-grain brown rice

2 cups water

1 bunch collard greens (about 6 medium leaves)

½ cup finely chopped dry-toasted almonds

½ teaspoon sea salt

½ teaspoon lemon zest

¼ teaspoon ground dried rosemary

⅓ cup halved dried cranberries (cut in half with scissors)

½ cup feta or goat cheese

Combine rice and water, place in a 2-quart saucepan, and bring to a boil. Reduce heat, cover, and simmer on low heat for 45 minutes or until done.

Meanwhile, wash the collard greens and blanch for 30 seconds. Cool and set aside. When rice is slightly cooled, stir in almonds, salt, lemon zest, rosemary, cranberries, and feta cheese.

Gently cut large stems from collard leaves. Lay flat on a cutting board. Place a scoopful of the rice mixture in the center of the leaf. Roll up like a burrito, tucking in the sides of the leaf. Repeat for all leaves.

PER SERVING: 222 CALORIES; 10G FAT (38.6% CALORIES FROM FAT); 7G PROTEIN; 28G CARBOHYDRATE; 2G DIETARY FIBER; 11MG CHOLESTEROL; 302MG SODIUM.

Health Note ♥

COLLARD GREENS ARE AN EXCELLENT SOURCE OF CALCIUM, NEEDED FOR BONE HEALTH; VITAMIN K, NEEDED FOR NORMAL BLOOD CLOTTING; VITAMIN A, NEEDED FOR GOOD VISION; AND VITAMIN C, WHICH HELPS TO FIGHT INFECTION, HEAL WOUNDS, AND KEEP TISSUES HEALTHY. EAT YOUR GREENS!

Spring Rolls with Peanut Sauce

Kids love to make these fun and delicious appetizers, which can be altered numerous ways to accommodate whatever's in season. Typically the sauce is made with peanuts, but if you're not allergic, feel free to substitute almond butter for the peanut butter.

SERVES 12

Spring Rolls

2 small cucumbers, seeded

2 medium carrots

12 rice paper wrappers

8 leaves butter lettuce, torn into small pieces

12 fresh mint leaves, chopped

12 sprigs fresh cilantro, stems removed

Peanut Sauce

Two 1" pieces ginger root, peeled

5 cloves garlic

1 to 2 teaspoons red chile paste

1 cup peanut butter or almond butter

¼ cup low-sodium tamari or other low-sodium soy sauce

¼ cup sugar

⅓ cup vegan Worcestershire sauce

¼ cup rice vinegar

1 lime, juiced, to taste

2 tablespoons fresh lemon juice

Water, if too thick

Slice the cucumbers and carrots into matchsticks, along with any other vegetables you'd like to add.

Set up a shallow bowl of warm water. A pie pan will work. Slip a spring roll wrapper into the water, pressing so that the wrapper is covered with water. When the wrapper becomes pliable, after about 30 seconds, remove and lay it flat on a piece of waxed paper. Place lettuce on the bottom half of the wrapper. Arrange vegetable mixture over the lettuce along with mint and cilantro.

Roll up the wrapper, tucking in the ends as you roll, and rolling as tightly as possible. Serve with peanut dipping sauce.

To make the dipping sauce: In a blender or food processor, place the ginger, garlic, and chile paste. Blend until smooth. Add remaining ingredients and continue to blend, adjusting the water to desired consistency.

PER SERVING: 200 CALORIES; 13G FAT (53.0% CALORIES FROM FAT); 6G PROTEIN; 36G CARBOHYDRATE; 3G DIETARY FIBER; 0MG CHOLESTEROL; 287MG SODIUM.

Variations

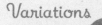

USING DIFFERENT NUTS IN THE DIPPING SAUCE WILL CHANGE THE FLAVOR SLIGHTLY—AND THIS KIND OF EXPERIMENTING IS ONE OF THE MOST ENJOYABLE ASPECTS OF COOKING. TRY IT WITH ALMONDS, CHANGE IT UP WITH CASHEWS, OR EVEN USE PINE NUTS.

Eating Seasonally

PRACTICE EATING SEASONALLY BY ADDING ANY OF THE VEGETABLES BELOW, OR SUBSTITUTING THEM FOR THE MAIN INGREDIENTS IN THE ROLLS, DEPENDING ON THE TIME OF YEAR.

Spring: PEAS, AVOCADOS, GREEN ONIONS, MUSTARD GREENS, RAW GRATED BEETS

Summer: RED PEPPERS, JICAMA, RADISHES, LETTUCES, ZUCCHINI, SUMMER SQUASHES

Autumn: BELL PEPPERS, BROCCOLI, CARROTS, CABBAGES

Winter: DAIKON RADISHES, BOK CHOY, CARROTS

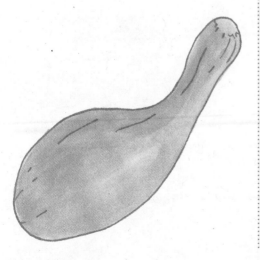

Red Pepper Strips with Artichoke and Caper Filling

Be sure to make this appetizer during the summer months, when red peppers are at their peak. The sweet red peppers and tangy filling are a wonderful combination.

SERVES 6

One 13-ounce jar water-packed artichoke bottoms

⅓ cup minced red onion or shallots

2 tablespoons capers, minced

¼ cup finely minced parsley, stems removed

1 tablespoon Dijon mustard

1 tablespoon olive oil

2 tablespoons apple cider or white balsamic vinegar

1 tablespoon minced fresh basil

1 teaspoon paprika

½ teaspoon freshly ground black pepper

2 red bell peppers, washed and dried

Fresh basil leaves, for garnish

Drain the artichoke bottoms and mince very finely. Put in bowl with onions, capers, and parsley.

In a small bowl, stir together the mustard, oil, vinegar, basil, paprika, and pepper. Toss with artichoke mixture. Set aside.

Cut the bell peppers in half lengthwise and discard stems, seeds, and white membranes. Cut in half again then slice each quarter into 3 strips. Spoon artichoke mixture onto the pepper and garnish with basil leaves. If basil is not in season, you may substitute fresh parsley. These may be served cold or at room temperature.

PER SERVING: 56 CALORIES; 3G FAT (39.3% CALORIES FROM FAT); 2G PROTEIN; 7G CARBOHYDRATE; 3G DIETARY FIBER; 0MG CHOLESTEROL; 301MG SODIUM.

Health Note ♥

ONE CUP OF RAW BELL RED PEPPERS PROVIDES YOUR DAILY VALUE OF BOTH VITAMINS C AND A. THEY ARE ALSO HIGH IN B6, WHICH IS NEEDED FOR MORE THAN 100 ENZYMES INVOLVED IN PROTEIN METABOLISM. ARTICHOKES ARE AN EXCELLENT SOURCE OF DIETARY FIBER, VITAMIN C, MAGNESIUM, AND POTASSIUM.

Hummus

Serve hummus with lots of brightly colored veggies, which are called crudités when served this way. You may eat the veggies raw, or for broccoli, cauliflower, and green beans or peas, lightly steam them first, if desired.

YIELDS 2 CUPS

2 cups cooked garbanzo beans or one 15-ounce can

1 lemon, juiced

½ teaspoon sea salt

¼ teaspoon black pepper

2 tablespoons tahini

2 cloves garlic

½ teaspoon ground cumin

¼ teaspoon cayenne pepper

¼ cup extra-virgin olive oil, plus more for garnish

¼ teaspoon paprika

Rinse and drain garbanzos and place them in a food processor. Add the lemon juice, salt, black pepper, tahini, garlic, cumin, and cayenne pepper. Turn on the processor and slowly add the oil in a thin stream until the mixture is smooth. Taste and adjust seasonings, if needed. Place in a bowl, drizzle with a little oil, and sprinkle with paprika.

Per serving (4 tablespoons): 356 calories; 16g fat (38.5% calories from fat); 14g protein; 43g carbohydrate; 12g dietary fiber; 0mg cholesterol; 200mg sodium.

Cooking Tip

To cook your own garbanzo beans, also known as chickpeas, soak 1 cup beans and a piece of kombu seaweed in cold water for 8 hours. (Another way is the quick-soak method: Place 1 cup beans, a piece of kombu, and 2 cups water in a saucepan, bring to a boil, and boil for 2 minutes. Next, cover, turn off the heat, and let sit for 2 hours.) After soaking, the beans take about an hour to cook at a simmer on the stove. The kombu in the soaking liquid and in the cooking water makes the beans more digestible and less likely to cause gas.

Variations

Try adding a handful of washed and dried spinach leaves into the processor. Also, you can chop some red bell pepper into small pieces and add it to the hummus after you have processed it. We like seeing the little red pieces in the hummus! Want to give this a Latin flavor? Substitute cooked black beans for the garbanzos, and then experiment with adding a jalapeño or other chile to taste, if you like.

Sprouted Garbanzo Hummus

This version is not as smooth in texture as the hummus you are used to, but it's very good just the same. Serve as you would "regular" hummus.

YIELDS 2 CUPS

1 cup dried garbanzo beans, sprouted

1 tablespoon lemon juice

½ teaspoon sea salt

½ teaspoon black pepper

1 tablespoon tahini

1 clove garlic

1 tablespoon extra-virgin olive oil, plus more for garnish

Paprika, for garnish

Place sprouted garbanzo beans in a food processor. Add the lemon juice, salt, pepper, tahini, and garlic. Turn on the processor and slowly add the oil in a thin stream until the mixture is smooth. Use more oil, if desired, for taste and texture. Taste and adjust seasonings, if needed. Place in a bowl, drizzle with a little oil, and sprinkle with paprika.

PER SERVING (4 TABLESPOONS): 109 CALORIES; 3G FAT (24.7% CALORIES FROM FAT); 5G PROTEIN; 16G CARBOHYDRATE; 5G DIETARY FIBER; 0MG CHOLESTEROL; 126MG SODIUM.

Health Note

MANY BELIEVE THAT SPROUTED FOODS ARE ONE OF THE MOST NUTRITIOUS FOODS YOU CAN EAT. WHEN A SEED SPROUTS, PROTEIN CONTENT INCREASES UP TO 30 PERCENT AS THE CARBOHYDRATE FOOD SOURCE GETS CONVERTED. CHLOROPHYLL AND FIBER CONTENT ALSO INCREASES. ALSO, SPROUTS ARE LIVING FOODS THAT CONTAIN ACTIVE ENZYMES THAT HELP WITH DIGESTION AND ASSIMILATION.

Cooking Tip

TO SPROUT THE GARBANZO BEANS, SOAK THEM IN COLD WATER OVERNIGHT. IN THE MORNING, DRAIN THE BEANS AND PLACE IN A SPROUTER. IF YOU DON'T HAVE A STORE-BOUGHT SPROUTER, SIMPLY USE A WIDE-MOUTH MASON JAR AND COVER THE OPENING WITH A PIECE OF CHEESECLOTH THAT HAS BEEN SECURED WITH A RUBBER BAND; KEEP THE JAR AT AN ANGLE SO THAT THE EXCESS WATER CAN DRAIN, AND DO NOT PLACE IN DIRECT LIGHT. RINSE THEM 2–3 TIMES A DAY UNTIL THEY SPROUT, ABOUT 3–4 DAYS. IT'S FUN TO WATCH THE BEANS START TO SPROUT. SEE OUR SPROUTING INSTRUCTIONS ON PAGE 23.

Roasted Garlic and White Bean Dip

This dip is great for raw vegetables or as a sandwich spread. Try spreading on halved cherry tomatoes for a wonderful appetizer.

YIELDS 2¼ CUPS

1 head garlic

2 teaspoons plus 2 tablespoons extra-virgin olive oil, divided

1 medium yellow onion, diced

1 tablespoon finely chopped fresh sage

2 cups cooked white beans or one 15-ounce can, rinsed and drained

½ teaspoon balsamic vinegar

1 teaspoon sea salt

½ teaspoon freshly cracked black pepper

Preheat oven to 400°F. To roast garlic, remove papery outer layer of skin and trim a small portion off the top of the head to expose cloves. Place on a square of parchment paper or aluminum foil and set on a baking sheet. Drizzle with 2 teaspoons of the oil, seal package, and bake for 40 minutes. Remove from oven and let cool.

While the garlic is roasting, heat the remaining 2 tablespoons of the oil in a skillet over medium heat. Cook the onion and sage together until the onions are soft. Set aside.

In a food processor or in a bowl using a potato masher or a fork, combine the onion mixture, beans, vinegar, salt, and pepper. Squeeze the roasted garlic from each clove and add to the mixture. Process until smooth, adding water if necessary to create a smooth mixture. Serve warm or at room temperature.

PER SERVING (3½ TABLESPOONS): 98 CALORIES; 4G FAT (33.8% CALORIES FROM FAT); 4G PROTEIN; 13G CARBOHYDRATE; 3G DIETARY FIBER; 0MG CHOLESTEROL; 191MG SODIUM.

Health Note ♥

BEANS ARE HIGH IN DIETARY FIBER, FOLATE, PROTEIN (SERVE WITH A GRAIN FOR A COMPLETE PROTEIN), AND IRON. THE IRON IN BEANS IS MORE DIGESTIBLE WHEN MIXED WITH A FOOD HIGH IN VITAMIN C SUCH AS TOMATOES.

Guacamole

How simple is this to make? There's only one step! Try dipping peeled and sliced jicama into this familiar dip for a tasty snack. Almost any sliced veggie will work well. Of course, you can also purchase whole-grain pita bread, cut it like a pie, and bake the wedges in a 375°F oven until toasted, about 15 minutes or so.

YIELDS APPROXIMATELY 2 CUPS

2 ripe avocados, peeled

Juice of 1 lemon or lime

½ small red onion, diced

1 tomato, diced

Sea salt, to taste

Hot pepper sauce, to taste

Fresh cilantro, chopped (optional)

Minced garlic (optional)

In a medium bowl, mash the avocados, add the other ingredients, and mix.

PER SERVING (½ CUP): 179 CALORIES; 16G FAT (70.3% CALORIES FROM FAT); 3G PROTEIN; 12G CARBOHYDRATE; 3G DIETARY FIBER; 0MG CHOLESTEROL; 14MG SODIUM.

Health Note ♥

AVOCADOS ARE HIGH IN THE HEART-HEALTHY MONOUNSATURATED FAT KNOWN AS OLEIC ACID. THEY ARE ALSO AN EXCELLENT SOURCE OF POTASSIUM, A MINERAL THAT REGULATES BLOOD PRESSURE.

Baba Ghanoush

This is a puréed and often-roasted eggplant dish that is popular in Middle Eastern cooking. Use it as a dip for veggies and/or toasted pita bread. Also try spreading it on toasted whole-grain bread or in a wrap and then adding grated carrots, fresh seasonal greens, and a nice thick slice of a fresh tomato, if it is summer, for a healthy sandwich. If it's winter, top slices of steamed or roasted butternut squash with baba ghanoush and then sprinkle on a little Parmesan. You'll love it.

YIELDS 2 CUPS

1 large eggplant

¼ cup extra-virgin olive oil, plus more for brushing on, divided

1 teaspoon ground cumin

2 cloves garlic

¼ teaspoon cayenne pepper

½ teaspoon sea salt, or to taste

½ teaspoon black pepper, or to taste

2 teaspoons chopped fresh parsley, stems removed

1 teaspoon chopped fresh chives

1 tablespoon pine nuts, toasted

Halve eggplant lengthwise and brush with oil. Set on grill, close cover, and cook until flesh is soft (or you may also broil it 6" from burner). Let eggplant cool.

Scoop flesh into food processor. Discard peels. Add cumin, garlic, cayenne pepper, salt, and pepper. While processing, add ¼ cup of the oil in a slow stream until it emulsifies.

Garnish with parsley and chives and sprinkle with toasted pine nuts.

PER SERVING (5 TABLESPOONS): 111 CALORIES; 10G FAT (76.8% CALORIES FROM FAT); 1G PROTEIN; 5G CARBOHYDRATE; 2G DIETARY FIBER; 0MG CHOLESTEROL; 160MG SODIUM.

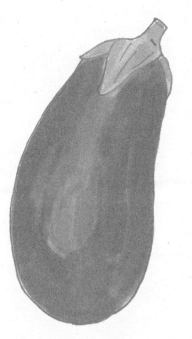

Health Note

FOR ADDED DEPTH OF FLAVOR, DRY-TOAST 1 TEASPOON WHOLE CUMIN SEEDS, THEN GRIND AND ADD INSTEAD OF THE 1 TEASPOON REGULAR GROUND CUMIN.

Spinach Dip

As a dip, you'll want to serve this with plenty of sliced fresh vegetables. Also try spreading it onto a whole-grain tortilla, then grate some carrots and slice some celery, red bell peppers, tomatoes, and anything else you like, and wrap up. You can even cut the wrap into small slices and serve as an appetizer or lunch sushi roll–style.

YIELDS 1½ CUPS

One half of 12-ounce package silken tofu

2 teaspoons lime zest

¼ cup fresh lime juice

1½ teaspoons Dijon mustard

1 teaspoon sugar or agave nectar

½ teaspoon sea salt

½ teaspoon black pepper

10 ounces frozen spinach, thawed, drained, and squeezed dry

⅔ cup chopped red onions or scallions

In a food processor, purée the silken tofu, lime zest, lime juice, mustard, sugar, salt, and pepper. Process until smooth.

Add the spinach and purée, then add onions and pulse until blended but not puréed.

PER SERVING (4 TABLESPOONS): 38 CALORIES; 1G FAT (24.8% CALORIES FROM FAT); 3G PROTEIN; 5G CARBOHYDRATE; 2G DIETARY FIBER; 0MG CHOLESTEROL; 211MG SODIUM.

Health Note

TOFU IS A VERY GOOD SOURCE OF PROTEIN, CALCIUM (FORTIFIED), AND IRON. IT IS ALSO HIGH IN TRYPTOPHAN, AN ESSENTIAL AMINO ACID THAT IS A BUILDING BLOCK OF PROTEIN, AND MANGANESE, A TRACE MINERAL THAT WORKS WITH MANY ENZYME SYSTEMS IN YOUR BODY.

Red Pepper "Cheese" Dip

When Patty's son Russell sampled this dip for the first time at age 12, he immediately asked for more "cheese" dip. There's no dairy in this recipe—it's the nutritional yeast that gives it the cheesy flavor! For a richer flavor, you may roast the red peppers if you like.

YIELDS 2½ CUPS

1 medium red bell pepper, washed and seeded

1½ cups raw cashews

¼ cup sesame seeds

½ cup water

⅓ cup nutritional yeast

¼ cup freshly squeezed lemon juice

1 tablespoon soy sauce

Blend all ingredients in a blender until smooth, about 3–4 minutes. Put in a bowl, cover, and place in the refrigerator until it's set, about 2 hours. Serve cold or at room temperature with sliced veggies or as a sandwich spread.

PER SERVING (ABOUT ⅓ CUP): 170 CALORIES; 14G FAT (67.7% CALORIES FROM FAT); 5G PROTEIN; 10G CARBOHYDRATE; 2G DIETARY FIBER; 0MG CHOLESTEROL; 135MG SODIUM.

Cooking Tip

IF YOU REMEMBER, SOAK THE RAW CASHEWS IN COLD WATER FOR 30 MINUTES OR LONGER, THEN DRAIN. THIS SOFTENS THEM, MAKING THEM EASIER TO BLEND.

Health Note

NUTRITIONAL YEAST (NOT TO BE CONFUSED WITH BREWER'S YEAST) IS AN EXCELLENT SOURCE OF B-VITAMINS AND AMINO ACIDS. NEXT TIME YOU MAKE POPCORN, SPRINKLE ON SOME OLIVE OIL, NUTRITIONAL YEAST, MINCED FRESH GARLIC OR GARLIC POWDER, SEA SALT, AND A PINCH OF CAYENNE PEPPER. EVERYONE LOVES THE WONDERFUL FLAVORS! WE WISH ALL MOVIE THEATERS WOULD CONVERT!

Chapter 6
Salads and Dressings

Salads are an excellent way to add more vegetables, please (MVP) to your diet. Salads are so versatile and nutritious; serve them for lunch, dinner, or even as a snack. A salad doesn't need to be anything but some beautiful fresh greens, a few seasonal and colorful vegetables, and fresh herbs or flower petals (make sure they're edible!). Add kidney or garbanzo beans for added flavor and protein. Then, all can be easily tossed with a little lemon juice and olive or flaxseed oil. Fresh green salads are the epitome of health.

There are two main types of salads: tossed and composed. A composed salad is one in which the ingredients are artfully arranged on a platter or plate and the dressing is drizzled on top. One famous example is *salade niçoise*, which consists of potatoes, green beans, hard-boiled eggs, anchovies, and tuna layered beautifully on a plate, drizzled with vinaigrette, and topped with, of course, niçoise olives. Keep in mind that in your version, you might toss the ingredients and then compose the salad, which is perfectly fine. For those with children, have them "compose" the salad—they'll love it!

A tossed salad is just that: greens and veggies—grains and beans, too—tossed together in a bit of dressing and served. If you are using heavier pieces of vegetables, mix them separately and place them on top of the salad. Be sure to choose the freshest seasonal greens you can and eat a wide variety of these greens for good health. There are many types with different flavors, and very few people have any reactions to leafy greens or green vegetables; thus, they can be plentiful in your diet.

Be sure to wash your lettuce well. If you have picked spinach out of the garden, it is often very dirty and may need to be washed several times. Place the spinach in a sink (use less water by not filling the sink too full) or in a large bowl of water and move the greens around with your hands. Lift out the spinach and you will see that most of the dirt is in the bottom of the bowl.

A salad spinner works quite nicely to dry your greens. Spinners don't operate as well when they're too full, so spin in batches if necessary. Also, empty the water out of the spinner occasionally. You can roll up your greens in a flour sack–type towel and store in the refrigerator or in a sealed plastic bag (though we are trying to use less plastic).

To make preparing and serving salads simple for you, we have included a salad dressing recipe for almost every salad in this chapter. This is not to say you can't mix and match, but sometimes you want someone else to decide for you—so we have. On the other hand, if you're feeling adventurous, use the Salad Seasonings list on page 95 to come up with your own dressing!

Eating Seasonally

Spring and Summer:	BABY SPINACH, ARUGULA, BUTTER LETTUCE, RED AND GREEN OAK LEAF, MÂCHE, ROMAINE, BEET GREENS, DANDELION GREENS, RAW KALE, AND CHARD
Autumn and Winter:	ESCAROLE (DID YOU KNOW YOU CAN LIGHTLY GRILL IT?), RADICCHIO, ENDIVE, FRISÉE, AND MIXED LETTUCES (IN MOST AREAS)

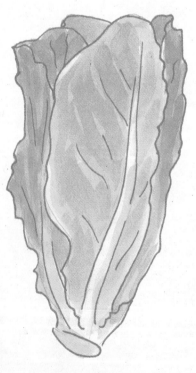

SEASONINGS FOR SALADS

Here is a summary of common spices and flavorings that go with various vegetables, greens, fruits, and meats typically found in salads. Add some olive oil and vinegar to these spices, and you're good to go! Keep in mind that these spice combinations are just as tasty in cooked dishes as well:

ASPARAGUS: marjoram, orange or other citrus, dill

AVOCADO: dill seed, oregano, garlic, chiles, lemon or lime

BEAN: oregano, summer savory, cumin, bay

BEET: caraway seed, chervil, green dill, thyme, garlic

CARROT: celery seed, ginger, dill

CELERY: fennel seed, mint, green onions

CHICKEN: basil, chives, marjoram, saffron, tarragon, thyme, curry, parsley

COLESLAW: caraway seed, chervil, chives, green dill, mint, mustard seed, tarragon, thyme, ginger

CUCUMBER: basil, chervil, chives, green dill

FRUIT, MIXED: basil, chervil, cinnamon, ginger, marjoram, mint, nutmeg, parsley, rosemary, tarragon

GREENS, MIXED: chervil, coriander, fennel seed, marjoram, oregano, parsley, summer savory, tarragon, basil, mint

ORANGE: cardamom

PEAR: cardamom, nutmeg, poppy seed

POTATO: celery seed, chives, dill seed, green dill, mustard, parsley, sesame seed, summer savory, curry

SEAFOOD: basil, celery seed, chives, fennel seed, green dill, marjoram, oregano, parsley, saffron, tarragon

SPINACH OR KALE: basil, chives, marjoram, garlic

TOMATO: basil, chervil, chives, parsley, summer savory, thyme

TUNA: celery seed, chives, marjoram, onions, pickles

VEGETABLES, MIXED: green dill, celery seed, chives, parsley, summer savory

Arugula, Beet, and Sunflower Seed Salad

This is a beautiful, delicious salad with ingredients seasonal in the fall and early winter. A little of the creamy dressing goes a long way, so you can go light when you drizzle it on. If you have dairy allergies, use the Basic Vinaigrette (page 108) or Mustard Vinaigrette (page 102) instead.

SERVES 4

8 cups washed and dried arugula leaves

1 cup grated raw beets

1 peeled and segmented tangerine

½ cup toasted sunflower seeds

Buttermilk and
Blue Cheese Dressing

YIELDS APPROXIMATELY 1 CUP

⅔ cup buttermilk

¼ cup crumbled blue cheese

Dash of sea salt

⅛ teaspoon freshly ground black pepper

Divide arugula into 4 servings and place each on a small plate. Place freshly grated raw beets in a mound on the arugula and then arrange the tangerine segments around the mound of beets.

To make the dressing: Place buttermilk, blue cheese, salt, and pepper in a jar and shake well. Yields 1 cup.

Drizzle each salad with some Buttermilk and Blue Cheese Dressing and sprinkle with toasted sunflower seeds.

PER SERVING (SALAD): 136 CALORIES; 10G FAT (66.2% CALORIES FROM FAT); 6G PROTEIN; 11G CARBOHYDRATE; 3G DIETARY FIBER; TRACE CHOLESTEROL; 38MG SODIUM.

PER SERVING (DRESSING, ¼ CUP): 42 CALORIES; 2G FAT (51.7% CALORIES FROM FAT); 3G PROTEIN; 2G CARBOHYDRATE; TRACE DIETARY FIBER; 7MG CHOLESTEROL; 201MG SODIUM.

Health Note

BEETS ARE AN EXCELLENT SOURCE OF FOLATE, IRON, POTASSIUM, VITAMIN C, AND DIETARY FIBER. RAW BEETS ARE DELICIOUS, AS ARE BEET GREENS. TRY MIXING RAW GRATED BEETS WITH GRATED APPLES AND A BIT OF FRESH GINGER. DRIZZLE WITH OLIVE OIL AND A LITTLE RICE WINE VINEGAR FOR A DELICIOUS SALAD.

Cooking Tip

BUY SUNFLOWER SEEDS (OR ANY NUTS AND SEEDS FOR THAT MATTER) RAW AND TOAST THEM YOURSELF. SIMPLY PLACE THEM IN A SMALL SKILLET AND HEAT ON LOW, UNTIL LIGHTLY BROWNED, STIRRING FREQUENTLY. IF YOU BUY THEM ALREADY ROASTED, YOU DON'T KNOW WHAT KIND OF OIL THEY HAVE BEEN ROASTED IN.

Southwestern Caesar Salad

Always a kid's favorite, this salad is a winner. Kids love to cut the tortillas into strips. Be sure to toast your own pumpkin seeds (see Cooking Tip for previous recipe). If you have fresh corn, you can use it raw; just slice the kernels off the cob.

SERVES 8

3 hearts romaine lettuce, washed and dried

6 corn tortillas

¼ cup extra-virgin olive oil

1 tomato, sliced

½ cup grated cheddar cheese

1 avocado, peeled and sliced

½ cup roasted pumpkin seeds

½ cup fresh corn

⅓ cup diced jicama

Dressing

2 to 3 cloves garlic

1 lemon, juiced

1 teaspoon Dijon mustard

1 teaspoon chili powder (for dressing), plus 1 teaspoon more (for strips)

½ cup extra-virgin olive oil

Chop and place the romaine lettuce in a large salad bowl; refrigerate until needed.

To make the dressing: Whisk together the garlic, lemon juice, mustard, and 1 teaspoon of the chili powder in a small bowl. Continue whisking while you slowly pour in a thin stream of ½ cup of the oil. You may use a blender instead of a whisk if you like, slowly adding the oil.

Cut the corn tortillas into thin strips and toss with remaining ¼ cup oil and the remaining 1 teaspoon chili powder. Bake at 350°F for 15–20 minutes or sauté in a skillet until lightly golden.

Dress the salad and toss well. Garnish with tomatoes, cheese, avocado, pumpkin seeds, corn, jicama, and tortillas. Toss again and serve immediately.

PER SERVING (SALAD): 161 CALORIES; 6.5G FAT (36.5% CALORIES FROM FAT); 10G PROTEIN; 24G CARBOHYDRATE; 8G DIETARY FIBER; 7MG CHOLESTEROL; 117MG SODIUM.

PER SERVING (DRESSING): 23 CALORIES; 2.5G FAT (96.5% CALORIES FROM FAT); TRACE PROTEIN; TRACE CARBOHYDRATE; TRACE DIETARY FIBER; 0MG CHOLESTEROL; 1.8MG SODIUM.

Cooking Tip

IF YOU'D PREFER TO USE LESS OIL, YOU COULD BUY A NONAEROSOL PUMP SPRAYER AND SPRAY THE TORTILLAS WITH JUST A FEW TEASPOONS OF OLIVE OIL. THEY ARE AVAILABLE AT WILLIAMS-SONOMA AND OTHER COOKWARE RETAILERS. YOU SIMPLY OPEN THE SPRAYER AND PUT IN YOUR CHOICE OF OIL, PLACE THE LID BACK ON, PUMP (WHICH BUILDS UP THE PRESSURE INSIDE), AND THEN SPRAY! AEROSOL SPRAYS ARE NOT GOOD FOR THE EARTH'S ATMOSPHERE.

Cobb Salad with Carrot-Ginger Dressing

Two of Patty's favorite restaurants in New York are Joy Pierson and Bart Potenza's The Candle Cafe and Candle 79. This recipe is adapted from their wonderful book, *The Candle Cafe Cookbook*. This is a terrific salad for special guests. We like to sprinkle the top with chopped kalamata olives, sliced tempeh bacon, and perhaps some croutons. For those who eat cheese, a little bleu cheese is nice sprinkled on top.

SERVES 4

1 pound firm tofu, cubed

4 tablespoons chopped fresh parsley
(or 2 tablespoons chopped fresh parsley
plus 1 tablespoon chopped fresh basil
and 1 tablespoon chopped fresh dill)

6 scallions, sliced

1 tablespoon miso

⅓ cup tahini

1 teaspoon sea salt

½ teaspoon black pepper

2 teaspoons fresh lemon juice

½ cup shredded carrots

2 stalks celery, sliced

6 shiitake mushrooms, sliced, sautéed
in a little oil or steamed, and cooled

4 handfuls lettuce, spring mix,
or mesclun

2 medium tomatoes, quartered

Toasted sunflower seeds,
for garnish (optional)

Carrot-Ginger Dressing

YIELDS 3 CUPS

2 cups grated carrots

¼ cup freshly grated ginger

3 cloves garlic, chopped

¼ cup chopped red onion

2 tablespoons apple juice

1½ teaspoons toasted sesame oil

1 cup sunflower oil
(or sesame oil, not toasted)

½ cup apple cider vinegar

Blanch the tofu (see "Blanch or Parboil," page 52) for 1 minute and drain.

In a medium bowl, place the fresh herbs, scallions, miso, tahini, salt, pepper, and lemon juice. Mix well and fold in tofu, carrots, celery, and cooked mushrooms.

Wash and dry lettuce, then place on a large platter. In the center place the tofu mixture and place the quartered tomatoes around the edge.

To make the dressing: Grate the carrots by hand or in a food processor. In a food processor, place the carrots, ginger, garlic, and onions and process until finely chopped. Add the apple juice, sesame oil, sunflower oil, and vinegar and blend until well combined.

Drizzle dressing onto composed salad and sprinkle with toasted sunflowers seeds and any other additions you might like. So beautiful! This dressing will keep in the refrigerator for up to 10 days.

PER SERVING (SALAD): 275 CALORIES; 17G FAT (50.5% CALORIES FROM FAT); 16G PROTEIN; 22G CARBOHYDRATE; 7G DIETARY FIBER; 0MG CHOLESTEROL; 702MG SODIUM.

PER SERVING (DRESSING, 4 TABLESPOONS): 181 CALORIES; 18G FAT (88.5% CALORIES FROM FAT); TRACE PROTEIN; 5G CARBOHYDRATE; 1G DIETARY FIBER; 0MG CHOLESTEROL; 9MG SODIUM.

The Best Kale Salad Ever

This is one of Patty's favorite salads. In the summer, slice some beautiful tomatoes and serve this salad on top of them. You can also stuff pita bread with this salad. Delicious! And if you have kids, ask them to wash their hands and then do the mixing.

SERVES 6

2 bunches washed and dried kale

2 tablespoons fresh lemon juice

1 whole ripe avocado, peeled and chopped

½ medium red onion, chopped

1 medium apple, cored and chopped

2 teaspoons minced fresh garlic

2 teaspoons peeled and grated fresh ginger

2 tablespoons extra-virgin olive oil

2 teaspoons tamari or Bragg Liquid Aminos

½ cup raw, chopped cashews

Remove the large stems and then chop the kale; place in large bowl. Add lemon juice and avocado. With your hands, mix together until the avocado is smooth. Add the remaining ingredients and mix well. Serve immediately.

PER SERVING: 190 CALORIES; 15G FAT (66.6% CALORIES FROM FAT); 4G PROTEIN; 13G CARBOHYDRATE; 3G DIETARY FIBER; 0MG CHOLESTEROL; 127MG SODIUM.

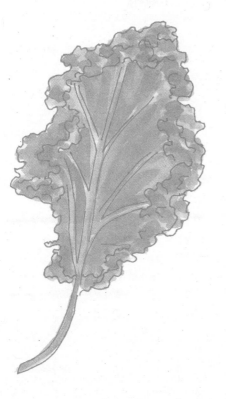

Health Note ♥

LEAFY GREEN VEGETABLES ARE WONDER FOODS. WE WOULD ALL BE SO MUCH HEALTHIER IF WE ATE DARK GREEN LEAFY GREENS EVERY DAY. KALE IS HIGH IN VITAMINS K, A, AND C AS WELL AS AN EXCELLENT SOURCE OF MANGANESE AND DIETARY FIBER. KALE IS THOUGHT TO BE PROTECTIVE AGAINST CERTAIN TYPES OF CANCER SUCH AS LUNG, COLON, BLADDER, BREAST, AND OVARIAN.

Spicy-Sweet Lime Slaw

Even people who don't like "regular" coleslaw like this recipe, a modified version of Dr. Ed Bauman's of Bauman College. The sweetness of the dates and the tang of the limes are so refreshing. Remember to zest the lime before juicing. Another time try adding raw, grated kohlrabi.

SERVES 12

1 medium green cabbage, finely shredded

½ medium red cabbage, finely shredded

4 medium carrots, grated

6 radishes, thinly sliced

½ cup toasted and chopped almonds

½ cup minced cilantro

Dressing

⅓ cup water

4 limes, juiced

1 tablespoon lime zest

¾ cup mayonnaise or nondairy mayonnaise

1 teaspoon seeded and minced jalapeño

4 cloves garlic, minced

3 to 4 dates, pitted and chopped

Sea salt to taste

Freshly ground black pepper to taste

Toss the cabbages, carrots, and radishes in a large bowl.

To make the dressing: In a blender combine the water, lime juice, lime zest, mayonnaise, jalapeño, garlic, and dates; blend well. Taste the dressing and add salt and pepper if you like. Toss with the slaw mixture.

Stir in the almonds and cilantro or sprinkle on the top.

PER SERVING (SALAD): 77 CALORIES; 3G FAT (35% CALORIES FROM FAT); 3G PROTEIN; 11G CARBOHYDRATE; 3G DIETARY FIBER; 0MG CHOLESTEROL; 27MG SODIUM.

PER SERVING (DRESSING): 112 CALORIES; 12G FAT (85.1% CALORIES FROM FAT); TRACE PROTEIN; 4G CARBOHYDRATE; TRACE DIETARY FIBER; 5MG CHOLESTEROL; 79MG SODIUM.

Health Note

CABBAGE IS A MEMBER OF THE CANCER-FIGHTING CRUCIFEROUS FAMILY, ALONG WITH KALE, BROCCOLI, CAULIFLOWER, AND BRUSSELS SPROUTS. IT IS VERY HIGH IN VITAMINS K AND C. CABBAGE IS ALSO AN EXCELLENT SOURCE OF DIETARY FIBER.

Asparagus Salad with Orange Vinaigrette

You know it's spring when you see asparagus at your farmer's market! Present this salad as is, or place on a butter lettuce leaf or some fresh spinach leaves and garnish with thinly sliced carrots and orange wedges. This may be served cold or at room temperature. Asparagus is high in vitamins K, A, and C as well as folate and dietary fiber.

SERVES 2

½ pound asparagus, cut into 1" pieces

Orange Vinaigrette

1 tablespoon freshly squeezed orange or lemon juice

½ teaspoon white wine vinegar

½ teaspoon Dijon mustard

1 clove garlic, minced

½ teaspoon honey

2 teaspoons orange or lemon zest

¼ cup toasted sesame oil

1 teaspoon whole cumin seeds, toasted and ground

Sea salt to taste

Black pepper to taste

Place a steamer into a pot of water and bring to a boil. Add the asparagus pieces and steam 2–3 minutes or until al dente. Plunge into ice water to stop cooking. Drain and cool in the refrigerator.

To make the dressing: In a small bowl, combine the orange juice, vinegar, mustard, garlic, honey, and zest. Whisk in the oil. Stir in the cumin.

Immediately before serving, drizzle the vinaigrette over the asparagus pieces. Season with salt and pepper if desired.

PER SERVING: 273 CALORIES; 28G FAT (88.2% CALORIES FROM FAT); 2G PROTEIN; 7G CARBOHYDRATE; 1G DIETARY FIBER; 0MG CHOLESTEROL; 19MG SODIUM.

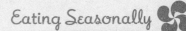

Eating Seasonally

Summer and Early Autumn:
TRY THIS RECIPE USING GREEN BEANS.

Edamame Salad with Mustard Vinaigrette

This salad is as easy to make as it is good.

SERVES 6

1 pound edamame, frozen and shelled

1 cup thinly sliced red onion

½ cup chopped celery

1 tablespoon minced fresh parsley, stems removed

Mustard Vinaigrette

1½ tablespoons brown rice vinegar

1 teaspoon Dijon mustard

½ teaspoon sea salt

1 tablespoon flax oil or extra-virgin olive oil

Cook frozen edamame in boiling water for 3–4 minutes. Drain well.

To make the dressing: Combine vinegar, mustard, and salt in a medium bowl. Add the oil, stirring with a whisk. Add edamame to bowl. Add onion, celery, and vinaigrette and toss well to coat. Stir in parsley and serve.

PER SERVING: 272 CALORIES; 1G FAT (4.1% CALORIES FROM FAT); 19G PROTEIN; 49G CARBOHYDRATE; 20G DIETARY FIBER; 0MG CHOLESTEROL; 196MG SODIUM.

Arame Salad

Think of arame—and all edible seaweeds for that matter—as the herbs of our great oceans. This nutritious salad has a warm, toasty flavor. You can enhance that flavor by sprinkling a little gomasio (see page 63) on top.

SERVES 8

1¾ ounces arame

2 tablespoons brown-rice vinegar

2 teaspoons toasted sesame oil

1 red bell pepper, diced

1 bunch scallions, diced

1 tablespoon sesame seeds, toasted

Soak the arame for 15 minutes in cold water and drain well. In a bowl, combine the vinegar and oil. Add the arame, vegetables, and sesame seeds and toss to coat. Serve immediately.

PER SERVING: 12 CALORIES; 1G FAT (40.5% CALORIES FROM FAT); TRACE PROTEIN; 2G CARBOHYDRATE; TRACE DIETARY FIBER; 0MG CHOLESTEROL; 1MG SODIUM.

To Soy or Not to Soy?

Soybeans, or edamame, are a great protein source, contain B-vitamins, healthy fats, and dietary fiber, and contain no cholesterol. They also contain phytoestrogens that can both support or disrupt endocrine function, so soymilk for babies is not a good choice. Other research has found that high levels of phytic acid in soy reduce assimilation of calcium, magnesium, copper, iron, and zinc, and they may affect the assimilation of the thyroid hormone, especially for those who are taking hormone replacement. Phytic acid is, however, reduced by the fermentation process, so soy products like tempeh or miso are the healthiest soy choices. That being said, edamame in moderation is a healthy food.

Potato Salad

Everyone's favorite barbecue salad has been reinvigorated
with the addition of fresh herbs.

SERVES 6

5 cups cubed red potatoes, boiled until al
dente and drained

¼ cup Mustard Vinaigrette (page 102) or
Basic Vinaigrette (page 108)

½ cup chopped celery

½ cup minced red onion

2 hard-boiled eggs, chopped

2 tablespoons minced dill pickle

1 tablespoon chopped fresh parsley,
stems removed

1 tablespoon chopped fresh dill

⅓ cup mayonnaise (optional)

2 teaspoons mustard (optional)

½ teaspoon sea salt

½ teaspoon black pepper

Let the warm potatoes marinate in the
vinaigrette in a large bowl for an hour or
so. Add the remaining ingredients (leave
out the 2 teaspoons mustard if you're using
the mustard vinaigrette) and toss gently.

PER SERVING: 265 CALORIES; 17G FAT (56.4% CALO-
RIES FROM FAT); 5G PROTEIN; 25G CARBOHYDRATE; 3G
DIETARY FIBER; 67MG CHOLESTEROL; 325MG SODIUM.

Variations

YOU CAN ADD SO MANY MORE VEGETA-
BLES TO THIS SALAD IF YOU LIKE: RAW OR
STEAMED BROCCOLI, CHOPPED SPINACH
LEAVES, PEAS, GRATED CARROTS, AND
SUNFLOWER SPROUTS. YOU MAY LEAVE
THE MAYONNAISE OUT ALTOGETHER AND
ADD A BIT OF OLIVE OIL.

Health Nut Brown Rice Salad

Patty's favorite rice to use in this recipe is long grain brown basmati rice. But you may also use farro, the ancient Italian grain. This is a great dish as a main course served on top of a lettuce leaf, or you can serve with grilled fish, chicken, tempeh, or tofu. Try using roasted red bell peppers for added depth of flavor. You may also add black beans if you like; beans and rice together have all the amino acids to make a complete protein.

SERVES 8

3 cups cooked and cooled long-grain brown rice (see Cooking Tip)

⅓ cup sliced almonds

⅓ cup sunflower seeds

1 tablespoon sesame seeds

½ cup shredded carrots

½ cup sliced celery

½ cup chopped red bell pepper

3 tablespoons Basic Vinaigrette (page 108), or to taste

2 tablespoons chopped fresh parsley, stems removed

Place the brown rice in a medium bowl. Lightly toast the almonds and add to the brown rice along with the sunflower and sesame seeds, carrots, celery, and bell pepper. Pour vinaigrette over all and toss. Top with the parsley and serve.

PER SERVING: 368 CALORIES; 12G FAT (28.0% CALORIES FROM FAT); 8G PROTEIN; 59G CARBOHYDRATE; 3G DIETARY FIBER; 0MG CHOLESTEROL; 14MG SODIUM.

Cooking Tip

TO MAKE 3 CUPS COOKED BROWN RICE, BRING 2 CUPS WATER, ½ TEASPOON SEA SALT, AND 1 TEASPOON OF OLIVE OIL TO A BOIL IN A MEDIUM SAUCEPAN. ADD 1 CUP BROWN RICE AND STIR. BRING BACK TO A BOIL, COVER, AND TURN THE HEAT TO A SIMMER. BROWN RICE TAKES ABOUT 45 MINUTES TO COOK. NEVER STIR THE RICE WHEN IT'S SIMMERING OR IT WILL GET GUMMY.

Eating Seasonally

PRACTICE EATING SEASONALLY BY ADDING ANY OF THE VEGETABLES BELOW, OR SUBSTITUTING THEM FOR THE MAIN INGREDIENTS IN THIS SALAD, DEPENDING ON THE TIME OF YEAR.

Spring: PEAS, RADISHES, SUGAR PEAS, GREEN GARLIC, GREEN ONIONS

Summer: CHERRY TOMATOES, CORN, ZUCCHINI, CUCUMBERS, BASIL

Autumn: DAIKON RADISHES, COOKED YAMS, BROCCOLI

Winter: WINTER SQUASHES, BROCCOLI, CAULIFLOWER

Pasta Salad

You certainly don't need a recipe for pasta salad—these salads are so simple to make and the variations are infinite. But here are our basic guidelines to get you—and your children, since this is a great way to build their confidence and creativity in the kitchen—going. Have fun!

SERVES 4–6

5–6 cups of your favorite chopped seasonal vegetables

8 ounces of your favorite pasta, uncooked

Buttermilk and Blue Cheese Dressing (page 96), Carrot-Ginger Dressing (page 98), or Basic Vinaigrette (page 108)

Your favorite garnishes (olives, chopped fresh parsley, chopped red bell pepper, toasted sunflower seeds or pine nuts, cheese, etc.)

White beans (optional)

Chop, slice, and/or dice your favorite vegetables. Lightly steam some of them and leave others raw. Place in a large bowl.

Cook your favorite pasta according to the directions. Add the cooked pasta to vegetables. Add dressing and toss all together, then sprinkle with your favorite accoutrements. Add white beans to the salad for additional protein and fiber, if you like.

Zesty Marinated Vegetables

This salad makes a very beautiful presentation, leaving a lasting impression on both the eyes and the taste buds. Because the veggies are blanched they retain their colors and are fresh tasting. Kids really like to help out with this salad; older kids can cut the veggies and younger children can shake the dressing. This marinade is also very good as a dressing on fish, poultry, or tempeh; place the marinade ingredients in a jar and shake!

Serves 6

2 cups bite-size broccoli florets

2 cups bite-size cauliflower florets

2 cups sliced carrots

2 tablespoons extra-virgin olive oil

1 large red bell pepper, cut into ½" cubes

Lettuce leaves (optional)

Zesty Marinade

¼ cup rice wine vinegar

3 tablespoons soy sauce

2 tablespoons fresh lemon or orange juice

2 cloves garlic, minced

5½ teaspoons peeled and minced or grated fresh ginger

½ teaspoon honey or agave nectar

Bring 10 cups of water to a boil in a large pot. Add the broccoli, cauliflower, and carrots. Blanch for 1 minute. Remove and plunge into ice water (or very cold water), then drain immediately. Toss with oil and let cool.

To make the marinade: In a small bowl, mix together the vinegar, soy sauce, lemon juice, garlic, ginger, and honey.

Add marinade and bell pepper to cooled vegetables. Marinate for a few hours or up to 24 hours. Serve on lettuce leaves if desired.

Per serving: 90 calories; 5g fat (43.7% calories from fat); 3g protein; 11g carbohydrate; 3g dietary fiber; 0mg cholesterol; 546mg sodium.

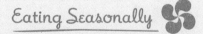

Eating Seasonally

Practice eating seasonally by adding any of the vegetables below, or substituting them for the main ingredients in this recipe, depending on the time of year.

Spring: Asparagus, carrots

Summer: Asparagus, carrots, jicama, green beans, tomatoes, zucchini, red bell pepper

Autumn and Winter: All of the above are often available in autumn, plus butternut or other winter squashes

Basic Vinaigrette

Most people have their own recipe for what they consider their best vinaigrette. This one is Patty's. It's excellent tossed with salad greens or vegetables, or as a marinade. Feel free to change the fresh herbs with the seasons. For example, in the summer use fresh basil and in the winter use fresh parsley.

YIELDS 1 CUP

1 teaspoon Dijon mustard

⅓ cup white wine vinegar (or your favorite vinegar)

½ teaspoon sea salt

½ teaspoon black pepper

⅔ cup extra-virgin olive oil or flaxseed oil (or a combination thereof)

1 tablespoon minced fresh tarragon

Place mustard, vinegar, salt, and pepper in a bowl. Slowly whisk in oil. Add tarragon and serve!

PER SERVING (ABOUT 1½ TABLESPOONS): 130 CALORIES; 14G FAT (97.1% CALORIES FROM FAT); TRACE PROTEIN; 1G CARBOHYDRATE; TRACE DIETARY FIBER; 0MG CHOLESTEROL; 101MG SODIUM.

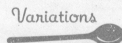

Variations

USING WHITE BALSAMIC VINEGAR IS ALSO A TERRIFIC OPTION IN PLACE OF THE WHITE WINE VINEGAR. YOU MAY ALSO USE LEMON OR ORANGE JUICE (TRY A BLOOD ORANGE SOMETIME). TRY ADDING 1–2 TEASPOONS TOASTED SESAME OIL. ALSO, ADD 1 CLOVE GARLIC, MINCED.

Cooking Tip

REMEMBER THAT IF YOU USE FLAXSEED OIL IN THIS RECIPE DO NOT HEAT THE DRESSING AS A MARINADE, AS FLAXSEED OIL IS EASILY DAMAGED BY HEAT.

Avocado Dressing

This hearty dressing is very versatile. It can be used with the Zesty Marinated Vegetables (page 107), on other firmer salads, and as a dip, much like a variation of guacamole. It's too heavy a dressing for light spring lettuces but works well for heartier fare. Also try it on a baked potato or spread it on a sandwich.

YIELDS 1 CUP

1 medium tomato, or ¼ cup salsa (page 75)

Juice of 1 large lemon

¼ cup water

1 large avocado, peeled

2 cloves garlic, coarsely chopped

2 tablespoons chopped fresh parsley, stems removed

2 tablespoons chopped fresh cilantro, stems removed.

1 teaspoon miso (optional)

Sea salt to taste

Black pepper to taste

Place all of the ingredients except salt and pepper into a blender and blend until smooth. Add salt and pepper if needed. You may add a little water if it's too thick.

PER SERVING (¼ CUP): 96 CALORIES; 8G FAT (65.4% CALORIES FROM FAT); 2G PROTEIN; 8G CARBOHYDRATE; 2G DIETARY FIBER; 0MG CHOLESTEROL; 62MG SODIUM.

Chipotle Dressing

This dressing is wonderful on a taco salad, baked potato, or potato salad. Give it a try on a sandwich, as a dip for veggies, or on the Health Nut Brown Rice Salad (page 105).

YIELDS 2 CUPS

½ pound silken tofu

¼ cup sunflower or olive oil

1 tablespoon nutritional yeast

2 tablespoons drained capers

1½ tablespoons lemon juice

1 teaspoon honey or agave nectar

1 tablespoon apple cider vinegar

1 whole chipotle chile canned in adobo, or to taste (start with ½ chile if you prefer)

3 tablespoons chopped red onion

½ teaspoon sea salt

½ teaspoon black pepper

½ teaspoon chili powder

½ teaspoon paprika

3 cloves garlic, minced

Place all ingredients in a blender or food processor and blend until smooth.

PER SERVING (¼ CUP): 90 CALORIES; 8G FAT (78.1% CALORIES FROM FAT); 3G PROTEIN; 3G CARBOHYDRATE; 1G DIETARY FIBER; TRACE CHOLESTEROL; 152MG SODIUM.

Creamy Lemon-Ginger Dressing

Flax oil contains the essential building blocks for both omega-6 and omega-3 fatty acids. Do not heat this dressing, as the mild-flavored healthy oil can be easily damaged. It's excellent, however, as a dressing for lettuce or vegetable salads or drizzled cold onto fish or chicken.

YIELDS 6–8 OUNCES

2 teaspoons ginger juice

3 tablespoons lemon juice

3 tablespoons extra-virgin olive oil

3 tablespoons flax oil

2 tablespoons water

½ teaspoon sea salt

4 ounces soft tofu

2 tablespoons minced scallions or shallots

Place all ingredients except the scallions in a blender and blend until smooth and creamy. Add the scallions and mix well.

PER SERVING (2 TABLESPOOONS): 102 CALORIES; 6G FAT (92% CALORIES FROM FAT); 1G PROTEIN; 1G CARBOHYDRATE; TRACE DIETARY FIBER; 0MG CHOLESTEROL; 236MG SODIUM.

Cooking Tip

GINGER JUICE CAN BE BOUGHT, BUT IT'S RATHER EXPENSIVE. AN ALTERNATIVE IS TO JUICE GINGER ROOT USING A JUICER, IF YOU HAVE ONE. OR YOU CAN ALSO PRESS A LITTLE RAW GINGER ROOT WITH A GARLIC PRESS. IF YOU HAVE ANY JUICE LEFT OVER, ADD A FEW DROPS TO MINERAL WATER TO MAKE A VERSION OF GINGER AID. IT'S VERY REFRESHING.

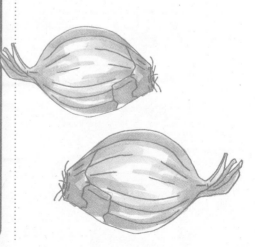

Chinese Chicken Salad with Mandarin Dressing

This is an excellent summer salad and a favorite with adults and children alike. Patty has been making this recipe for so many years that she can't recall its origins. The dressing can be used as a marinade for fish, chicken, or tempeh.

SERVES 4

1/3 cup chopped almonds

1 pound shiitake mushrooms, sliced

2 tablespoons extra-virgin olive oil

1 head Napa cabbage

1 cup sliced scallions

1 cup fresh snow pea pods

1 cup bean sprouts

1 cup water chestnuts

1 pound boneless, skinless chicken breasts, cooked and shredded or cubed

1/2 cup total sliced red and/or green bell peppers (optional)

Mandarin Dressing

YIELDS 1½ CUPS

1/2 cup rice wine vinegar

3 tablespoons toasted sesame oil

1 tablespoon soy sauce

6 ounces frozen concentrate pineapple juice

1 tablespoon peeled and freshly grated ginger

2 cloves garlic, minced

1/4 teaspoon red pepper flakes

Toast almonds until golden; set aside.

Sauté mushrooms in a bit of oil; set aside.

Shred cabbage and place in a large bowl with scallions, pea pods, sprouts, water chestnuts, and chicken.

To make the dressing: Combine all dressing ingredients and mix well. Refrigerate any leftover dressing.

Add dressing to bowl of vegetables and toss well. Place in salad bowls, topped with almonds. You may place the sliced bell peppers on top of the salad if you like.

PER SERVING (SALAD): 598 CALORIES; 16G FAT (21.4% CALORIES FROM FAT); 34G PROTEIN; 95G CARBOHYDRATE; 17G DIETARY FIBER; 58MG CHOLESTEROL; 84MG SODIUM.

PER SERVING (DRESSING): 72 CALORIES; 4G FAT (49.8% CALORIES FROM FAT); TRACE PROTEIN; 9G CARBOHYDRATE; TRACE DIETARY FIBER; 0MG CHOLESTEROL; 104MG SODIUM.

Health Note ♥

ALMONDS CONTAIN HEART-HEALTHY FATS, B-VITAMINS, AND A SIGNIFICANT AMOUNT OF VITAMIN E AS WELL AS MAGNESIUM, COPPER, ZINC, POTASSIUM, AND IRON!

Mediterranean Tuna Salad

Don't you love delicious, healthy recipes that have only one line of directions? To serve, place a lettuce leaf on a plate and mound the tuna salad on top. Or try stuffing it into pita bread or inside a slightly hollowed-out tomato.

SERVES 4

2 cans (6 ounces each) tuna, drained

One half of a 14-ounce can water-packed artichoke hearts, drained and chopped

¼ cup finely chopped red bell pepper

⅓ cup sliced Kalamata olives

¼ cup minced red onion

1 tablespoon chopped fresh parsley, stems removed

1 tablespoon chopped fresh basil

1 clove garlic, minced

½ teaspoon dried oregano, or 1½ teaspoons fresh oregano

1½ tablespoons fresh lemon juice

⅓ cup mayonnaise

Freshly ground black pepper to taste

Combine all ingredients in a medium bowl; mix together well.

PER SERVING: 339 CALORIES; 25G FAT (64.3% CALORIES FROM FAT); 22G PROTEIN; 9G CARBOHYDRATE; 3G DIETARY FIBER; 39MG CHOLESTEROL; 307MG SODIUM.

Cooking Tip

IF YOU HAVE FRESH TUNA, THEN BY ALL MEANS USE IT! IF NOT, A GOOD-QUALITY CANNED TUNA WILL BE FINE. FOR FURTHER INFORMATION ABOUT WHICH FISH TO EAT FOR YOUR HEALTH AND THE HEALTH OF THE OCEANS AND FISH POPULATIONS, VISIT WWW.OCEANSALIVE.ORG.

Chapter 7
Soups and Sandwiches

When making soup, a cook with a stockpot is like an artist with an empty palette: The possibilities are endless as long as you let your creative energy flow.

What really makes a good soup? The answer is a great base, made up of a good broth or stock, fresh vegetables, and fresh herbs. When you begin to put together a soup and you make or have on hand your own homemade broth, your work is half done. Nothing beats a flavorful broth. Now here is where some take the wrong path. Making a soup is not simply throwing leftovers into a pot and stirring in some salt and pepper. A wonderful soup also ideally uses some fresh vegetables and, whenever possible, fresh herbs.

Most soups begin with a little butter or olive oil in a stockpot and, when hot, chopped onions of some kind are added. The onions are simmered for a bit until soft, then other seasonal vegetables and water or broth, or even a bit of wine, are added. The soup is simmered until the veggies are tender, but not mushy, and then fresh herbs are added. Puréed vegetables can make a nice flavor addition and act as a thickener. For a soup with some kind of meat, you cook the meat separately and then add it to the pot with the veggies, or you can brown the chopped meat in the stockpot first and then add the onions and veggies. That's it!

SEASONINGS FOR SOUPS

BEAN SOUP: bay leaves, ground cumin, dill seed, green dill, mint, oregano, summer savory, tarragon

BEEF STOCK: bay leaves, chervil, parsley

BORSCHT: ground cumin, dill seed, green dill, thyme

BOUILLABAISSE: bay leaves, saffron, parsley

CABBAGE SOUP: anise seed, caraway seed, celery seed

CHICKEN SOUP: ground cumin, green dill, ginger, marjoram, rosemary, summer savory, tarragon

CHICKEN STOCK: chervil, marjoram, parsley, saffron, sage

CLAM CHOWDER (NEW ENGLAND STYLE): marjoram, thyme, caraway seed, parsley

CORN SOUP: bay leaves, chiles, garlic, basil, parsley, cilantro

FISH AND SEAFOOD CHOWDERS: green dill, saffron, parsley, cilantro, garlic, bay, thyme, curry

GAZPACHO: celery seed, garlic, green dill, Tabasco sauce, cayenne pepper, cilantro

GUMBO: thyme, chiles, bay leaves, Creole spice mix, parsley

LENTIL SOUP: summer savory, curry, cumin, paprika, parsley, cilantro

MINESTRONE: basil, bay leaves, garlic, marjoram, oregano, sage, thyme, onions, parsley

MUSHROOM SOUP: oregano, tarragon, parsley

ONION SOUP (FRENCH STYLE): marjoram, oregano

PARSNIP SOUP: thyme, parsley, garlic, onions

PEA SOUP: basil, cardamom seed, coriander seed, ground cumin, curry powder, green dill, mint, rosemary, sage, summer savory, tarragon, thyme

POTATO SOUP: mustard seed, rosemary, sage, curry, chiles, almost anything

SPINACH SOUP: basil, marjoram, rosemary, garlic

TOMATO SOUP: basil, bay leaves, green dill, marjoram, oregano, sage, tarragon

VEGETABLE SOUP: basil, chervil, oregano, sage, summer savory, thyme

SOUP GARNISHES: chervil, chives, fennel seed, paprika, parsley, poppy seed, sesame seed, sour cream

Vegetable Broth

Starting with cold water allows more of the flavor of the vegetables to be extracted during the cooking process.

YIELDS 2 QUARTS

4 quarts cold water

2 medium onions, coarsely chopped

1 medium potato or parsnip (optional)

3 large carrots, cut into chunks

4 ribs celery, with tops, cut into chunks

2 inches kombu or other seaweed

1 tablespoon black peppercorns

2 whole bay leaves

½ cup parsley, stems and leaves

2 sprigs fresh thyme

Combine the water, onions, potato, carrots, and celery in a large stockpot over high heat. Bring to a boil, then lower the heat, add the kombu, peppercorns, and bay leaves and simmer, partly covered, for 40 minutes. Add the parsley and thyme and simmer 20 minutes longer.

Let the stock cool, then strain it through a fine-mesh sieve. Press on the solids to extract as much of the flavorful and nutrient-rich liquid as possible, but don't press so hard that the solids start to come through. Store in an airtight container; it will keep up to 5 days in the refrigerator or up to 3 months in the freezer.

PER RECIPE: 387 CALORIES; 3G FAT (5.4% CALORIES FROM FAT); 12G PROTEIN; 90G CARBOHYDRATE; 24G DIETARY FIBER; 0MG CHOLESTEROL; 418MG SODIUM.

Variations

YOU MAY ROAST THE VEGETABLES IN A BIT OF OLIVE OIL IN A 375°F OVEN FOR ABOUT 45 MINUTES BEFORE YOU SIMMER WITH WATER AND HERBS IF YOU LIKE. ANOTHER DIRTY PAN, BUT A REALLY NICE RICH FLAVOR.

Mushroom Broth

This broth can be modified in many ways to suit your tastes: You may use any one mushroom or combination of mushrooms, and you may also add other flavorings depending on the broth's intended use—fresh sage or thyme are excellent additions, as is a tablespoon (or more!) of sherry. Simply discard the mushrooms after they have been (over)cooked, or find a way to eat them in something that day, like scrambled with eggs and spinach or over chicken or tofu.

YIELDS 1 QUART

2 tablespoons extra-virgin olive oil

3 cups sliced fresh shiitake mushrooms

3 cups sliced fresh portobello mushrooms

2 medium shallots, chopped

3 cloves garlic, chopped

¼ teaspoon sea salt

¼ teaspoon black pepper

4 cups water

1 tablespoon stems removed and chopped fresh parsley

Put the oil in a heavy-bottomed pan over medium heat. Add the mushrooms and sauté, stirring occasionally, for about 20 minutes or until slightly browned. Add the shallots, garlic, salt, and pepper the last 5 minutes. Add the water and parsley and bring to a boil. Reduce heat and simmer for 30 minutes. Let cool slightly and strain. Discard mushrooms (or reuse—see above). The broth can be stored in the refrigerator or frozen just like vegetable broth.

PER RECIPE: 635 CALORIES; 9G FAT (11.0% CALORIES FROM FAT); 21G PROTEIN; 143G CARBOHYDRATE; 22G DIETARY FIBER; 0MG CHOLESTEROL; 156MG SODIUM.

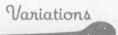

Variations

TO MAKE A REDUCTION, SIMPLY SIMMER THIS BROTH UNTIL IT REDUCES TO ABOUT 2 CUPS. THEN ADD IT TO A PASTA DISH OR SAUTÉED VEGGIES. TRY THIS PAIRING: STIR A LITTLE MUSHROOM REDUCTION INTO SOME STEAMED CHOPPED CABBAGE AND SERVE WITH BAKED SALMON.

Chicken Broth

Use the broth and some of the reserved meat for a soup. You can use the breast meat for another meal.

Yields 2 quarts

1 whole free-range chicken (about 3½ pounds), rinsed, giblets discarded

2 whole carrots, cut into large chunks

3 stalks celery, cut into large chunks

1 medium white onion, quartered

1 small potato, halved

1 whole bay leaf

1 tablespoon whole black peppercorns

6 sprigs parsley

1 tablespoon fresh thyme

Combine the chicken, carrots, celery, onion, and potato in a large stockpot over medium heat. Pour in only enough cold water to cover, then add the bay leaf and peppercorns. Let the stock slowly come to a boil, still over medium heat. (This is better than using high heat because it extracts more flavors from the ingredients.)

Turn down the heat to medium-low and gently simmer, partly covered, for 1 hour. As it cooks, skim off any impurities that rise to the surface. Add the parsley and thyme and simmer 30 minutes longer.

Carefully remove the chicken to a cutting board. As soon as it's cool enough to handle, discard the skin. Remove the meat from the bones and store in the refrigerator; discard the bones.

Strain the stock through a fine-mesh sieve into another pot, pressing on the solids to extract as much of the flavorful and nutrient-rich liquid as possible, but not so hard that the solids start to come through. If you won't be using the stock immediately, place the pot with the strained stock in a sinkful of ice water and stir to cool the stock quickly. Store in an airtight container; it will keep 3–4 days in the refrigerator or up to 3 months in the freezer.

Per recipe: 2,515 Calories; 158g fat (56.4% calories from fat); 189g protein; 86g carbohydrate; 27g dietary fiber; 895mg cholesterol; 1,061mg sodium.

Cooking Tip

There is nothing like a homemade broth as the base for a soup or a sauce. Homemade broth adds flavor that can't be replaced with purchased broth. We never add sea salt to broth, as it reduces slightly and can become too salty. Salt the broth, if necessary, after you make your soup or sauce.

Mineral Broth

Adapted from a recipe by Dr. Ed Bauman of Bauman College, this delicious broth is high in minerals and can be very fortifying for people undergoing chemotherapy, which tends to deplete minerals. Sip a cup of this broth warm, or add it to soup, grains, and other dishes in place of stock. Instead of spinach, you can use a similar amount of a combination of kale, collard greens, and Swiss chard, and in place of the parsley you can use a combination of cilantro, basil, thyme, and oregano.

SERVES 9

2½ pounds winter squash or yams

1½ pounds broccoli or string beans

1 pound spinach or a combination of kale, collard, *and* chard

½ bunch parsley or a combination of cilantro, basil, thyme, *and* oregano

5 shiitake mushrooms

2 pieces kombu

¼ cup flaxseeds

Chop the winter squash into 3-inch chunks, leaving the skins on, and put it in a large stockpot. Coarsely chop the broccoli, layer it atop the squash, then coarsely chop the spinach and parsley and layer them atop the broccoli.

Halve the mushrooms and add to the pot, along with the kombu. Fill the pot with water up to 2 inches from the top. Bring to a boil over high heat, and then lower the heat, cover, and simmer for 4 hours.

Allow the broth to cool for 30 minutes, then add the flaxseeds and let sit for another 15 minutes.

Strain the broth through a large colander set over a large pot or mixing bowl, pressing the solids to extract more of the mineral-rich broth, but don't press so hard as to push the solids through the colander. Once it's completely cool, store the broth in airtight containers. It will keep for 5 days in the refrigerator or up to 3 months in the freezer.

Drink warm. Can be added to soup and grains or puréed with vegetable pulp from the original soup pot.

PER SERVING: 172 CALORIES; 2G FAT (10.4% CALORIES FROM FAT); 8G PROTEIN; 37G CARBOHYDRATE; 9G DIETARY FIBER; 0MG CHOLESTEROL; 69MG SODIUM.

Variations

To make a mineral-rich soup, simply remove the kombu and purée all of the ingredients once they're cooked, rather than straining and discarding the pulp. An immersion blender is the best tool for this job, but you can also purée it in batches in a blender or food processor.

Health Note ♥

Kombu is a type of seaweed that contains protein, calcium, iodine, magnesium, iron, and folate. If you soak and cook your beans with a piece of kombu they become more digestible and are less likely to cause gas.

What's the Difference Between Stock and Broth?

Chicken stock is generally made from mostly bones, whereas broth is made from meat. Chicken stock has a richer flavor due to the gelatin released by long-simmering bones. Feel free to use bones and not the whole chicken in this recipe, and you'll have stock. Broth is nice in sauces since it's a little lighter in flavor.

Minestrone Soup with Farro

Farro, an ancient form of wheat, is lower in gluten than its hybridized modern cousin, so some people who have difficulty with wheat find that they can tolerate farro. In addition to being great in soups, this hearty grain is also wonderful in salads. Just add vinaigrette and seasonal raw veggies, and you're set!

SERVES 8

2 tablespoons extra-virgin olive oil, plus more for garnish

1 whole onion, diced

6 cloves garlic, chopped

3 cups diced carrots

1½ cups sliced celery

1 bunch kale, chopped

3 cups diced tomatoes, fresh or canned

1 tablespoon chopped fresh sage

One 2" sprig fresh rosemary

1 tablespoon fresh oregano

2 cups cooked cannellini beans (or one 15-ounce can), drained

2 quarts vegetable broth (page 117) or chicken broth (page 119)

3 cups cooked farro (follow the directions on the package)

Sea salt to taste

Black pepper to taste

1 cup grated Parmesan cheese (optional)

Heat the oil in a soup pot over medium-high heat, then add the onion, garlic, carrots, and celery and sauté for 5 minutes. Add the kale and sauté for an additional 5 minutes, then add the tomatoes, sage, rosemary, and oregano and cook 10 minutes longer. Add the beans and broth; lower the heat and simmer, covered, for 30 minutes.

Stir in the farro and season to taste with salt and pepper. Serve garnished with a drizzle of oil and a sprinkle of cheese, if you like.

PER SERVING: 610 CALORIES; 13G FAT (18.6% CALORIES FROM FAT); 22G PROTEIN; 104G CARBOHYDRATE; 11G DIETARY FIBER; 10MG CHOLESTEROL; 1,865MG SODIUM.

Variations

IF YOU'D LIKE A CREAMIER SOUP, ADD THIS STEP: AFTER THE SOUP HAS FULLY COOKED AND BEFORE ADDING THE FARRO, PURÉE ONE-THIRD OF THE SOUP IN AN IMMERSION BLENDER OR FOOD PROCESSOR. THEN POUR THE PURÉE BACK INTO THE POT. CONTINUE FOLLOWING THE DIRECTIONS. FOR A MORE SOPHISTICATED FLAVOR, SUBSTITUTE 1 CUP RED WINE FOR 1 CUP BROTH.

Eating Seasonally

MINESTRONE IS A VERSATILE DISH, MAKING IT PERFECT FOR SEASONAL COOKING. ADD ANY OF THE VEGETABLES BELOW, OR SUBSTITUTE THEM FOR VEGETABLES IN THIS RECIPE, ADDING THE FIRM, HEARTY VEGETABLES EARLY IN THE PROCESS AND MORE DELICATE VEGETABLES LATER.

Spring: DANDELION GREENS, GREEN GARLIC, GREEN PEAS, SPINACH

Summer: FRESH BASIL, TOMATOES, ZUCCHINI, BELL PEPPERS, LEAFY GREENS, CELERY, CARROTS

Autumn: BELL PEPPERS, PUMPKIN, BROCCOLI

Winter: BOK CHOY, BROCCOLI, CABBAGES, KALE, CARROTS, WINTER SQUASHES

Golden Tofu Cauliflower Soup

This soup is from Patty's mom's good friend, Caroline Ognebene, a wonderful soup maker and all-around good cook! According to Mark Twain, "Cauliflower is nothing but cabbage with a college education," but we think cauliflower is a bit more refined, having a lower content of sulfurous compounds and therefore less odor.

SERVES 4

1 tablespoon sesame oil

1 medium onion, sliced

2 cloves garlic, minced or pressed

2 teaspoons ground coriander

2 teaspoons cumin powder

1 teaspoon curry powder

4 cups vegetable broth (page 117) or chicken broth (page 119)

2 cups coarsely chopped cauliflower

½ pound medium tofu, cubed

3 tablespoons lemon juice

1 teaspoon sea salt

3 tablespoons chopped fresh parsley, stems removed, for garnish

Heat the oil in a soup pot over medium heat, then add the onions and cook, stirring occasionally, for about 10 minutes, until translucent. Stir in the garlic, coriander, cumin, and curry powder and continue to cook and stir for another minute. Add the broth, cauliflower, tofu, lemon juice, and salt; bring to a boil; then lower the heat, cover, and simmer for 8 minutes.

Allow the soup to cool a bit, then purée it slightly with an immersion blender. Alternatively, you can use a regular blender or food processor, but be careful if using a blender. Don't put the lid on tightly, as the pressure from the hot soup can cause it to pop off and spurt out hot soup! It's a good idea to hold a kitchen towel over the blender lid just in case this happens. If necessary, reheat the puréed soup, then serve garnished with the parsley.

PER SERVING: 126 CALORIES; 7G FAT (48.0% CALORIES FROM FAT); 7G PROTEIN; 9G CARBOHYDRATE; 3G DIETARY FIBER; 0MG CHOLESTEROL; 2,702MG SODIUM.

Health Note

CAULIFLOWER IS A MEMBER OF THE CANCER-FIGHTING CRUCIFEROUS FAMILY. CAULIFLOWER HAS MANY VITAMINS, INCLUDING C AND K AS WELL AS FOLATE.

Split Pea Soup

You can use lentils in place of the split peas. In either case, this soup lends itself well to incorporating a wide variety of veggies. Split peas and lentils are legumes and are great blood-sugar regulators.

SERVES 10

3 cups dry split peas or lentils

8 cups vegetable broth (page 117)

4 carrots, diced

3 stalks celery, diced

2 yams, peeled and diced

½ pound shiitake mushrooms, sliced

⅓ cup miso

1 cup warm water or broth

Combine the split peas and stock in a large soup pot and bring to a boil over high heat. Lower the heat, cover, and simmer for 45 minutes, stirring often. Add more broth if the split peas get too dry, but not too much, as the soup should be thick. Add the carrots, celery, yams, and mushrooms. Cover and simmer about 30 minutes longer, until the split peas are falling apart and the vegetables are tender.

Mix the miso with the warm water, then stir it into the soup and serve right away.

PER SERVING: 462 CALORIES; 4G FAT (8.3% CALORIES FROM FAT); 23G PROTEIN; 87G CARBOHYDRATE; 23G DIETARY FIBER; 2MG CHOLESTEROL; 1,584MG SODIUM.

Eating Seasonally

ADD ANY OF THE FOLLOWING VEGETABLES IN ADDITION TO OR IN PLACE OF VEGETABLES CALLED FOR IN THIS RECIPE. WITH THE AUTUMN AND WINTER VEGETABLES, YOU MAY NEED TO SIMMER THE SOUP A BIT LONGER.

Spring: GREEN PEAS, CELERY, GREEN GARLIC, BEET GREENS

Summer: TOMATOES, CORN, CARROTS, RED BELL PEPPER

Autumn: YAMS, PUMPKIN, CARROTS, TOMATOES

Winter: WINTER SQUASHES, POTATOES, CARROTS, PARSNIPS

Health Note

THE AVERAGE AMERICAN CONSUMES TOO MUCH SALT. YOUR SODIUM INTAKE SHOULD BE ABOUT 2,300 MG PER DAY OR ABOUT 1¼ TEASPOONS. BECAUSE OF THE NATURALLY SALTY MISO IN THIS RECIPE, YOU ARE DONE WITH SALT FOR THE DAY!

Tuscan Tomato Soup

This is a wonderful Italian soup. It is better passed through a food mill, but a food processor, blender, or immersion blender will do in a pinch.

SERVES 6

6 tablespoons extra-virgin olive oil, plus more for garnish

6 cloves garlic

1 bunch fresh basil (reserve 6 basil leaves for garnish)

1½ cups thinly sliced stale Italian bread

4 cups diced fresh tomatoes, or one 28-ounce can

2 small medium-hot dried chiles

2 cups warm chicken broth (page 119) or vegetable broth (page 117)

Sea salt to taste

Black pepper to taste

Place the oil, garlic, and about ⅓ of the basil in a soup pot over medium heat. Simmer for several minutes, but don't brown the garlic. Remove the garlic and set it aside.

Add the sliced bread to the pan and cook, stirring continuously, for 10 minutes to allow the bread to absorb the flavor of the garlic. Add the tomatoes, chiles, another one-third of the basil, and the reserved garlic. Lower the heat, add about ½ cup of the broth, and simmer for at least 1 hour, adding the remainder of the broth in small increments during the cooking.

Add the remaining one-third of the basil and then purée the soup using an immersion blender. Alternatively, if using a regular blender, don't put the lid on tightly, as the pressure from the hot soup can cause it to pop off and spurt out hot soup! It's a good idea to hold a kitchen towel over the blender lid just in case this happens.

Reheat the soup if necessary, then serve drizzled with a bit of oil and garnished with a leaf of basil. Add salt and pepper to taste.

PER SERVING: 328 CALORIES; 16G FAT (44.5% CALORIES FROM FAT); 8G PROTEIN; 38G CARBOHYDRATE; 3G DIETARY FIBER; 0MG CHOLESTEROL; 612MG SODIUM.

Variations

OKAY, THIS IS A BOOK ABOUT ADDING MORE VEGETABLES, AND THIS RECIPE CONTAINS ONLY ONE VEGETABLE (IF WE DON'T COUNT THE CHILES, GARLIC, AND BASIL). YOU CAN SAUTÉ A MINCED SHALLOT WITH THE OLIVE OIL AND GARLIC. THEN, AFTER THE SOUP IS PURÉED, ADD ABOUT ½ CUP OF PEAS. THAT'S ALL WE CAN THINK OF WITHOUT MAKING THIS WONDERFUL SOUP TOO FUSSY.

Winter Broccoli Soup

How simple is this? This soup is a wonderful accompaniment to a piece of grilled salmon served on lettuce leaves and garnished with a slice of lemon. When you make this soup, save the broccoli stems—they make a nice side dish if peeled, chopped finely, and sautéed in a bit of olive oil with minced garlic.

SERVES 4

1 bunch broccoli, florets only, coarsely chopped

2 small parsnips, peeled and sliced

1 medium onion, chopped

1 large celery rib, thinly sliced

4 cups vegetable broth (page 117) or chicken broth (page 119)

½ teaspoon freshly ground black pepper, or to taste

1 tablespoon lemon juice (optional)

½ teaspoon sea salt, or to taste

Chopped fresh parsley, for garnish

Combine the broccoli, parsnips, onion, celery, broth, and pepper in a soup pot over medium-high heat. Cover and bring to a boil, then lower the heat and simmer until the vegetables are tender, about 20 minutes.

Purée soup with an immersion blender until smooth. Alternatively, you can use a regular blender or food processor, but be careful if using a blender. Don't put the lid on tightly, as the pressure from the hot soup can cause it to pop off and spurt out hot soup! It's a good idea to hold a kitchen towel over the blender lid just in case this happens.

Add the lemon juice, if desired, and then season to taste with salt. Serve hot, garnished with parsley.

PER SERVING: 179 CALORIES; 2G FAT (10.6% CALORIES FROM FAT); 11G PROTEIN; 32G CARBOHYDRATE; 11G DIETARY FIBER; 0MG CHOLESTEROL; 825MG SODIUM.

Aztec Stew

This recipe calls for fresh carrot juice. If you don't have a juicer, you can likely buy fresh carrot juice at a natural-foods store or juice bar. If you do juice the carrots at home, save the pulp and add it to muffins to enhance their fiber content. Experiment with other varieties of beans in place of the kidney beans; azuki beans are especially good in this recipe. Pair this dish with a mixed-greens salad with lemon vinaigrette, which brings out the flavor of the carrots nicely. If you like, place baby spinach leaves in the bottom of the soup bowl before pouring in the hot soup, let sit for a minute before serving, and garnish with a lemon wedge.

SERVES 12

2 tablespoons extra-virgin olive oil

1 medium onion, coarsely chopped

4 cloves garlic, coarsely chopped

1½ cups sliced shiitake mushrooms

6 cups low-sodium tomato juice

4 cups fresh carrot juice

2 cups yams or other winter squash, peeled and cubed in ½" pieces

½ cup quinoa, thoroughly rinsed

1½ tablespoons chili powder

1½ cups zucchini, cut into ½" inch slices

2 cups cooked kidney beans (or one 15-ounce can), drained

1½ cups corn, fresh or frozen

Freshly squeezed lemon juice to taste

Chopped cilantro or parsley, for garnish

Heat the oil in a soup pot over medium-high heat, then add the onion, garlic, and mushrooms and sauté for about 5 minutes. Stir in the tomato and carrot juices, yams, quinoa, and chili powder, bring to a boil, then lower the heat, cover, and simmer for 15 minutes.

Check the yams. As soon as they're just starting to get tender, add the zucchini, cover, and continue simmering until the vegetables are tender, about 10 minutes longer. Add the beans and corn and continue simmering until heated through. Season to taste with fresh lemon juice and serve garnished with cilantro.

PER SERVING: 271 CALORIES; 3G FAT (7.8% CALORIES FROM FAT); 9G PROTEIN; 59G CARBOHYDRATE; 10G DIETARY FIBER; 0MG CHOLESTEROL; 485MG SODIUM.

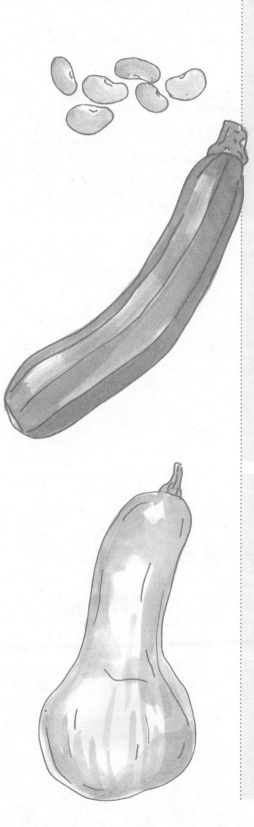

Eating Seasonally

THIS WONDERFUL STEW CAN ACCOMMODATE A WIDE RANGE OF SEASONAL VEGETABLES. OTHER THAN FOR TENDER GREENS, ADD THE VEGETABLES TO THE SAUTÉING STEP. ADD FIRMER, DENSER VEGETABLES FIRST, AND THEN ADD MORE TENDER VEGETABLES LATER IN THE SAUTÉ. ADD TENDER GREENS WITH THE BEANS AND CORN.

Spring: PEAS, GREEN BEANS

Summer: TOMATOES, ZUCCHINI, CORN, EDAMAME, CELERY, CARROTS

Autumn: PUMPKIN, BROCCOLI, KALE, PARSNIPS

Winter: WINTER SQUASHES, SUCH AS BUTTERNUT SQUASH OR YAMS, SPINACH

Health Note ♥

QUINOA (PRONOUNCED KEEN-WAH) ISN'T TECHNICALLY A GRAIN; IT'S ACTUALLY THE SEED OF A PLANT RELATED TO BEETS AND SPINACH. IT HAS AN EXCELLENT AMINO ACID PROFILE AND IS CONSIDERED A COMPLETE PROTEIN. YAMS ARE AN EXCELLENT SOURCE OF VITAMIN C AS WELL AS VITAMIN B6, WHICH THE BODY NEEDS TO BREAK DOWN HOMOCYSTEINE, A METABOLIC BYPRODUCT THAT CAN DAMAGE BLOOD VESSEL WALLS.

Borscht with Sautéed Carrots

Thanks to Caroline Ognebene, you too can prepare this wonderful recipe, which is chock-full of healthful vegetables.

SERVES 4

2 tablespoons extra-virgin olive oil

2 cups chopped onions

2 cups peeled and grated beets

1 cup coarsely grated carrots

4 cups vegetable broth (page 117) or chicken broth (page 119)

2 cups shredded green cabbage

1 medium Yukon gold potato, cut into ½" pieces

½ cup chopped green bell pepper

¼ cup chopped celery

2 large garlic cloves, minced

3 tablespoons freshly squeezed lemon juice

1 pinch sugar

Sea salt to taste

Black pepper to taste

Sour cream, for garnish

Chopped fresh dill, for garnish

Heat the oil in soup pot over medium heat. Add the onions, beets, and carrots and sauté until the vegetables are tender, about 10 minutes. Add the broth and bring to a boil, then add the cabbage, potato, bell pepper, celery, and garlic. Lower the heat, cover, and simmer until all of the vegetables are tender, about 30 minutes.

Remove the soup from the heat and stir in lemon juice and sugar. Thin with more broth if the soup is too thick. Season to taste with salt and pepper, then serve garnished with a dollop of sour cream and a sprinkling of dill.

PER SERVING: 201 CALORIES; 7G FAT (34.0% CALORIES FROM FAT); 5G PROTEIN; 28G CARBOHYDRATE; 6G DIETARY FIBER; 0MG CHOLESTEROL; 2,584MG SODIUM.

Health Note

BEETS ARE HIGH IN FOLATE, MANGANESE, POTASSIUM, AND VITAMIN C. THEY ARE ALSO HIGH IN CHROMIUM AND FIBER. PATTY'S FAVORITE WAY TO EAT BEETS IS TO PEEL AND THEN GRATE THEM, THEN SERVE RAW ATOP A SPINACH SALAD. IT'S REALLY GOOD! FOR THOSE WITH DIABETES, RAW BEETS ARE LOWER ON THE GLYCEMIC INDEX AND ARE HIGHER IN CHROMIUM.

Gazpacho

This is one recipe that doesn't lend itself to eating seasonally. Only make it in the summer, when vine-ripened tomatoes at the peak of their flavor are available.

SERVES 6

2 cups chopped tomatoes

1 cup peeled and coarsely chopped cucumber

¼ cup extra-virgin olive oil

⅓ cup freshly squeezed lemon juice

½ teaspoon sea salt

½ jalapeño, seeded and minced (you may use 1 whole jalapeño if you like)

1 large garlic clove, chopped

2 cups finely chopped tomatoes

⅔ cup peeled and finely chopped cucumbers

½ red bell pepper, finely chopped

¼ cup finely chopped red onion

½ cup chopped fresh parsley or cilantro, stems removed

To make the vegetable purée, place the first 7 ingredients in a food processor and process until smooth. Pour into a serving bowl. Add the remaining ingredients into the bowl and stir. Serve right away while the dish is at the peak of its flavor, though, like most gazpachos, it can also be served chilled.

PER SERVING: 18 CALORIES; 9G FAT (67.1% CALORIES FROM FAT); 1G PROTEIN; 9G CARBOHYDRATE; 2G DIETARY FIBER; 0MG CHOLESTEROL; 169MG SODIUM.

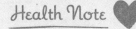

Health Note

WE CAN'T SAY ENOUGH GOOD THINGS ABOUT TOMATOES! THEY ARE HIGH IN VITAMINS C, A, AND K AND ARE ALSO RICH IN LYCOPENE, A POWERFUL ANTI-OXIDANT. IF THAT'S NOT ENOUGH, THEY ARE DELICIOUS JUST THE WAY THEY ARE. (THOUGH NOT COMMON, SOME PEOPLE REACT TO TOMATOES, FOR EXAMPLE, WITH JOINT ACHES.)

Cioppino

More of a stew than a soup, cioppino is a very delicious (and messy!) dish. You can freely substitute the seafood, using shrimp, scallops, mussels, or whatever you like. Serve with crusty garlic bread.

SERVES 6

¼ cup extra-virgin olive oil

2 large onions, chopped

4 cloves garlic, chopped

3 large carrots, chopped

2 ribs celery plus leaves, sliced

2 cups chopped tomatoes (or one 15-ounce can diced tomatoes)

2 cups tomato sauce

1 cup white wine

1 cup water

2 teaspoons fresh thyme

1 tablespoon chopped fresh basil

1 bay leaf

Sea salt to taste

Freshly ground black pepper to taste

Pinch of cayenne pepper

¼ cup chopped parsley, plus ¼ additional cup for garnish, stems removed

3 pounds clams, in shell and scrubbed well

1 pound halibut fillets, or other white fish, cut into bite-size pieces

1 whole crab, cooked and cracked

6 lemon wedges for garnish

Heat the oil in a soup pot over medium-high heat. Add the onions, garlic, carrots, and celery and sauté until the onion is transparent and all of the vegetables are limp, about 10 minutes. Add the chopped tomatoes, tomato sauce, wine, water, thyme, basil, bay leaf, salt, black pepper, cayenne pepper, and half of the parsley. Bring to a boil, then lower the heat and simmer for 30 minutes, partly covered.

Add the clams and simmer for 10 minutes and then add the halibut and crab and simmer 15 minutes longer. Discard any clams that haven't opened. Stir in a bit of water if the soup is too thick, then serve garnished with the remaining parsley and the lemon wedges.

PER SERVING: 456 CALORIES; 14G FAT (29.0% CALORIES FROM FAT); 52G PROTEIN; 24G CARBOHYDRATE; 5G DIETARY FIBER; 119MG CHOLESTEROL; 768MG SODIUM.

Chicken Vegetable Soup with Noodles

This is comfort food in a bowl. Chicken noodle soup is renowned for its healing properties. We'd venture to say that this version, with added vegetables, will provide an even greater boost to the immune system.

SERVES 4

2 tablespoons extra-virgin olive oil

1 medium onion, chopped

3 cloves garlic, minced

2 medium carrots, cut diagonally into ½" thick slices

2 ribs celery, halved lengthwise and cut into ½" thick slices

1 cup chopped broccoli

2½ quarts warm chicken broth (page 119)

1½ cups cooked and shredded chicken

4 sprigs fresh thyme

1 whole bay leaf

1 large tomato, chopped

4 ounces uncooked whole-wheat pasta

Sea salt to taste

Black pepper to taste

1 handful fresh flat-leaf parsley, stems removed and finely chopped, for garnish

Heat the oil in a soup pot over medium heat. Add onions, garlic, carrots, celery, and broccoli and cook, stirring, until the vegetables are al dente. Add the broth, chicken, thyme, and bay leaf and simmer, covered, for 10 minutes.

Add the tomatoes and noodles and simmer until the noodles are tender, about 7–8 minutes. Season with salt and pepper to taste. Place in serving bowls, sprinkle with chopped parsley, and serve.

PER SERVING: 364 CALORIES; 11G FAT (30.3% CALORIES FROM FAT); 50G PROTEIN; 36G CARBOHYDRATE; 4G DIETARY FIBER; 72MG CHOLESTEROL; 1,389MG SODIUM.

Variations

TO MAKE A VEGETARIAN VERSION, SUBSTITUTE THE CHICKEN BROTH FOR VEGETABLE BROTH (PAGE 117) AND SUBSTITUTE THE CHICKEN FOR CUBED, FIRM TOFU ADDED THE LAST 5 MINUTES OF SIMMERING.

Eating Seasonally

LIKE MOST SOUPS, THIS ONE OFFERS ENDLESS OPTIONS FOR SEASONAL VARIATIONS. MOST OF THE VEGETABLES LISTED BELOW CAN BE ADDED IN THE SAUTÉING STEP, BUT ADD HERBS OR TENDER GREENS AT THE END.

Spring: PEAS, ASPARAGUS, BEET GREENS, CARROTS, CELERY, COLLARD GREENS, CHIVES, PARSLEY, GREEN GARLIC

Summer: TOMATOES, GREEN BEANS, CORN, RED BELL PEPPER (NOT TOO MUCH SUMMER SQUASHES, BASIL

Autumn: POTATOES, CORN, JERUSALEM ARTICHOKES, LEEKS, BROCCOLI, PUMPKIN, SHALLOTS, TURNIPS, PARSNIPS

Winter: BROCCOLI, CABBAGE, CHARD, KALE, PARSNIPS, WINTER SQUASHES, TURNIPS, YAMS

Sandwiches Galore

What speaks to a family more than soups and sandwiches? We think these two types of dishes are by far the easiest ways to and more vegetables, please (MVP) into your diets. So let's get busy creating a variety of sandwiches with a veggie slant! And, yes, they make a nice meal when paired with any of our nutritious and tasty hot soups in this chapter. Although we have not listed sliced cheese for our sandwiches, partly because we are focused on veggies and want people to generally reduce their animal fats, any of the following recipes can use cheese if you believe it's an important part of your diet.

Asian Inspired

Peanut sauce (page 82)

Whole wheat wrap

Sprouts

Thinly sliced celery

Thinly sliced radishes

Sautéed tofu

This wrap is a tasty follow-up to our Spring Rolls (page 82). Simply spread leftover peanut sauce onto a whole-wheat wrap. Add sprouts, celery, radishes, and tofu and roll up. Yum!

Italian Inspired

Whole-wheat roll, foccacia, or sourdough roll

Red bell pepper spread (see Roasted Red Pepper Sauce, page 73)

Thickly sliced fresh tomatoes

Arugula or romaine lettuce

Fresh basil or parsley

The trick to this sandwich is making enough room for all the veggies. Slice the roll in half lengthwise then scoop out some of the soft bread in the middle of the roll. Spread halves with a basic red bell pepper spread. Then layer on tomatoes, arugula, and basil. Delizioso!

Greek Inspired

Hummus (page 85) or baba ghanoush (page 89)

Whole-wheat wrap

Fresh tomato slices

Thinly sliced red onions

Chopped kalamata olives

Shredded carrots

Chopped parsley, stems removed

Spread a generous amount of hummus onto the wrap. Then layer the remaining ingredients and roll.

Mexican Inspired

Tortilla

Black bean hummus (page 85)

Avocado

Fresh cilantro

Grated carrots

Diced red bell peppers

Shredded chicken

Shredded romaine lettuce

Chopped tomatoes

Make a healthy burrito by spreading the tortilla with black bean hummus. Layer the remaining ingredients in a strip and roll. ¡Olé!

Grilled Cheese

Sliced bread

Sliced cheese

Puréed yams

Watercress, arugula, or lettuce

Sliced tomato

Adding MVP to the classic grilled cheese sandwich is easy. Layer one slice of cheese onto each slice of bread. Then spread with puréed yams (or leftover Yam Casserole, page 189) and watercress for a little zip. Grill in skillet. In a separate skillet, grill the tomato slices then add them to the sandwich.

The Californian

Sliced sourdough bread

Pesto

Turkey

Sliced tomatoes

Sliced cucumbers

Thinly sliced red onions

Sprouts

Mesclun mix

Blue cheese

Sliced avocado

Spread slices of bread with pesto, then layer on the other ingredients. Enjoy!

Tuna with a Twist

Tuna salad

Thinly sliced celery

Fresh corn

Diced red bell pepper

Diced red onion

Whole-grain bread

Fresh spinach leaves

Start with you favorite tuna salad recipe. Then add celery, corn, red pepper, and red onion to the tuna salad. Spread it on some bread and add spinach. You can also place our Mediterranean Tuna Salad (page 113) between bread for a classic sandwich with MVP. Remember that tuna salad doesn't have to include mayonnaise—try a little olive oil instead!

Salad Sandwich

Lettuce

Grated raw fresh beets

Grated fresh carrots

Whatever is in season

Italian dressing (or the dressing of your choice)

Whole-wheat wrap

This is a salad in a wrap! In a bowl mix together lettuce, beets, carrots, and anything else that's seasonal. Toss with dressing and place in your favorite wrap.

Grilled Vegetable Sandwich

Seasonal vegetables

Extra-virgin olive oil

Your favorite bread

Pesto

Grill some seasonal vegetables of your choice with a little olive oil. Then simply place on the bread of your choice that has been spread with pesto.

136

Chapter 8

Entreés

Welcome to our main course chapter! Each dish has been selected to provide a complete focus on vegetables. Even our fish, poultry, and meat dishes have been modified to include more vegetables, please (MVP). You will learn how to add MVP to a variety of common and new tasty meals. For many people, vegetables are thought of as a side dish (and we agree—see chapter 9 Vegetable Side Dishes, page 181), yet there are so many truly exquisite and delectable vegetable main dishes, like the ones in the following pages. We would like for you to think about a meal being "vegetables and baked chicken" rather than the other way around.

We have organized the recipes in this chapter from purely vegetarian main courses to entrees incorporating seafood, then poultry, and ending with a few beef and pork dishes. We want to emphasize that we support a vegetarian and vegetable-focused diet, and we believe it is a healthy way to eat. You can still eat your favorite meats, you just need to rethink their position on your plate (and in your cookbook) as secondary to vegetables!

Enjoy the new adventure of eating a more vegetarian diet. It will be a very tasty, nutritious, and healthy step to take!

Vegetarian Main Dishes

Ratatouille

Ratatouille can be served cold, warm, or hot. It's very nice served with crusty whole-wheat French bread and baked halibut. Try it with polenta sometime. You may also place some spinach leaves in the bottom of a soup bowl and serve the ratatouille on top; the leaves will wilt slightly and be wonderful. Leftover ratatouille can be warmed in a pan and served with a poached egg for breakfast, or, for a tasty lunch, roll some up in a romaine-lined whole-grain wrap and sprinkle with a bit of Parmesan.

SERVES 6

3 tablespoons extra-virgin olive oil

1 large onion, peeled and chopped

5 cloves garlic

4 medium tomatoes, stems removed and diced

⅓ cup dry red wine

1 tablespoon fresh thyme, or 1 teaspoon dried

¼ cup chopped fresh basil leaves, or 2 teaspoons dried

2 whole bay leaves

1 teaspoon sea salt

1 teaspoon freshly ground black pepper

1 medium eggplant, peeled and cut into 1" chunks

3 small zucchini, cut into ½"-thick slices

1 large green bell pepper, cut into 1" squares

1 large red bell pepper, cut into 1" squares

Juice from ½ lemon (optional)

Heat the oil in a large heavy pot like a Dutch oven. Sauté the onions until they are translucent, stirring occasionally. Next add the garlic and sauté for another 2 minutes, then add the tomatoes with juice, wine, thyme, basil, bay leaves, salt, and pepper. Simmer uncovered for 30 minutes. Add the eggplant, zucchini, and green and red bell peppers and simmer, covered, for about 20 minutes or until the vegetables are tender, carefully stirring occasionally. Squeeze lemon juice into the ratatouille if you like. Serve warm, cold, or hot.

PER SERVING: 144 CALORIES; 7G FAT (44.8% CALORIES FROM FAT); 3G PROTEIN; 17G CARBOHYDRATE; 5G DIETARY FIBER; 0MG CHOLESTEROL; 337MG SODIUM.

Variations

PATTY LIKES TO MAKE RATATOUILLE IN A CLAY POT. SHE SIMPLY PLACES ALL INGREDIENTS IN THE CLAY POT, FORGOING THE SAUTÉING, THEN COVERS AND SIMMERS ON LOW HEAT ON THE STOVETOP UNTIL DONE. WHEN USING A CLAY POT, A HEAT DIFFUSER BETWEEN THE BURNER AND THE POT IS A GOOD IDEA, AS IT ADDS A BUFFER BETWEEN THE TWO TO PROTECT THE CLAY FROM TOO MUCH HEAT.

Tomato and Squash Tart

This summertime tart is great served with some crusty French bread. You may use whatever herbs you like in this recipe. Our favorite is a mix of basil, parsley, and thyme. Be sure to not use all rosemary or the flavor will overpower the dish.

SERVES 8

2 large vine-ripened tomatoes (about 1 pound)

1 medium zucchini (about 8 ounces)

1 medium summer squash (about 8 ounces)

1 large Yukon gold potato

½ cup chopped onion

1 cup grated Swiss cheese, divided

2 lightly beaten eggs

1 teaspoon sea salt, optional

¼ cup chopped fresh herbs (basil, parsley, thyme, rosemary, etc.), stems removed

½ teaspoon black pepper

Preheat oven to 400°F. Butter a 9" pie plate or shallow casserole dish.

Remove the stem ends from tomatoes. Cut in half through stem ends then thinly slice crosswise. Cut zucchini, summer squash, and potato in half lengthwise, then thinly slice crosswise.

In a large bowl, combine the zucchini, summer squash, potato, onion, ¾ cup of the cheese, eggs, salt, fresh herbs, and pepper until well mixed. Arrange half of the tomato slices on the bottom of the pie plate. Next, evenly spoon the vegetable mixture over the tomatoes, pressing slightly to flatten and to make even around the pan. Arrange the remaining tomato slices on the top.

Bake until the vegetables are tender, about 50 minutes. Sprinkle with the remaining ¼ cup of cheese the last 10 minutes of cooking.

PER SERVING: 108 CALORIES; 5G FAT (42.2% CALORIES FROM FAT); 7G PROTEIN; 9G CARBOHYDRATE; 2G DIETARY FIBER; 60MG CHOLESTEROL; 294MG SODIUM.

Health Note ♥

TOMATOES ARE HIGH IN VITAMINS C AND A (AS BETA-CAROTENE) AS WELL AS LYCOPENE, A POWERFUL ANTIOXIDANT THAT SUPPORTS MEN AND PROSTATE HEALTH AND MAY HAVE ANTICANCER EFFECTS AS WELL. TOMATO SAUCE IS A GOOD LOW-CALORIE, FLAVORFUL ADDITION FOR GRAINS AND VEGETABLES.

Kids in the Kitchen

BE SURE TO LET YOUR KIDS HELP WITH THE LAYERING PART. THEY DO TEND TO SMASH RATHER THAN LIGHTLY PRESS, SO YOU MIGHT WANT TO SUPERVISE.

Thai Tofu and Squash Stew

This vegetable-packed dish may be served over brown rice or quinoa and garnished with additional cilantro and lime wedges. You may use 1 tablespoon of curry powder instead of the curry paste and increase the jalapeño to 1 whole, seeded and minced, if you like. You may also use other winter squash.

SERVES 4

2 tablespoons extra-virgin olive oil

2 medium leeks, white and light green parts only, washed and chopped

3 cloves garlic, minced

½ jalapeño pepper, seeded and minced

1 tablespoon peeled and grated fresh ginger

1 teaspoon (or to taste) green curry paste

1 teaspoon sugar

3 tablespoons tamari or other soy sauce

3 cups vegetable broth (page 117)

One 15-ounce can unsweetened coconut milk

1½ pounds butternut squash, peeled and diced into ½" cubes

1 medium carrot, thinly sliced

1 stalk celery, thinly sliced

2 cups spinach leaves

1 cup frozen peas

One 10-ounce package firm tofu

Juice of 1 freshly squeezed lime

½ to 1 teaspoon sea salt, optional

Cooked brown rice or quinoa

¼ cup chopped cilantro, for garnish

⅓ cup raw peanuts, optional, for garnish

Heat the oil in a soup pot over medium heat then add the leeks and sauté for about 3 minutes, stirring occasionally. Next, add the garlic, jalapeño, and ginger; cook for 1 minute more. Add curry paste, sugar, and tamari. Reduce heat to medium and cook for about 2 more minutes. Add the broth, coconut milk, squash, carrot, and celery. Bring to a boil, lower to simmer, cover, and simmer for 15 minutes. Add the spinach, peas, tofu, and lime juice. Add salt to taste. Serve over your choice of grain with a garnish of cilantro and peanuts, if you like.

PER SERVING: 356 CALORIES; 23G FAT (54.1% CALORIES FROM FAT); 10G PROTEIN; 35G CARBOHYDRATE; 7G DIETARY FIBER; 0MG CHOLESTEROL; 793MG SODIUM.

Kids in the Kitchen

LEARNING TO COOK AND BAKE HELPS CHILDREN TO LEARN ABOUT MANY DIFFERENT SKILLS OTHER THAN PREPARING A DISH. WHEN YOU MAKE THIS RECIPE, HAVE A MAP OF THE WORLD HANDY TO SHOW YOUR CHILDREN WHERE THAILAND IS. WHEN THEY BEGIN TO STUDY GEOGRAPHY, THEY WILL BE ABLE TO POINT TO THAILAND ON A MAP! KIDS LIKE TO CUT THE TOFU INTO CUBES, AND THEY DON'T HAVE TO USE A SHARP KNIFE.

Sesame-Crusted Tofu Stuffed with Vegetables

This is a very pretty dish and is easy to make. It's wonderful with some protein-rich quinoa and sautéed bok choy.

SERVES 4

1 small fennel bulb, leaves and stems removed, finely chopped·

1 small carrot, grated

2 cloves garlic, minced

½ lemon, zested and then juiced

2 tablespoons chopped fresh dill

One 18-ounce tofu block, drained and cut into 4 slices

½ teaspoon sea salt

½ teaspoon pepper

¼ cup sesame seeds

Preheat the oven to 400°F.

Place the fennel, carrot, and garlic in a medium bowl. Mix well. Finely chop the lemon zest, then add it to the bowl along with the lemon juice and dill.

Cut a pocket lengthwise along one side of each tofu slice. Be careful not to cut all the way through. Carefully fill the pockets with the vegetable mixture. Close each pocket with a toothpick.

Season the tofu slices with salt and pepper and dip in the sesame seeds. Place on a lightly oiled baking sheet and bake in oven until golden brown, about 25 to 30 minutes, turning them over after 15 minutes. You may also sauté these over medium heat in a bit of sesame oil (not toasted sesame oil).

PER SERVING: 183 CALORIES; 11G FAT (48.1% CALORIES FROM FAT); 13G PROTEIN; 13G CARBOHYDRATE; 5G DIETARY FIBER; 0MG CHOLESTEROL; 285MG SODIUM.

Kids in the Kitchen

HAVE YOUR CHILD WASH AND DRY THE LEMON. IF YOU HAVE A MICROPLANE USE IT FOR ZESTING; IF NOT, A GRATER WILL WORK FOR ZESTING AND JUICING. EXPLAIN THAT HE HAS TO BE VERY CAREFUL NOT TO HAVE HIS FINGERS TOO CLOSE TO THE GRATER. HAVE HIM GRATE THE LEMON FIRST WHILE IT'S STILL WHOLE, THEN YOU WILL CUT IT IN HALF. YOUR CHILD CAN THEN JUICE IT. KIDS LIKE THIS PROCESS.

Vegetarian Jambalaya with Smoked Tempeh

This is an amazing special-occasion meal. This dish is beautiful and packed full of vegetables. Be sure to soak the farro for at least an hour if you are using it in this dish, as it speeds the cooking time. Serve this with a fresh spinach salad for a delicious and nutritious meal.

SERVES 6

6 cups vegetable broth (page 117)

¼ cup extra-virgin olive oil

1 medium yellow onion, chopped

½ cup chopped green bell pepper

½ cup chopped red bell pepper

1 cup chopped carrots (about 1 medium carrot)

1½ cups finely sliced celery (about 2 stalks)

4 cloves garlic, minced

2 cups farro, soaked and drained, or 2 cups uncooked brown rice

2 cups diced fresh tomatoes (or one 15-ounce can)

2 cups quartered shiitake mushrooms (about 10 mushrooms)

¼ pound okra, halved lengthwise

¾ cups sliced zucchini (about 1 small zucchini)

One 6-ounce package smoked tempeh, cut into ½" slices

2 whole bay leaves

1 tablespoon chopped fresh thyme leaves, stems removed

½ teaspoon sea salt

½ teaspoon black pepper

⅛ teaspoon cayenne pepper

⅓ cup chopped fresh parsley, stems removed, for garnish

In a medium saucepan, bring the vegetable broth to a simmer. Then lower the heat so that the broth is kept warm.

In a medium sauté pan, heat the oil over medium-high heat. Add the onions, peppers, carrots, and celery and cook until soft, 4–5 minutes, stirring occasionally. Add the garlic and farro and cook, stirring, for 2 to 3 minutes. Add the tomatoes, mushrooms, okra, zucchini, tempeh, bay leaves, and thyme. Cook, stirring, for about 2 minutes. Next add 2 cups of the warm broth, the salt, black pepper, and cayenne pepper, and bring to a boil. Reduce the heat to medium-low and simmer, stirring, until the liquid is absorbed.

Continue adding the broth, 2 cups at a time, as the previous addition is absorbed, cooking and stirring, until all the broth is absorbed and the grains are plump and tender. Serve sprinkled with fresh parsley.

PER SERVING: 817 CALORIES; 18G FAT (18.5% CALORIES FROM FAT); 26G PROTEIN; 151G CARBOHYDRATE; 17G DIETARY FIBER; 2MG CHOLESTEROL; 1,828MG SODIUM.

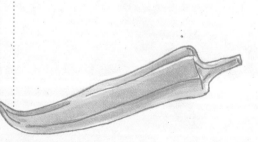

Variations

SMOKED TEMPEH IS ALSO KNOWN AS FAKIN' BAKIN' (SOY-BASED "BACON"). IF YOU CAN'T FIND EITHER, PURCHASE PLAIN TEMPEH AND STEAM IT FOR 10 MINUTES. COOL AND CUT INTO ½" SLICES AND ADD AS YOU WOULD THE SMOKED TEMPEH. ADD ½ TEASPOON LIQUID SMOKE WHEN YOU ADD THE OTHER SPICES. FARRO IS AN ANCIENT GRAIN AND IS RELATED TO SPELT. IF YOU CAN'T FIND IT USE BROWN RICE.

Kids in the Kitchen

KIDS LOVE TO STIR! HAVE THEM DO ALL THE STIRRING IN THIS DISH. IT'S A GOOD IDEA TO HAVE THEM PUT ON A POT HOLDER THAT FITS OVER THEIR HANDS AND UP THEIR ARMS, AS SOMETIMES THEIR ARMS WILL RELAX WHILE STIRRING AND CAN BURN ON THE EDGE OF THE PAN.

Yam Shepherd's Pie

This is not a busy-day dish, as it is rather time-consuming, but do make it for Sunday dinner and have your children spread the yams on top. For variations, add some black or azuki beans or chopped walnuts atop the millet; toasted pine nuts on top of the yams is also an option. Beans and millet make this dish a complete protein.

SERVES 8

2½ pounds yams (about 7 small to medium yams), peeled and diced

2 quarts water

2½ to 3 cups yam cooking liquid

2 tablespoons miso

1½ cups millet

2 tablespoons extra-virgin olive oil (for sautéing), plus 1½ tablespoons extra-virgin olive oil or unsalted butter (for blending)

1 medium onion, diced

1 cup diced shiitake mushrooms, tough stems removed

1 teaspoon sea salt

1 tablespoon fresh thyme

½ cup water or vegetable broth (page 117) (for cooking), plus 6 tablespoons water or broth (for blending)

1 large carrot, diced (or about 1 cup diced carrot)

2 cups chopped broccoli florets

3 cups chopped cauliflower florets (or about ½ head)

2 cups diced zucchini

1 pound spinach leaves, chopped

½ teaspoon paprika

Preheat the oven to 350°F. Generously oil a 13" x 9" baking dish.

Cook yams in 2 quarts boiling water until al dente, about 10 minutes. Drain, reserving liquid.

In a medium saucepan, bring 2½ cups of the yam cooking liquid to a boil with the miso. Add millet and simmer, covered, about 30–35 minutes. (Add the remaining ½ cup of the yam cooking liquid in increments only if the millet has absorbed all the liquid but is not yet fully cooked.)

In a sauté pan, heat 2 tablespoons of the oil over medium-high heat and then add the onion and cook until translucent, stirring occasionally. Add the mushrooms, salt, and thyme and sauté until the liquid is released. Add ½ cup of the water carrots, broccoli, and cauliflower. Cover and simmer 8–10 minutes or until al dente. Place the zucchini and spinach on top of the vegetables and cover, simmering about 5 minutes or until barely cooked.

144

Blend yams in food processor or with an immersion blender with the remaining 1½ tablespoons oil, the remaining 6 tablespoons of water, and the salt.

With wet hands, press millet into pan forming a bottom crust. Add the vegetables over the millet and then, with a spatula or wooden spoon, spread the puréed yams on top. Sprinkle with paprika and bake 20 minutes or until heated through.

PER SERVING: 326 CALORIES; 6G FAT (15.1% CALORIES FROM FAT); 8G PROTEIN; 64G CARBOHYDRATE; 10G DIETARY FIBER; 0MG CHOLESTEROL; 465MG SODIUM.

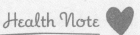

Health Note ♥

YAMS ARE AN EXCELLENT SOURCE OF DIETARY FIBER AND ARE HIGH IN VITAMIN C, VITAMIN A AS BETA-CAROTENE, FOLATE, POTASSIUM, AND MANGANESE.

Barley and Winter Vegetable Risotto

Risotto is an Italian dish that generally uses a short-grain rice, such as Arborio rice or short-grain brown rice, because of their starchier consistency. When you slowly stir in broth, the short-grain rice becomes creamy and delicious. Risotto is typically served with grated cheese. This unique version uses barley instead of rice.

SERVES 6

2 tablespoons extra-virgin olive oil

1 large onion, finely chopped

3 cloves garlic, minced

1½ cups pearl barley

2 cups white wine

2 cups vegetable broth (page 117)

1 cup cubed butternut squash

1 small red bell pepper, chopped

1 cup chopped broccoli

2 medium tomatoes, chopped

2 tablespoons minced mint leaves, stems removed

3 tablespoons minced fresh parsley, stems removed, plus more for garnish

1 teaspoon sea salt, or to taste

1 teaspoon black pepper, or to taste

3 tablespoons grated Parmesan cheese, plus more for garnish

Pine nuts, toasted, for garnish

Place the oil in a large pan over medium heat. When the oil is hot, add the onion and cook until transparent, then add the garlic and barley and cook, stirring often, for 2–3 minutes. Next, add the wine and continue to cook until the wine has evaporated.

Meanwhile, warm the broth in a small saucepan.

Lightly steam the squash, red bell pepper, and broccoli and set aside.

Gradually add the broth to the barley, stirring it regularly until barley is cooked, approximately 50 minutes. Add additional wine or broth if need be.

Stir in the cooked vegetables and continue stirring for 5–10 minutes. Remove risotto from heat and stir in tomatoes, mint, parsley, salt, pepper, and cheese.

To serve, place the risotto in a bowl and garnish with additional cheese, pine nuts, and parsley.

PER SERVING: 374 CALORIES; 7G FAT (19.9% CALORIES FROM FAT); 10G PROTEIN; 57G CARBOHYDRATE; 11G DIETARY FIBER; 3MG CHOLESTEROL; 921MG SODIUM.

Variations

TRY USING SHORT-GRAIN BROWN RICE INSTEAD OF BARLEY, CUBED PUMPKIN OR OTHER WINTER SQUASHES INSTEAD OF BUTTERNUT SQUASH, ROASTED RED PEPPERS INSTEAD OF FRESH, AND CHOPPED KALE IN ADDITION TO THE MINT AND PARSLEY.

Kids in the Kitchen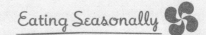

SHOW YOUR CHILDREN THAT THE STEMS OF FRESH MINT ARE SQUARE. MAKE EACH OF YOU A CUP OF MINT TEA TO SIP ON WHILE YOU'RE PREPARING THIS DISH. SIMPLY WASH THE FRESH MINT, PLACE IN A CUP OR TEAPOT, AND COVER WITH BOILING WATER. WONDERFUL! THEY WILL LEARN THAT FRESH HERBS ARE SO AROMATIC.

Eating Seasonally

MAKE THIS SOUP YEAR-ROUND BY SUBSTITUTING THE FOLLOWING VEGETABLES FOR THE WINTER ONES IN THIS RECIPE.

Spring: PEAS, ASPARAGUS

Summer: ZUCCHINI, PEPPERS, CORN

Cooking with Alcohol

A study in 1992 conducted by the U.S. Department of Agriculture's Nutrient Data Laboratory calculated the percentage of alcohol remaining in a dish based on various cooking methods.* The results are as follows:

PREPARATION METHOD PERCENT OF ALCOHOL RETAINED

Alcohol added to boiling liquid and removed from heat:............... 85%
Alcohol flamed:...75%
No heat, stored overnight: 70%
Baked for 25 minutes, alcohol not stirred into mixture:................45%
Baked or simmered for 15 minutes, alcohol stirred into mixture: 40%
Baked or simmered for 30 minutes, alcohol stirred into mixture: 35%
Baked or simmered for 1 hour, alcohol stirred into mixture:........ 25%
Baked or simmered for 1.5 hours, alcohol stirred into mixture: ... 20%
Baked or simmered for 2 hours, alcohol stirred into mixture: 10%
Baked or simmered for 2.5 hours, alcohol stirred into mixture:..... 5%

*(Augustin et al. 1992)

Brown Rice Sushi

Vegetarian sushi is always a favorite with kids, and it's a great way to have them eat more raw vegetables. They love to cut the veggies in julienne. Try many different veggies, but don't fill the rolls too full or they won't stay closed.

SERVES 12

2 cups brown rice, short grain

5 tablespoons brown rice vinegar

2 tablespoons sugar or agave nectar

24 sheets nori seaweed

4 whole cucumbers, cut into matchstick-size pieces

12 sprigs cilantro

5 carrots, julienned

3 red bell peppers, julienned

4 avocados, peeled and thinly sliced

2 tablespoons wasabi powder

Tamari or other soy sauce for dipping

Combine rice with four cups water in a heavy saucepan and bring to a boil. Reduce heat to low and cook, covered, for 45-50 minutes until liquid is absorbed and the rice is tender. Allow the rice to cool by spreading it out on a sheet pan. When it's cooled, but is still slightly warm, place the rice into a medium-size bowl.

Combine rice vinegar and sugar in a small bowl, stirring until sweetener dissolves. Fold mixture into the warm cooked rice.

Place 1 sheet of nori on the counter or cutting board. Dampen hands with water. Pat a thin layer of rice onto the nori, about ¼" thick, leaving a ½" plain nori border around the 4 edges. Arrange pieces of cucumber, cilantro, carrots, bell pepper, and avocado together at one lengthwise edge. Carefully roll up. Repeat with remaining ingredients. Slice and serve with wasabi and tamari.

To prepare wasabi, mix 2 tablespoons wasabi powder with enough water to create a paste.

PER SERVING: 271 CALORIES; 12G FAT (36.3% CALORIES FROM FAT); 6G PROTEIN; 40G CARBOHYDRATE; 5G DIETARY FIBER; 0MG CHOLESTEROL; 71MG SODIUM.

Kids in the Kitchen

WHILE MAKING THIS SUSHI ROLL, SHOW THE YOUNGSTERS JAPAN ON A MAP. OLDER KIDS CAN HELP JULIENNE, WHILE KIDS OF JUST ABOUT ANY AGE CAN HELP PAT DOWN THE RICE AND THEN ROLL THE SUSHI. *MISE EN PLACE* (PRONOUNCED MEE-ZAHN-PLAS), A FRENCH TERM MEANING "PUT IN PLACE," IS IMPORTANT HERE—YOU'LL WANT EVERYTHING AT THE READY WHEN YOU'RE READY TO ROLL.

Eating Seasonally

PRACTICE EATING SEASONALLY BY ADDING ANY OF THE VEGETABLES BELOW, OR SUBSTITUTING THEM FOR THE MAIN INGREDIENTS IN THIS RECIPE, DEPENDING ON THE TIME OF YEAR.

Spring: ASPARAGUS, PEAS, RADISH SLICES

Summer: RAW ZUCCHINI, JICAMA, CELERY, GREEN BEANS

Autumn: CELERIAC, FENNEL

Vegetarian Chili

A wonderful veggie-packed chili! Be sure to serve with lots of garnishes like avocado, cilantro, and cheese. In the summer, fresh tomato salsa (page 75) is a good choice. You can serve over brown rice to make a more complete protein.

SERVES 8

¼ cup extra-virgin olive oil

1 cup chopped celery

2 onions, chopped

1 jalapeño, seeded and minced

1 cup chopped shiitake mushrooms

1 medium red bell pepper, chopped

6 cloves garlic, minced

3 tablespoons chili powder

2½ tablespoons ground cumin

1 teaspoon ground oregano

Dash cayenne pepper

2 cups cooked pinto beans

2 cups cooked kidney beans

2 cups cooked black beans

Two 28-ounce cans crushed Italian tomatoes

Sea salt to taste

Black pepper to taste

Fresh cilantro or parsley for garnish

Grated cheese for garnish (optional)

Avocado slices for garnish (optional)

In a large, heavy saucepan over medium heat, warm the oil. Add the celery, onions, and jalapeño and sauté until tender, about 10 minutes, stirring occasionally. Add the mushrooms, red bell pepper, garlic, chili powder, cumin, oregano, and cayenne pepper and stir for about 5 minutes. Next add the pinto, kidney, and black beans and tomatoes; stir and bring to a boil. Reduce heat, cover, and simmer for about 20 minutes. Stir occasionally.

Season to taste with salt and black pepper. Serve hot garnished with cilantro and, if you like, cheese and avocado.

PER SERVING: 676 CALORIES; 10G FAT (12.2% CALORIES FROM FAT); 36G PROTEIN; 120G CARBOHYDRATE; 37G DIETARY FIBER; 0MG CHOLESTEROL; 136MG SODIUM.

Eating Seasonally

PRACTICE EATING SEASONALLY BY ADDING ANY OF THE VEGETABLES BELOW, OR SUBSTITUTING THEM FOR THE MAIN INGREDIENTS IN THIS RECIPE, DEPENDING ON THE TIME OF YEAR.

Spring: GREEN GARLIC, CARROTS, CELERY, PEAS (ADD AT THE VERY END)

Summer: BELL PEPPERS, CELERY, SUMMER SQUASHES, TOMATOES

Autumn: BELL PEPPERS, CARROTS, JERUSALEM ARTICHOKES, PARSNIPS

Winter: CARROTS, LEEKS, POTATOES, RUTABAGAS, WINTER SQUASHES

Variations

YOU MAY SUBSTITUTE 6 CUPS OF BEANS THAT YOU HAVE COOKED FOR THE CANNED BEANS.

Baked Beans

This is a wonderful old-fashioned baked beans recipe with three vegetables added. To make this dish even more MVP-worthy, stir in some corn, green bell peppers, or some cubed winter squash the last hour of cooking—even better! Try adding some smoked tempeh the last hour of cooking for a smoky flavor. Put the beans in the oven on Sunday morning, go play, come back, and dinner's ready.

SERVES 8

1 pound dry navy beans

One 2" piece kombu seaweed

4 cups cold water

1 medium onion, chopped

4 cloves garlic, minced

½ teaspoon sea salt

2 teaspoons cider vinegar

½ teaspoon prepared mustard

1 tablespoon brown sugar

¼ cup molasses

½ cup tomato ketchup

½ teaspoon black pepper

Hot water, as needed

Discard any beans that are discolored then rinse the beans to remove dirt. Place the cleaned beans in a 6-cup Dutch oven or other heavy pan with a lid. Soak the beans and kombu, covered, in the cold water for at least 4 hours or overnight. On the stovetop, heat to boiling then turn down to low and simmer, covered, for 30 minutes.

Preheat the oven to 300°F.

Stir in the onions and garlic, cover, and bake, stirring occasionally, for 3 hours. If necessary, add a little more hot water.

In a small bowl, mix the salt, vinegar, mustard, sugar, molasses, ketchup, and pepper. When the beans have baked for 3 hours, stir these seasonings into the pot, add any vegetables you like, cover and continue to bake for another 4 hours or so, adding a little more liquid if necessary.

PER SERVING: 133 CALORIES; TRACE FAT (2.9% CALORIES FROM FAT); 6G PROTEIN; 28G CARBOHYDRATE; 5G DIETARY FIBER; 0MG CHOLESTEROL; 455MG SODIUM.

Health Note ♥

BEANS ARE AN EXCELLENT SOURCE OF THE B-VITAMINS THIAMIN, RIBOFLAVIN, AND FOLATE, AS WELL AS VITAMIN E, IRON, AND MAGNESIUM. THEY ARE ALSO A GOOD SOURCE OF PHOSPHORUS AND ZINC AND ARE NATURALLY HIGH IN DIETARY FIBER.

SEAWEED MAKES THE BEANS MORE DIGESTIBLE AND ADDS IMPORTANT MINERALS.

Vegan Patties

This dish is adapted from a recipe by Julia Ross, author of *The Diet Cure*. Serve them with grated carrots, sprouts, lettuce, and sliced tomatoes on a whole-grain bun for a delicious vegan burger. The patties are very easy to handle and won't fall apart like some others you may have tried.

SERVES 6

One 14-ounce can garbanzo beans, drained

1 red onion, chopped

½ cup chopped red bell pepper

½ cup grated carrots

½ cup cooked quinoa (page 196)

½ cup chopped fresh parsley, stems removed

2 tablespoons nutritional yeast

1 teaspoon cumin seed, toasted and ground

1 teaspoon ground coriander

1 teaspoon sea salt

Dash cayenne pepper

1 to 2 tablespoons extra-virgin olive oil

Place beans in a food processor and process until smooth. Remove and place in a medium bowl. Place onion and bell pepper in food processor and pulse until finely chopped, or chop by hand. Add to the bean mixture along with the carrots. Add cooked quinoa, parsley, yeast, cumin, coriander, salt, and cayenne pepper. Mix well. Form into patties and sauté in oil for 3 minutes on each side or bake in a 375°F oven for about 20 minutes.

PER SERVING: 317 CALORIES; 5G FAT (14.2% CALORIES FROM FAT); 15G PROTEIN; 55G CARBOHYDRATE; 14G DIETARY FIBER; 0MG CHOLESTEROL; 340MG SODIUM.

Variations

CHANGE THE HERBS IF YOU LIKE: USE CILANTRO INSTEAD OF PARSLEY AND SKIP THE CORIANDER POWDER. YOU MIGHT ALSO TRY ADDING 1 TEASPOON OF CURRY POWDER.

Kids in the Kitchen

HAVE YOUR CHILDREN WASH THEIR HANDS AND HELP MAKE THE PATTIES. THIS RECIPE IS GREAT FOR LITTLE FINGERS, AS THE MIXTURE DOESN'T STICK MUCH, IF AT ALL, TO THEIR HANDS. ALSO, TAKE THE OPPORTUNITY TO EXPLAIN THAT DIFFERENT-SIZE FOODS COOK DIFFERENTLY. HAVE THEM MAKE ALL THE PATTIES ABOUT THE SAME SIZE.

Spaghetti Squash Supreme

This is an all-vegetable meal containing one of our favorite veggies: spaghetti squash. Its seeds, when baked, are also edible and have some protein and oils. When you bite them, the seeds pop out into your mouth; we discard the shells unless they have been toasted, making them more edible and crunchy with a roasted flavor. This very low-calorie dish can be served as a side; or add some cannellini or fava beans for added protein. For a richer flavor, you may sauté the onions in the olive oil before adding the remaining vegetables.

SERVES 4

½ to 1 medium to large spaghetti squash

1 small eggplant, sliced into half circles

1 small to medium onion, chopped

4 large button mushrooms, sliced

1 red bell pepper sliced into strips

1 to 2 tablespoons extra-virgin olive oil

2 to 4 tablespoons water

2 cups tomato or pasta sauce

¼ teaspoon sea salt

½ to 1 teaspoon mixed dried Italian seasoning, or ground oregano and basil

Parmesan cheese, for garnish

Fresh basil or parsley, chopped, for garnish

Preheat oven between 325°F–350°F. Place spaghetti squash on a baking sheet and bake 30–40 minutes, depending on size. Let it cool and slice open. Remove the seeds then scoop out the noodley squash and place in a bowl. Set aside.

In a large skillet, layer in the eggplant, onion, mushrooms, and red bell pepper; add the oil and water. Turn on the heat to medium and let the vegetables cook 5–10 minutes until they begin to soften. Add the spaghetti squash on top and cover with tomato sauce, salt, and herbs, and cover and cook on low to medium heat for another 5–10 minutes, stirring midway to mix all the foods and flavors together. Serve in bowls garnished with cheese and basil, if you like.

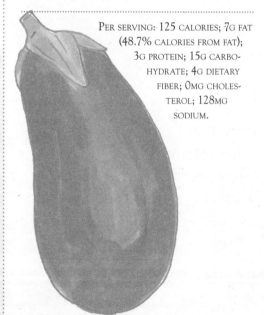

PER SERVING: 125 CALORIES; 7G FAT (48.7% CALORIES FROM FAT); 3G PROTEIN; 15G CARBO-HYDRATE; 4G DIETARY FIBER; 0MG CHOLES-TEROL; 128MG SODIUM.

Variations

THIS DISH CAN ADAPT TO ALL KINDS OF VEGETABLES. YOU CAN USE GREEN ZUC-CHINI (ADDING IT LATER IN THE COOKING STEP SO IT DOESN'T GET TOO SOFT) AND EVEN SPINACH, CHARD, OR KALE TOWARD THE END OF THE COOKING (WITH THE SPAGHETTI SQUASH). YOU CAN ALSO ADD CARROTS, BOK CHOY, CELERY, AND CHOPPED NUTS OR WHOLE CASHEWS.

Stuffed Baked Potatoes

Most people fill their baked potatoes with butter and sour cream.
But since this book is about MVP, this recipe gives you some
options for changing things up.

SERVES 4

4 medium to large russet potatoes

Your favorite veggies (bell peppers, onions, garlic, zucchini, corn, etc.)

Your favorite toppings (raw broccoli, parsley or cilantro, salsa, grated cheese, etc.)

Chipotle Dressing (page 110) (optional)

Scrub potatoes and bake for about an hour in a 375°F oven. No, you cannot use your microwave! While they're baking, sauté some of your favorite veggies or whatever is in season, then place in a bowl. Arrange each topping—and the Chipotle Dressing, if using—in small bowls, too. Your family will love creating their own potato from the potato bar. And hopefully they'll ask for MVP!

PER SERVING: NUTRITIONAL DATA WILL VARY DEPENDING ON THE TOPPINGS.

Baked Penne Pasta with Roasted Vegetables

Everyone loves pasta, and this will soon become a family favorite.
Serve with a fresh green salad.

SERVES 6

2 medium red bell peppers, cut into 1"-wide strips

2 medium zucchini, quartered lengthwise and cut into 1" cubes

2 medium summer squash, quartered lengthwise and cut into 1" cubes

6 medium shiitake mushrooms, halved

1 medium yellow onion, sliced into 1" pieces

¼ cup extra-virgin olive oil

1½ teaspoon sea salt, divided

1 teaspoon freshly ground black pepper, divided

1 tablespoon dried Italian seasoning

4 cloves garlic, minced

1 pound uncooked whole-wheat penne pasta

3 cups marinara sauce

1 cup grated Fontina or Provolone cheese

½ cup grated smoked mozzarella cheese

¼ cup grated Parmesan cheese, plus ⅓ cup for topping

1½ cups frozen peas, thawed

2 tablespoons unsalted butter, cut into small pieces

Preheat the oven to 450°F. On a baking sheet, toss the bell peppers, zucchini, squash, mushrooms, and onions with oil. Mix in ½ teaspoon of the salt, ½ teaspoon of the black pepper, and Italian seasonings. Roast in a single layer, so as to avoid steaming, until al dente, about 15–20 minutes. Add the garlic the last 5 minutes of cooking.

Meanwhile, bring a large pot of salted water to a boil over high heat. Add the pasta and cook for about 6 minutes. Drain. It won't be cooked all the way, as it will finish cooking in the oven.

In a large bowl, toss the pasta with the roasted vegetables, marinara sauce, Fontina and mozzarella cheeses, ¼ cup of the Parmesan cheese, peas, the remaining 1 teaspoon salt, and the remaining ½ teaspoon pepper. Gently mix until all the pasta is coated with the sauce and the ingredients are combined.

Pour the pasta mixture into a greased 9" by 13" pan. Top with the remaining 1/3 cup Parmesan cheese and butter pieces. Bake until top is golden and cheese melts, about 25 minutes.

PER SERVING: 561 CALORIES; 20G FAT (30.2% CALORIES FROM FAT); 21G PROTEIN; 82G CARBOHYDRATE; 13G DIETARY FIBER; 21MG CHOLESTEROL; 1,043 MG SODIUM.

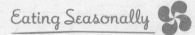

Eating Seasonally

PRACTICE EATING SEASONALLY BY ADDING ANY OF THE VEGETABLES BELOW, OR SUBSTITUTING THEM FOR THE MAIN

INGREDIENTS IN THIS RECIPE, DEPENDING ON THE TIME OF YEAR.

Summer: EGGPLANT, GREEN BEANS
Autumn: PARSNIPS, TURNIPS
Winter: WINTER SQUASHES

Macaroni and Cheese

Most everyone loves macaroni and cheese. This recipe still calls for cheese and butter (don't eat often!), but it also has four different vegetables. When Patty ran Summer Camp for Kids, it was always a favorite with the children.

SERVES 12

1 teaspoon extra-virgin olive oil

1 pound elbow macaroni

2 teaspoons sea salt, divided

8 tablespoons (1 stick) unsalted butter, divided

½ cup all-purpose flour

1 quart whole milk, heated

2½ cups grated Gruyere cheese (about 10 ounces)

2 cups grated extra-sharp cheddar cheese (about 6 ounces)

½ teaspoon freshly ground black pepper

½ teaspoon grated nutmeg

2 cups chopped broccoli, lightly steamed

1½ cups peas (if frozen, run under hot water and drain)

1 cup diced carrots, steamed

¾ pound fresh tomatoes (about 4 small), cut into ¼" slices

1 cup fresh bread crumbs (about 4 slices, cut or torn into small pieces)

Preheat the oven to 375°F.

Drizzle oil into a large pot of boiling salted water. Add the macaroni and 1 teaspoon of the salt and cook according to the directions on the package, about 6–8 minutes. Drain well.

Melt 6 tablespoons of the butter in a 4-quart pot and slowly whisk in the flour. Cook over low heat for 2 minutes, stirring constantly. Slowly add the hot milk and cook 1–2 minutes, until smooth and thickened. Turn off the heat and add the cheeses, the remaining 1 teaspoon salt, pepper, and nutmeg. Add the cooked macaroni and stir well. Stir in the broccoli, peas, and carrots. Pour into a buttered 3-quart baking dish.

Arrange the tomatoes on top. Melt the remaining 2 tablespoons of butter, combine them with the bread crumbs, and sprinkle on top. Bake 30–35 minutes, or until the sauce is bubbly and the macaroni is browned on top.

PER SERVING: 488 CALORIES; 24G FAT (42.7% FROM FAT); 23G PROTEIN; 49G CARBOHYDRATE; 5G DIETARY FIBER; 71 MG CHOLESTEROL; 638 MG SODIUM.

Cooking Tip

TO MAKE AHEAD OF TIME, PUT THE MACARONI AND CHEESE IN THE BAKING DISH, COVER, AND REFRIGERATE UNTIL READY TO BAKE. PUT THE TOMATOES AND BREADCRUMBS ON TOP JUST BEFORE COOKING AND BAKE 40–50 MINUTES.

Egg Main Dishes

Egg, Rice, and Veggie Bake

This is a dish that your kids can assemble with just a little supervision from you. They can take all the credit and will be so proud that they did it all themselves! It's great for breakfast, lunch, or dinner.

SERVES 9

1½ cups chopped broccoli

1 cup chopped carrots

1 cup chopped red bell pepper

3 cups cooked wild rice, or any leftover grain

1 cup quartered water-packed artichoke hearts, drained

12 eggs

1½ cups milk (dairy, plain soy, or rice)

1 teaspoon sea salt

1 teaspoon black pepper

1 cup grated cheese (pepper jack is nice), for topping (optional)

Preheat oven to 375°F. Oil a 9" x 13" pan.

Steam or sauté the broccoli, carrots, and bell pepper until al dente.

Place cooked wild rice evenly into the oiled pan. Place the artichoke hearts and steamed vegetables onto the wild rice.

In a large bowl, whisk the eggs and milk. Add the salt and pepper to the egg mixture and pour atop the vegetable mixture. If desired, sprinkle with cheese. Bake for 50 minutes or until lightly browned.

PER SERVING: 327 CALORIES; 8G FAT (21.3% CALORIES FROM FAT); 18G PROTEIN; 48G CARBOHYDRATE; 5G DIETARY FIBER; 255MG CHOLESTEROL; 333MG SODIUM.

Variations

CHANGE THE VEGGIES WITH THE SEASONS. IN THE SUMMER, SAUTÉ ONIONS AND ZUCCHINI AND USE THEM INSTEAD OF ARTICHOKES. PLAY WITH SEASONINGS: TRY GARLIC WITH ZUCCHINI, TARRAGON WITH BLANCHED ASPARAGUS, AND SO FORTH. I LIKE THIS DISH WITH A COUPLE TEASPOONS OF CURRY POWDER AND ½ CUP OF MINCED FRESH CILANTRO. YOU CAN ADD SOME DRAINED BEANS AND USE CHILI POWDER AND TOP WITH PEPPER JACK CHEESE (AND SALSA!). THIS RECIPE CAN ALSO BE DAIRY FREE IF YOU SUBSTITUTE ANOTHER MILK FOR COW, SUCH AS RICE OR ALMOND OR OAT (IDEALLY THE UNSWEETENED VERSIONS) MILK AND AVOID USING THE CHEESE.

Eggs for Breakfast

We rarely eat eggs plain. Sauté some onions and garlic with potatoes, mushrooms, and spinach, then add them to your eggs for a delicious scramble to start the day off right. Almost every vegetable pairs nicely with eggs. One of Dr. Haas's hearty breakfasts is two organic eggs cooked over easy on corn tortillas with salsa and greens or sprouts. It lasts him easily till lunchtime. Another easy, delicious, and nutritious breakfast is to wash and chop some kale, chard, or collard greens and place them in a covered pan with a little bit of water or broth. When the greens are cooked, crack two eggs on the top, cover, and "poach" the eggs until they're how you like them. Using a slotted spoon, place the greens and eggs onto a plate, sprinkle with sea salt and pepper, and enjoy!

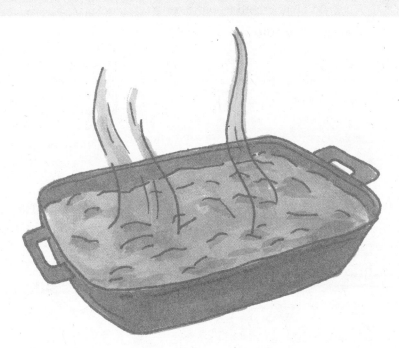

Frittata Primavera

Be sure to use a pan with an ovenproof handle, as the dish will be put under the broiler. You may use soymilk instead of dairy milk, and the cheese selection can be changed to whatever type you like as well. It's wonderful served with a fresh green or fruit salad.

SERVES 4

2 tablespoons extra-virgin olive oil

1 pound red potatoes, unpeeled and diced (about 3 cups)

Sea salt to taste

Black pepper to taste

1 red onion, sliced (about 2 cups)

¼ pound mushrooms, sliced (about 1½ cups)

1 red bell pepper, sliced (about 1 cup)

4 cloves garlic, minced

4 eggs

½ cup milk

½ cup chopped fresh basil, stems removed

½ cup grated Parmesan cheese

In a large sauté pan, place the oil over medium-high heat. When hot, add the potatoes in a single layer (so that they don't steam) and sauté until golden brown. Add a little salt and pepper to taste.

Meanwhile, prepare the vegetables. Add onion, mushrooms, bell pepper, and garlic to the pan and sauté another 5 minutes, stirring occasionally.

In a medium bowl, whisk the eggs and milk together, add basil, and pour egg mixture into frying pan. Gently toss egg mixture to spread throughout pan. Turn heat to low and cook for about 10 minutes. Sprinkle with cheese and place under a preheated broiler. Broil for 2 minutes.

PER SERVING: 359 CALORIES; 16G FAT (38.4% CALORIES FROM FAT); 17G PROTEIN; 41G CARBOHYDRATE; 11G DIETARY FIBER; 199MG CHOLESTEROL; 273MG SODIUM.

Eating Seasonally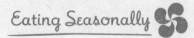

THE POTATOES ALWAYS REMAIN IN THE RECIPE, BUT OTHER VEGETABLES CAN BE CHANGED WITH THE SEASON.

Spring: ASPARAGUS, PEAS, SPRING ONIONS

Summer: ZUCCHINI, GREEN BEANS, CORN

Autumn: BROCCOLI, CARROTS

Winter: CELERIAC, BRUSSELS SPROUTS, SNOW PEAS

Variations

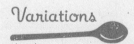

BASIL CAN BE SUBSTITUTED WITH PARSLEY, DILL, THYME, AND SO ON, FOR A DELIGHTFULLY DIFFERENT FLAVOR EACH TIME.

Eggs and Sprouts Burrito

Sprouts are such a nutritious food that we like to come up with lots of ways to use them in meals, even in a breakfast dish that could, of course, be used for lunch or dinner. We think you will like this one!

SERVES 4

1 tablespoon sesame oil

1½ teaspoons peeled and grated ginger

2 cloves fresh garlic, minced

1 cup thinly sliced shiitake mushrooms

2 green onions, chopped

2 cups chopped bok choy

6 whole eggs

1 tablespoon soy sauce

1 tablespoon dry sherry

1 teaspoon arrowroot or cornstarch

2 teaspoons water

1 cup bean sprouts

2 flour tortillas

In a medium sauté pan, heat the oil over medium heat. Add the ginger and garlic and sauté over low heat until fragrant, about 2 minutes. Add the mushrooms and green onions and cook, stirring, about 3 minutes. Add the bok choy and cook 2 minutes.

Break eggs into a bowl and whisk. Pour into the sauté pan and stir with the vegetables until eggs are almost set, about 3 minutes.

In a small bowl, mix together soy sauce, sherry, arrowroot, and water. Add bean sprouts and soy sauce mixture to sauté pan and stir together until slightly thickened. Spoon into warm flour tortillas and roll up. Cut in half and serve.

PER SERVING: 447 CALORIES; 13G FAT (25.2% CALORIES FROM FAT); 19G PROTEIN; 70G CARBOHYDRATE; 9G DIETARY FIBER; 281MG CHOLESTEROL; 546MG SODIUM.

Health Note ♥

EGGS ARE A COMPLETE PROTEIN AND ARE HIGH IN CHOLINE, WHICH APPEARS TO WORK WITH FOLATE AND THE AMINO ACID METHIONINE. CHOLINE IS PART OF A CELL'S STRUCTURE AND IS PARTICULARLY IMPORTANT FOR FETUSES AND INFANTS. HUMAN MILK HAS HIGH LEVELS OF THIS IMPORTANT NUTRIENT. EGGS ARE A VERY GOOD SOURCE OF CHOLINE, CONTAINING ROUGHLY 22 PERCENT OF AN ADULT'S DAILY REQUIREMENT IN ONE EGG.

Asparagus Quiche

This is a crust-less quiche that is wonderful served in the spring when asparagus are at their peak.

SERVES 12

1 cup shredded Swiss cheese

½ cup shredded cheddar cheese

1½ cups chopped asparagus

⅓ cup chopped green onions, white parts only, or shallots

1 cup sliced mushrooms

12 whole eggs

2 cups milk

½ teaspoon nutmeg, or to taste

1 teaspoon sea salt

½ teaspoon black pepper, or to taste

Chopped fresh parsley, stems removed, for garnish (optional)

Preheat oven to 375°F. Grease a 9" x 13" pan. Spread cheeses on bottom of pan and top with asparagus, onions, and mushrooms.

Whisk together eggs, milk, nutmeg, salt, and pepper. Pour over cheese and vegetables. Bake about 45 minutes or until knife inserted in center comes out clean. Garnish with parsley, if desired.

PER SERVING: 152 CALORIES; 10G FAT (59.4% CALORIES FROM FAT); 11G PROTEIN; 4G CARBOHYDRATE; 1G DIETARY FIBER; 206MG CHOLESTEROL; 287MG SODIUM.

Variations

FEEL FREE TO ADD MORE VEGETABLES TO THIS CLASSIC CUSTARD-LIKE QUICHE. PEAS AND CHOPPED BROCCOLI WOULD BE NICE ADDITIONS. OR SERVE WITH A MIXED-GREENS SALAD DRESSED WITH SOME OLIVE OIL AND FRESH LEMON JUICE. THAT'S ALL YOU NEED!

Kids in the Kitchen

THIS IS THE PERFECT RECIPE TO EXPLAIN TO YOUR CHILDREN THE IMPORTANCE OF SEASONAL EATING. NOTHING SAYS SPRINGTIME MORE THAN ASPARAGUS. HAVE THEM EAT A STALK FRESH WHILE THEY ARE HELPING TO PREPARE.

Fish Main Dishes

Salmon *en Papillote*

En papillote means "in paper" in French, and that's what you use to cook the fish in. You may use any kind of fish, or use tofu or a pounded chicken breast (bake for approximately 25 minutes for poultry) in this versatile dish. Change the vegetables with the season or simply use this same format with just vegetables! This may be prepared earlier in the day and kept in the refrigerator until ready to bake; it's great for parties—just multiply the recipe for the number of people you're serving. The salmon skin provides good oils and nutrients, so if its "sliminess" doesn't bother you, eat it right along with the fish.

SERVES 1

1 tablespoon white wine

½ teaspoon toasted sesame oil

½ teaspoon peeled and grated fresh ginger

⅛ teaspoon sea salt

Black pepper to taste

1 cup spinach leaves, washed and dried

6 ounces salmon fillet, skin removed, washed and dried

2 stalks asparagus, sliced in half lengthwise

2 thin slices red bell pepper

Preheat the oven to 375°F.

Mix the wine, oil, ginger, salt, and pepper to taste in a small bowl.

Cut a piece of parchment paper to about 18" long. Weight down the edges and place the spinach leaves on one side of the paper.

Place the salmon fillet atop the leaves. On top of the salmon place the asparagus and bell pepper. Drizzle with the sauce.

Bring up the parchment paper and crimp edges to close tightly. Place on baking sheet and bake for 20 minutes.

You may open at the table if you like (be careful of the steam when removing the wrapper) and serve with a tossed green salad. It's very pretty.

PER SERVING: 289 CALORIES; 7G FAT (20.7% CALORIES FROM FAT); 38G PROTEIN; 19G CARBOHYDRATE; 6G DIETARY FIBER; 88MG CHOLESTEROL; 379MG SODIUM.

Fish Burgers with Tomato Relish

You may broil or sauté these tasty burgers. Use whatever fish is fresh in your area, and be sure to check your fish guide for environmentally sound choices.

SERVES 4

4 whole-grain sourdough sandwich buns

1 pound fresh white fish, fillets or steaks, skin removed

Extra-virgin olive oil

Sprouts

Lettuce

1 avocado, peeled and sliced

Tomato Relish

YIELDS 2⅓ CUPS

½ cup chopped red bell pepper

1 cup chopped onion

4 cloves garlic, minced

1 medium jalapeño, seeded and minced

1 cup finely chopped tomatoes

Juice of 1 whole lemon or lime

1 tablespoon brown sugar or agave nectar

¼ teaspoon sea salt

Make an indentation in the bottom half of each bun by removing some of the bread (this will help keep the grilled seafood from falling out during serving and eating). Lightly brush buns and fish with oil. Warm or toast buns on the grill then set aside to keep warm.

Grill fish fillets to desired doneness, generally 5–10 minutes total per inch of thickness. Place on a plate and remove bones, if any. Pile grilled fish on the side of bun with the indentation and top with spicy tomato relish. Top with sprouts and/or lettuce.

To make the relish, combine all ingredients in a small saucepan and cook uncovered until thick, about 20 minutes. Serve warm.

PER SERVING: 562 CALORIES; 7G FAT (11.2% CALORIES FROM FAT); 37G PROTEIN; 87G CARBOHYDRATE; 6G DIETARY FIBER; 36MG CHOLESTEROL; 948MG SODIUM.

Kids in the Kitchen

FISH IS SOMETHING EITHER KIDS LIKE OR REALLY DON'T LIKE—OR SO THEY THINK! KEEP TRYING TO INTRODUCE FISH, AS KIDS' TASTES ARE CONSTANTLY CHANGING. FISH BURGERS JUST MIGHT DO IT...IF NOT, THE TUNA CASSEROLE RECIPE (PAGE 163) WILL! TO GET YOUR CHILDREN INVOLVED, HAVE THEM HOLLOW OUT THE BUNS AND PREPARE ANY ADDITIONAL CONDIMENTS FOR THE BURGERS, SUCH AS WASHING AND DRYING THE LETTUCE.

Tuna Casserole

When an old-fashioned recipe is spruced up with three vegetables and fresh herbs, and served with a green salad, you'll have an instant family favorite. You won't believe that the original recipe called for four cups of cheese and zero vegetables!

SERVES 4

2½ cups unsalted chicken broth (or if salted, omit the 1 teaspoon salt)

1 teaspoon sea salt

½ teaspoon black pepper

8 ounces uncooked egg noodles

½ cup diced red bell pepper

1 cup chopped green beans, cut into 1" pieces

1 cup milk

1 cup fresh or frozen peas

1½ cups grated cheddar cheese

One 6⅛-ounce can white albacore tuna packed in water, drained (or freshly poached tuna, cooled slightly and flaked)

¼ cup chopped fresh parsley, stems removed

1 tablespoon chopped fresh basil leaves

In a large (4-quart) pot, bring the broth to a boil. Then add salt (if needed), pepper, and noodles and return to a boil. Lower heat to medium, cover, and cook about 4 minutes, stirring occasionally

Stir diced bell pepper, beans, and milk into pot of noodles. Cover and simmer another 3–4 minutes or until pasta and beans are al dente. Stir in peas, cheese, tuna, and parsley until cheese is melted. (If you would like to bake this meal in a casserole dish, do not add the cheese during this step; instead, sprinkle it on top before baking. See below.) Add the basil at the last minute.

For easy cleanup, but not the prettiest presentation, you may serve directly from the pot as soon as the peas have been heated through. Or you may place the tuna and noodle mixture into a greased casserole dish, sprinkle with cheese (see note in previous paragraph), and bake in a 350°F oven until cheese melts. (You can also make the mixture ahead of time, store it in the refrigerator, and then bake it in the oven just before serving.) Add a nice green salad to round out your veggies.

PER SERVING: 450 CALORIES; 8G FAT (16.8% CALORIES FROM FAT); 37G PROTEIN; 55G CARBOHYDRATE; 4G DIETARY FIBER; 36MG CHOLESTEROL; 1,175MG SODIUM.

Health Note ♥

GREEN BEANS ARE A GOOD SOURCE OF VITAMINS K, C, AND A AS WELL AS MANGANESE, POTASSIUM, AND DIETARY FIBER.

Cooking Tip

IF YOU HAVE FRESH TUNA, THEN BY ALL MEANS USE IT! IF NOT, A GOOD-QUALITY CANNED TUNA WILL BE FINE.

Halibut or Salmon Sauté

This dish is wonderful served on basmati brown rice with a spinach salad. Halibut and salmon are both coldwater fish that are high in omega-3 fatty acids, which have numerous health benefits, particularly in maintaining good brain function.

SERVES 3

1 pound halibut or salmon

Sea salt to taste, plus ¼ teaspoon, divided

Black pepper to taste

2 tablespoons extra-virgin olive oil, divided

1 cup thinly sliced carrots

1 cup thinly sliced celery

1 cup thinly sliced green onions

1 cup broccoli florets

1 teaspoon peeled and grated fresh ginger root

¼ cup vegetable broth (page 117) or chicken broth (page 119)

2 teaspoons cornstarch or arrowroot

1 teaspoon grated lemon or lime peel

Remove and discard the skin and bones from the halibut or salmon. Cut into 1" cubes. Season fish with salt and pepper and set aside.

In a sauté pan, heat 1 tablespoon of the oil over medium-high heat. Add the fish and sauté until barely cooked, about 5 minutes. Remove fish from skillet.

Sauté carrots, celery, onions, and broccoli in remaining oil until al dente. Return fish to skillet. Add ¼ teaspoon salt and ginger. Combine broth, cornstarch, and lemon peel in a small bowl; add to fish mixture. Cook and stir until thickened and the fish flakes when tested with a fork.

PER SERVING: 295 CALORIES; 13G FAT (39.0% CALORIES FROM FAT); 34G PROTEIN; 11G CARBOHYDRATE; 4G DIETARY FIBER; 48MG CHOLESTEROL; 300MG SODIUM.

Health Note ♥

HALIBUT IS A GOOD SOURCE OF TRYPTOPHAN (REMEMBER HOW THAT THANKSGIVING TURKEY MAKES YOU SLEEPY? THAT'S THE TRYPTOPHAN, WHICH FORMS SEROTONIN, OUR FEEL-GOOD AND RELAXING NEURO-HOR-MONE), AS WELL AS SELENIUM, PROTEIN, VITAMIN B3, AND HEART-HEALTHY OMEGA 3 FATTY ACIDS.

Red Snapper Veracruz-Style

The state of Veracruz, in Mexico, stretches along the Gulf Coast, and the rich culinary heritage of the locals is reflected in the ingredients in this, their signature dish. For a beautiful color and added nutrients, add one 14-ounce can of black beans, rinsed and drained, to your meal. Heat the beans and place them on top of the rice, saving a few to sprinkle on the top of the dish.

SERVES 4

2 pounds red snapper or other firm white fish fillets

½ teaspoon sea salt

¼ cup fresh lime juice

1 medium yellow onion, thinly sliced

1 medium red bell pepper, thinly sliced, divided

2 cups diced tomatoes (about 2 large tomatoes)

One 4-ounce can green chiles, mild or hot, chopped

1 tablespoon capers, drained

½ cup chopped cilantro

Wash the fish, pat dry, and place in a glass bowl. Lightly salt and pour the lime juice evenly over the fillets. Cover and refrigerate for at least 1 hour.

Sauté the onion in a skillet over medium-low heat, covered, until tender, about 10 minutes. If necessary, add a tablespoon of water to prevent scorching. Add half the bell peppers and all of the tomatoes, chiles, and capers. Cook, covered, for about 10 minutes. There will be liquid in the bottom of the pan. Add the fish and the other half of the bell pepper and cook, uncovered, for about 5 minutes on each side. Sprinkle with cilantro and serve over quinoa or brown rice.

PER SERVING: 287 CALORIES; 4G FAT (11.5% CALORIES FROM FAT); 49G PROTEIN; 14G CARBOHYDRATE; 3G DIETARY FIBER; 84MG CHOLESTEROL; 418MG SODIUM.

Health Note ♥

THE ONION FAMILY INCLUDES GARLIC, LEEKS, SHALLOTS, AND CHIVES. THE ANTIOXIDANT QUERCETIN, FOUND IN ONIONS, HELPS TO DESTROY FREE RADICALS AND PROTECTS AND REGENERATES VITAMIN E. ONIONS MAY ALSO HAVE A BENEFICIAL EFFECT ON CHOLESTEROL LEVELS.

Halibut Marengo-Style

Marengo is an Italian dish named for the food that Napoleon ate after the battle of Marengo. Serve with brown basmati rice or quinoa and a simple spinach salad. That's it—an easy weeknight meal!

SERVES 4

Four 4-ounce halibut steaks

⅛ teaspoon sea salt, plus more for seasoning

White pepper for seasoning

1 medium tomato, diced

1 tablespoon extra-virgin olive oil

½ cup sliced mushrooms

½ cup sliced onions

½ cup diced celery

1 tablespoon lemon juice

1 teaspoon fresh thyme

½ teaspoon black pepper

Chopped fresh parsley, stems removed

Black olives, chopped or sliced

Preheat oven to 375°F.

Season halibut with a little salt and white pepper and place in a 9" x 9" glass baking dish that has been lightly rubbed with oil. Spoon tomato over halibut.

In a sauté pan, heat oil over medium heat. Add mushrooms, onions, celery, lemon juice, thyme, ⅛ teaspoon of the salt, and black pepper and sauté until vegetables are al dente, about 5 minutes. Spoon over halibut. Bake, covered, until halibut flakes when tested with a fork, about 20 minutes. Garnish with parsley and olives.

PER SERVING: 175 CALORIES; 6G FAT (32.3% CALORIES FROM FAT); 24G PROTEIN; 5G CARBOHYDRATE; 1G DIETARY FIBER; 36MG CHOLESTEROL; 137MG SODIUM.

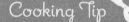

Cooking Tip

OFTENTIMES LEMON JUICE CAN "BRIGHTEN" A DISH. BEFORE YOU REACH FOR THE SALTSHAKER, TRY A BIT OF LEMON JUICE OR FRESH HERBS APPROPRIATE FOR THE DISH.

Poultry Main Dishes

Turkey Meatloaf

This recipe—one of Patty's most requested—can also be made with ground beef or chicken—and just about any vegetable combination. Be sure to have your kids help. They can add the ingredients, mix it with their hands, and shape it. If you are sensitive to oats, you may substitute leftover brown rice.

SERVES 10

3 pounds ground turkey

3 large eggs

1 cup rolled oats

1 red bell pepper, finely chopped

1 medium yellow onion, finely chopped

1 small carrot, grated (about ¾ cup)

1 stalk celery, finely chopped (¾ cup)

1½ teaspoons sea salt, black pepper, and dry mustard

Preheat oven to 375°F.

Place all ingredients in a large bowl and mix well. You may find it easier to mix with your hands. Place the mixture in a 9" x 9" pan and shape into a loaf. Bake for 1 ½ hours or until light brown.

PER SERVING: 267 CALORIES; 13G FAT (45.5% CALORIES FROM FAT); 27G PROTEIN; 8G CARBOHYDRATE; 2G DIETARY FIBER; 164MG CHOLESTEROL; 434MG SODIUM.

Variations

YOU MAY FORM THE MIXTURE INTO MEATBALLS AND BAKE ON A COOKIE SHEET FOR ABOUT 30 MINUTES AT 375°. YOU MAY ALSO SAUTÉ THEM IN A LITTLE OLIVE OIL OVER MEDIUM HEAT. AFTER THEY HAVE BROWNED ON ALL SIDES, REMOVE THEM FROM THE PAN AND KEEP THEM WARM ON A PLATE IN THE OVEN. INTO THE PAN WITH DRIPPINGS ADD 1 TABLESPOON FLOUR AND COOK FOR 1 MINUTE. WHISK IN ½ CUP OF WHITE WINE OR BROTH AND ¼ CUP FRESHLY MINCED PARSLEY AND COOK FOR ABOUT 3 MINUTES, OR UNTIL SOME OF THE WINE OR BROTH HAS EVAPORATED. SEASON WITH SEA SALT AND PEPPER AS DESIRED. POUR OVER MEATBALLS AND SERVE.

FOR A BEAUTIFUL PRESENTATION, TRY STUFFING THE MEATLOAF WITH MORE VEGETABLES. PLACE AN 18" PIECE OF WAXED PAPER OR PARCHMENT ON A HARD SURFACE. PRESS THE MEATLOAF MIXTURE INTO A 9" X 12" SIZE. INTO THE CENTER PLACE SOME GRATED CARROTS, COOKED AND DRAINED SPINACH, AND WHATEVER ELSE YOU CHOOSE. USING THE WAXED PAPER, ROLL UP THE MEATLOAF (LIKE A JELLY ROLL) AND PLACE IN PAN, SEAM SIDE DOWN. WHEN YOU SLICE THE BAKED MEATLOAF, YOU WILL SEE SPIRALS OF COLORS. YOU MAY ALSO SPRINKLE YOUR STUFFING MIXTURE WITH ABOUT ½ CUP OF GRATED CHEESE IF YOU LIKE.

Weeknight Turkey Marsala

This is a quick and easy dish perfect for a weeknight dinner. Serve with quinoa or brown rice and steamed broccoli. In the 1700s, Marsala wine was reputedly responsible for soldiers "fighting with more flair." We're not in any kind of position to confirm or deny that statement, but we'll emphatically affirm that this famous Italian wine does add flair to this dish (see the Cooking with Alcohol sidebar, page 147).

SERVES 4

2 tablespoons extra-virgin olive oil, divided

4 boneless turkey breast cutlets, lightly pounded

8 ounces mushrooms, sliced, preferably shiitake

1 cup sliced onion

½ cup Marsala wine

½ cup fresh or frozen peas

½ cup thinly sliced carrots

Sea salt to taste

Black pepper to taste

2 tablespoons chopped fresh parsley, stems removed

Heat a large skillet over medium-high heat until hot. Add 1 tablespoon of the oil and then add the turkey. Cook 2 minutes each side; remove from skillet and keep warm. Add remaining 1 tablespoon oil, mushrooms, and onion to skillet; cook and stir 5 minutes. Reduce heat to low. Add wine, peas, and carrots and simmer uncovered 2 minutes. Return cutlets to skillet and coat with sauce and season with salt and pepper if desired. Sprinkle with parsley and serve.

PER SERVING: 207 CALORIES; 8G FAT (38.4% CALORIES FROM FAT); 20G PROTEIN; 10G CARBOHYDRATE; 3G DIETARY FIBER; 45MG CHOLESTEROL; 172MG SODIUM.

Health Note

TURKEY IS LOW IN FAT AND HIGH IN PROTEIN AND CONTAINS IRON, ZINC, PHOSPHORUS, POTASSIUM, AND B-VITAMINS.

Wheat-Free Zucchini Pizza

Zucchini and rice are the primary ingredients in the crust of this unique pizza. Summer's bountiful zucchini is high in manganese, vitamin C, magnesium, vitamin A, and dietary fiber. For a vegetarian version, simply leave out the ground turkey.

SERVES 6

4 cups grated zucchini

2 cups cooked brown rice

1½ cups grated Monterey jack or mozzarella cheese

2 eggs, beaten

1 pound ground turkey

1 medium onion, chopped

3 tablespoons chopped fresh oregano

3 tablespoons chopped fresh basil

1½ cups marinara sauce (page 69)

2 cups grated cheddar cheese or other cheese

Preheat oven to 425°F.

In a bowl, combine the zucchini, rice, jack cheese, and eggs. Press into a greased 15" x 11" x 1" jelly roll pan. Bake for 20–25 minutes or until lightly browned.

In a medium skillet, brown the turkey with onion, oregano, and basil. Set aside.

Pour marinara over crust, sprinkle with turkey mixture, and top with cheddar cheese. Bake at 425°F for 15 minutes. Let stand 5 minutes before serving.

PER SERVING: 677 CALORIES; 32G FAT (42.6% CALORIES FROM FAT); 38G PROTEIN; 59G CARBOHYDRATE; 4G DIETARY FIBER; 187MG CHOLESTEROL; 739MG SODIUM.

Kids in the Kitchen

HAVE YOUR CHILD GREASE THE PAN, SPREAD THE ZUCCHINI MIXTURE IN THE PAN, AND THEN, AFTER THE CRUST IS BAKED, SPRINKLE THE REMAINING INGREDIENTS ON TOP. WATCH OUT FOR THE HOT PAN!

Adding MVP to Pizzas

Get out of your pepperoni rut and spread your pizza crust with puréed veggies or your vegetable-added marinara sauce (see Marinara Sauce for Spaghetti, Pizza, and More, page 48, for tips). Then sauté onions, garlic, shredded zucchini, and whatever else you like and add as toppings. We like fresh spinach or basil leaves on top, and add them at the end of the baking time so as not to overcook.

Dr. Haas uses a cornmeal pizza crust, one that has just a little wheat which can be found already prepared in some markets—spread with an organic garlic and basil tomato sauce. Then he cuts up onion, peppers, mushrooms, zucchini, and garlic and tosses it all in a bowl with some olive oil, balsamic vinegar, and seasoning herbs. Then he layers it on the crust and then adds more sauce on top. These pizzas can be up to 3 inches high! He bakes it at 325–350°F for 30–45 minutes or until done with a slightly crispy crust. Cheese is optional and can be added on top toward the end.

Chicken with Artichoke Pesto and Wilted Spinach

Serve this delicious dish with some sautéed red bell pepper slices placed next to the chicken on the plate for a nice splash of color.

SERVES 4

1 pound boneless, skinless chicken breast halves, 4 ounces per serving, lightly pounded

½ teaspoon sea salt, plus more to taste

½ teaspoon freshly ground black pepper, plus more to taste

2 tablespoons extra-virgin olive oil, divided

1 tablespoon lemon zest, grated

1 cup fresh basil leaves

3 cloves garlic

½ cup chicken broth (page 119)

One 14-ounce can artichoke hearts, in water, drained and minced

1 pound spinach leaves, washed

Toasted pine nuts, for garnish

Grated Parmesan cheese, for garnish

Wash the chicken breasts and pat dry. Sprinkle with ½ teaspoon of the salt and ½ teaspoon of the pepper. Heat 1 tablespoon of the oil in a medium skillet over medium heat. Add chicken and cook 3–4 minutes. Turn over and sprinkle with lemon zest. Cook another 3–4 minutes until done. Remove from pan and keep warm.

To make the artichoke pesto, place basil, garlic, broth, and remaining 1 tablespoon oil in a blender and process until smooth. Do not purée the artichoke hearts. Place mixture in a bowl and stir in the artichoke hearts.

In the skillet used to cook the chicken, place the spinach and stir for a minute until wilted over low heat. Season with salt and pepper to taste.

Place the spinach on a plate with the chicken and artichoke pesto on the top. Garnish with pine nuts and a grating of cheese.

PER SERVING: 263 CALORIES; 9G FAT (29.0% CALORIES FROM FAT); 33G PROTEIN; 15G CARBOHYDRATE; 8G DIETARY FIBER; 66MG CHOLESTEROL; 564MG SODIUM.

Variations

FOR A VEGETARIAN VERSION, SUBSTITUTE THE CHICKEN FOR FIRM TOFU CUT INTO THICK SLICES.

Baked Chicken and Veggie Taquitos

Almost everyone loves Mexican food, and it is an easy way to add MVP into your diet. This recipe calls for veggies of your choice. To make your taquitos spicier, add finely chopped jalapeños, minced garlic, or green onions. Garnish with guacamole (page 88) and chopped cilantro.

SERVES 6

3 cups assorted chopped seasonal vegetables

1 tablespoon extra-virgin olive oil

2 cups cooked white beans (if using canned beans, drain before use)

2 cups diced cooked chicken breast meat

1½ cups salsa (page 75)

1½ cups grated cheddar cheese or Monterey jack cheese

Six 10" flour (or nongluten) tortillas

Preheat oven to 450°F.

Sauté your choice of vegetables in oil for 5–6 minutes. Place in a medium bowl and add beans, chicken, salsa, and cheese and mix. Divide mixture among 6 tortillas, placing mixture on the bottom half of the tortilla. Begin to roll, tucking in the sides as you go. Place seam side down on a cookie sheet lined with parchment paper. Bake for 10–15 minutes or until golden and crispy.

PER SERVING: 558 CALORIES; 18G FAT (29.8% CALORIES FROM FAT); 37G PROTEIN; 61G CARBOHYDRATE; 7G DIETARY FIBER; 70MG CHOLESTEROL; 776MG SODIUM. (NOTE THAT NUTRIENTS CAN CHANGE BASED ON SEASONAL INGREDIENTS USED.)

Variations

TACOS AND BURRITOS ARE TWO OF THE EASIEST WAYS TO INCORPORATE HEALTHY VEGGIES INTO YOUR DIET. WHEN WE THINK OF TACOS AND BURRITOS, WE THINK OF ONIONS, GARLIC, PEPPERS, TOMATOES, LETTUCE...BUT START TO THINK ABOUT SHREDDED CARROTS AND ZUCCHINI OR CUBED WINTER SQUASH. YOU CAN MIX THESE IN OR LAYER ON TOP OF YOUR RICE AND WHOLE OR REFRIED BEANS. THINLY SLICED GREENS SUCH AS KALE, CHARD, MUSTARD GREENS, OR COLLARDS ARE ALSO NICE. YOUR SALSA COULD BE MADE FROM FRESH TOMATILLOS AND TOMATOES.

Kids in the Kitchen

BE SURE TO LET THE KIDS MAKE THESE TAQUITOS—THEY CAN'T SEEM TO RESIST THE ROLLING. FOR SMALLER CHILDREN, YOU CAN HAVE EVERYTHING PREPARED IN BOWLS AND THEN SIMPLY HAVE THEM ASSEMBLE.

Health Note

THIS BAKED VERSION OF THE TYPICALLY DEEP-FRIED TAQUITO IS AN EXCELLENT SOURCE OF NIACIN, FOLATE, PHOSPHORUS, AND MAGNESIUM AS WELL AS VITAMIN B6, VITAMIN B12, IRON, CALCIUM, ZINC, AND DIETARY FIBER.

Paella

This is such a dramatic dish! Open this for the first time at the table and listen for the oohs and aahs. You may use the three veggies this recipes calls for and also add artichoke hearts the last 10 minutes of cooking if you like.

Serves 8

2 teaspoons saffron

4 cups chicken broth (page 119), warm, plus 2 tablespoons more for saffron

2 cups chopped chicken, breast or thighs, cut into 1" pieces

1 teaspoon sea salt, plus more for seasoning

1 teaspoon freshly ground pepper, or to taste, plus more for seasoning

2 tablespoons extra-virgin olive oil

1 link chorizo, cut into 10 slices

1 medium yellow onion, thinly sliced

4 cloves garlic, chopped

2 cups brown rice

2 medium red bell peppers, thinly sliced

1 teaspoon paprika

1 teaspoon ground oregano

1 pound medium shrimp, peeled

12 clams, well scrubbed

1½ cups peas

½ cup chopped fresh parsley, stems removed

Black olives, for garnish

Preheat oven to 350°F.

Soak saffron in 2 tablespoons of the warm chicken broth.

Rinse chicken and pat dry. Sprinkle with salt and pepper. Heat olive over medium heat in a paellero or large skillet that has a lid, or a casserole dish that can go on the stove and in the oven. Add chicken and brown well on all sides. Remove from pan and set aside. Lightly brown the sausages in the same pan and then set aside.

Drain off all but 1 tablespoon fat and add the onions and garlic and cook, stirring occasionally, for 5 minutes. Add the rice, saffron, and 1 teaspoon of the salt and cook for 5 minutes, stirring frequently. Add the remaining 4 cups chicken broth, bring to a boil, reduce heat, cover, and cook on low heat for 30 minutes.

Take off cover, but do not stir the rice. Arrange the chicken, chorizo, and bell peppers attractively on top. Sprinkle with paprika and oregano. Cover and place in oven for 10 minutes. Remove from oven and place the shrimp, clams, and peas on top. Cover and cook for another 10 minutes or until clams are open. Discard any clams that haven't opened. Sprinkle with parsley, cracked pepper, olives, and serve!

Per serving: 456 calories; 16g fat (31.9% calories from fat); 30g protein; 46g carbohydrate; 3g dietary fiber; 139mg cholesterol; 1,534mg sodium.

Baked Chicken

Add cubed potatoes, yams, onions, peppers, sliced zucchini, and so on to your baked chicken. Remember that different vegetables take various times to bake, so put the cut carrots and potatoes in with the chicken before the sliced zucchini, as an example. Also, you can make and bake any one-dish animal proteins, as with fish or beef, and add vegetables to the dish, baking all together. It's all very tasty when the juices are mixed together.

Chicken Pot Pie

The vegetables called for in this recipe are this classic pot pie vegetables. For something different, try using parsnips and turnips, or add some broccoli and lima beans. You may even use all vegetables and vegetable broth to make this a veggie pot pie. Serve with a green salad. Make a double batch and freeze some for another time. You can make these in individual sizes if you like.

SERVES 8

1 pound chicken or turkey breast, cubed

1 onion, chopped

2 medium carrots, thinly sliced

2 large celery ribs, thinly sliced

1 cup peas, fresh or frozen

⅓ cup extra-virgin olive oil or unsalted butter

⅓ cup flour or other thickener

1 teaspoon sea salt, or to taste

1 teaspoon black pepper

2 teaspoons poultry seasoning

2 home-made (or ready-made) pie crusts

Place chicken and onion in a 2-quart saucepan. Pour in just enough water to cover. Bring to a boil over medium-high heat; reduce heat to medium and simmer until meat is cooked through, about 20 minutes. Add carrots and celery and simmer for 10 minutes. Add peas and simmer for 1 minute.

Drain water from pan, reserving 2 cups of the liquid. Set chicken and veggie mixture aside in a bowl.

Preheat oven to 375°F.

In the pan, heat the oil over medium-low heat until melted. Stir in flour and cook for 2 minutes. Slowly whisk in the reserved liquid and stir until the mixture thickens. Add salt, pepper, and poultry seasoning to taste, stirring into the chicken mixture.

Center one pie crust over a 9" pie pan. Place chicken mixture on crust and top with the second crust. Seal edges and prick holes in top of crust. Bake 45–50 minutes. Cool 10 minutes before slicing.

PER SERVING: 207 CALORIES; 13G FAT (58.5% CALORIES FROM FAT); 11G PROTEIN; 10G CARBOHYDRATE; 2G DIETARY FIBER; 29MG CHOLESTEROL; 280MG SODIUM.

Cooking Tip

NEVER SET HOT FOOD IN PLASTIC BOWLS; ALWAYS USE GLASS OR STAINLESS STEEL, AS HOT PLASTIC CAN RELEASE DANGEROUS CHEMICALS, SOME KNOWN TO CAUSE CANCER.

······· **Meat Main Dishes** ·······

Pot Roast with Carmelized Onions

This dish is very high in protein, but also very high in fat, so it's not something to eat often. Adding lots of vegetables is the key to making this old-fashioned pot roast a bit healthier. You may add 2 tablespoons tomato paste during the last half hour of cooking if you like.

SERVES 8

1 tablespoon extra-virgin olive oil

3½ pounds boneless chuck roast

1 ½ teaspoons sea salt

1 teaspoon black pepper

2 large yellow onions, chopped or sliced

5 cloves garlic, chopped

2½ cups wine, vegetable broth (page 117), or beef broth (or a combination thereof)

4 large carrots, thickly sliced

3 ribs celery, thickly sliced

1 medium turnip, peeled and chopped

1 large parsnip, peeled and choppped

2 medium potatoes, cubed

1 bay leaf

1 teaspoon ground rosemary

1 teaspoon ground oregano

Heat the oil in a thick-bottomed pot, such as a Dutch oven, over medium-high heat. Wash the meat and sprinkle it with salt and pepper. Brown roast in the oil until browned on all asides. Don't move the roast while it is browning or else it won't brown well. It generally takes 2–3 minutes on each side.

When the roast is browned, remove it and place on a plate and set aside. Add the onions and garlic to the pot and simmer until the onions are golden brown, or caramelized. Remove from the pot, place the roast back in the pot, and cover with the onions and garlic. Pour the wine over the roast, cover, and simmer for approximately 3 hours, adding more wine if necessary.

Add the remaining veggies and seasonings and simmer for another 30 minutes.

PER SERVING: 511 CALORIES; 33G FAT (58.6% CALO-RIES FROM FAT); 33G PROTEIN; 19G CARBOHYDRATE; 4G DIETARY FIBER; 115MG CHOLESTEROL; 494MG SODIUM.

Cooking Tip

USING A HEAT-DIFFUSER UNDER THE POT OR DUTCH OVEN IS HELPFUL. IF YOU DON'T HAVE A HEAT DIFFUSER, YOU CAN TAKE SOME ALUMINUM FOIL AND ROLL IT UP TIGHTLY INTO A COIL. PLACE THAT ON THE BURNER AND PLACE THE POT ON TOP OF THE COIL.

Beef Fajitas

Restaurants use a cast-iron pan so the fajitas can be served sizzling hot. Most households don't have these on hand, so a warm plate works just fine. You can use any kind of animal protein (chicken or shrimp come to mind), or grilled tofu, in fajitas. You can also use a variety of vegetables that you and your family enjoy.

SERVES 6

4 cloves garlic (for marinade) plus 2 more cloves

2 tablespoons lime juice

1 teaspoon sea salt

1½ teaspoons black pepper

2 teaspoons ground cumin

1½ teaspoons onion powder

2 pounds flank steak

2 tablespoons extra-virgin olive oil

1 medium red bell pepper, thinly sliced

1 medium yellow bell pepper, thinly sliced

1 medium green bell pepper, thinly sliced

1 medium onion, thinly sliced

1 cup thinly sliced radishes

6 corn or flour tortillas

Cilantro, for garnish

Grated cheese, for garnish

Guacamole (page 88), for garnish

Make the marinade by chopping and mashing 4 cloves of the garlic into a paste. In a medium bowl, combine the garlic paste with lime juice, salt, pepper, cumin, and onion powder. Set aside.

Trim the fat from the flank steak. Add the steak to the marinade, turning several times to coat all sides. Cover the steak and marinate in the refrigerator for at least 1 hour or overnight.

Grill the steak on a hot grill to the desired doneness. This can be 4–10 minutes per side, depending on thickness. Remove the steak and allow it to rest for 10 minutes.

Meanwhile, heat the oil in a large sauté pan over medium-high heat. Chop the remaining 2 cloves of garlic. Add the chopped garlic, peppers, onion, and radishes, and cook until tender, but not soft, about 5–6 minutes.

Slice the steak against the grain into thin slices. Arrange the steak and pepper mixture on warm flour or corn tortillas and garnish with the cilantro, cheese, and guacamole if desired.

PER SERVING: 345 CALORIES; 21G FAT (54.3% CALORIES FROM FAT); 30G PROTEIN; 9G CARBOHYDRATE; 2G DIETARY FIBER; 77MG CHOLESTEROL; 427MG SODIUM.

Cooking Tip

IF YOU DON'T HAVE A BARBECUE GRILL, JUST SAUTÉ THE BEEF IN A PAN. SAUTÉ IN BATCHES SO THAT THE BEEF CAN STAY IN A SINGLE LAYER, OR ELSE IT WILL BRAISE AND NOT BROWN PROPERLY.

Health Note

A HALF CUP OF RADISHES OFFERS ABOUT 25 PERCENT OF YOUR DAILY INTAKE OF VITAMIN C AS WELL AS FOLATE (FOLIC ACID, A B-VITAMIN).

Old-Fashioned Beef Stew

Have fun experimenting with this simple family favorite. You might like the vegetarian option of using all mushrooms. Serve with a simple salad and some cornbread. This is the epitome of comfort food with lots of great veggies.

SERVES 3–4

1 tablespoon extra-virgin olive oil

1 onion, chopped, for every pound of stew meat

Beef stew meat, cubed, or a combination of 1 pound mixed mushrooms (shiitake and portobellos), chopped

3 tablespoons unbleached flour

Beef broth or red wine to cover

Carrots, chopped

Celery, chopped

Potatoes, chopped

Parsnips, chopped

Turnips, chopped

2 cloves garlic, peeled and chopped

1 bay leaf

1 teaspoon dried oregano, or 1 tablespoon fresh

½ cup chopped fresh parsley, stems removed

Sea salt to taste

Black pepper to taste

Heat olive oil in a heavy-bottomed pan over medium heat. Simmer the onions until they are lightly browned. Remove from pan and add meat. Cook until the meat is browning. Sprinkle the meat with flour, stirring, and cook 2–3 minutes.

Slowly whisk in broth to cooked mixture until the liquid barely covers the meat. Simmer, covered, until meat is tender. If you are using mushrooms, add all the other veggies now, including the garlic, and simmer until veggies are almost tender. Then add herbs, salt, and pepper.

After meat is tender, add veggies and simmer until they are almost tender. Add herbs, salt, and pepper.

If need be, you may thicken the mixture with a little arrowroot or cornstarch mixed with a bit of water.

PER SERVING: NUTRITIONAL DATA WILL VARY DEPENDING ON THE INGREDIENTS USED.

Kids in the Kitchen

COOKING IS SUCH A CREATIVE ACTIVITY, AND VERSATILE STEWS SUCH AS THIS ONE ARE PERFECT FOR KIDS TO BEGIN TO SPREAD THEIR CULINARY WINGS. THIS DISH IS ALSO A GREAT WAY TO LEARN ABOUT SEASONAL EATING. IF YOU HAVE A GARDEN OR A FARMERS MARKET NEARBY, YOU CAN PICK THE VEGGIES AND THEN MAKE THIS RECIPE USING SEASONAL INGREDIENTS.

Eating Seasonally

PRACTICE EATING SEASONALLY BY ADDING ANY OF THE VEGETABLES BELOW, OR SUBSTITUTING THEM FOR THE MAIN VEGGIES IN THIS RECIPE, DEPENDING ON THE TIME OF YEAR.

Spring: PEAS, CARROTS, GREEN GARLIC, GREEN ONIONS

Summer: ZUCCHINI, FRESH TOMATOES, GREEN BEANS, BELL PEPPERS, CORN, CAULIFLOWER

Autumn: BROCCOLI, EGGPLANT, CORN, WINTER SQUASHES, PUMPKINS, POTATOES

Winter: WINTER SQUASHES, RUTABAGAS, PUMPKINS, PARSNIPS, TURNIPS

Hamburgers with a Twist

Veggies in the patty, veggies on the bun! You can find panko bread crumbs in the Asian-foods section of your market, or substitute any other type of bread crumb, leftover brown rice, or other grain or rolled oats. Serve on whole-grain buns with the condiments of your choice as well as lettuce, sprouts, and, in the summer, a thick slice of vine-ripened tomato. Yum!

Serves 6

½ large red onion, finely chopped

1 small carrot, grated (about ½ cup)

½ cup finely chopped celery (about ½ stalk)

3 cloves garlic, minced

1½ pounds lean, ground, grass-fed beef

1 teaspoon sea salt

1 teaspoon black pepper

2 teaspoons Dijon mustard

10 ounces frozen chopped spinach, thawed and squeezed dry

½ cup panko bread crumbs

In a sauté pan over low heat, cook the onion, carrot, celery, and garlic until tender. Let cool. Place the cooled veggies with all remaining ingredients in a bowl and mix well. Form into patties and grill, broil, or sauté until desired doneness.

Per serving: 339 calories; 24g fat (64.3% calories from fat); 22g protein; 7g carbohydrate; 2g dietary fiber; 85mg cholesterol; 462mg sodium.

Variations

You can add chopped zucchini and bell peppers into the burger mixture. Also, you can use ground turkey or chicken instead of beef. Serve sautéed bell peppers cooked in the onion pan as a side dish.

Pork Tenderloin and Roasted Vegetables

We would rather title this Roasted Vegetables with Pork Tenderloin to emphasize the veggies, but the pork really is the featured ingredient. This can be a one-dish meal or served with quinoa drizzled with pesto.

SERVES 3

3 tablespoons extra-virgin olive oil, divided

One 12-ounce pork tenderloin

2½ tablespoons dried herbs (rosemary, thyme, parsley, and/or sage), divided

8 ounces mushrooms, halved if large (about 3 cups)

8 ounces new potatoes, halved or quartered depending on size (about 3 cups)

1 medium red bell pepper, cubed (about 1½ cups)

1 medium yellow onion, peeled and cut into 8 wedges

Preheat oven to 450°F.

Coat a 15" x 12" inch roasting pan with 1 tablespoon of the oil. Rub pork with 2 teaspoons of the dried herbs; place in prepared pan.

In a large bowl, toss mushrooms, potatoes, bell pepper, and onion with remaining 2 tablespoons of oil and the remaining 5 ½ teaspoons of the dried herbs; add to roasting pan in a single layer.

Roast, uncovered, stirring vegetables occasionally, until meat thermometer inserted into the pork registers 160°F and the vegetables are tender, about 20 minutes. Cut pork into thin slices and serve immediately.

PER SERVING: 358 CALORIES; 18G FAT (44.4% CALORIES FROM FAT); 28G PROTEIN; 23G CARBOHYDRATE; 4G DIETARY FIBER; 74MG CHOLESTEROL; 1,566MG SODIUM.

Eating Seasonally

PRACTICE EATING SEASONALLY BY ADDING ANY OF THE VEGETABLES BELOW, OR SUBSTITUTING THEM FOR THE MAIN VEGGIES IN THIS RECIPE, DEPENDING ON THE TIME OF YEAR.

Spring: ASPARAGUS, PEAS, CELERY, GREEN GARLIC, GREEN ONIONS

Summer: GREEN BEANS, ZUCCHINI, EGGPLANT, BELL PEPPERS, JERUSALEM ARTICHOKES

Autumn: NEW POTATOES, WINTER SQUASHES, BROCCOLI, PARSNIPS, TURNIPS

Winter: WINTER SQUASHES, BOK CHOY, BRUSSELS SPROUTS

A side dish is just that, on the side of the main dish—in other words, it's secondary to the main dish. In the United States, main dishes are generally thought of as meat dishes. However, we think that vegetables should not be relegated to the role of a "side dish," as they are one of our most important foods. That said, since all the main dishes in this book are chock-full of vegetables, we will let the "side dish" label stand.

When you are eating fresh, locally grown, and seasonal vegetables, there is no need to get fancy with preparation, as they are most delicious cooked simply. Crispy stalks of asparagus in the spring can be eaten raw or lightly steamed and, if you like, sprinkled with a bit of butter and lemon juice. In the autumn, a yam baked in the oven is a wonderful side dish. No embellishments needed...well, maybe a little olive oil or butter.

Cooking methods generally vary with the seasons. Typically, foods that take longer to grow are generally more warming than foods that grow more quickly. The harder foods take more energy to cook and thus contain more heat for the body. This is part of the common sense of Nature, which provides different foods during different times of the year, essentially helping to keep our body in balance.

In the spring, the focus is on fresh, lighter fare representing the new growth of the season. Outside everything is fresh and green, and your plate could be the same. Spinach, tender kale leaves, Swiss chard, lettuce, parsley, and, of course, the bastion of spring, asparagus, need only light steaming, if cooked at all.

Summer brings light and heat—and, not coincidentally, cooling foods, which usually have a higher water content than foods available during the coldest times of the year. These foods include zucchini and other summer squash, peppers, broccoli, cauliflower, and corn. Fresh cilantro, basil, and mint are wonderful summer herbs. Summer vegetables, just like spring vegetables, need little if any cooking—which is perfect for those warm days when you don't want to heat up your kitchen. Lightly sauté or steam most summer vegetables.

In autumn, we look to more warming foods, including carrots, yams, hard squashes, onions, and garlic. These typically need more cooking with more heat and baking times. Seasonings might include ginger and dried peppers.

Winter takes us to even more warming foods. Root vegetables, including carrots, potatoes, winter squashes, onions, and garlic come to mind, and roasting these vegetables brings out their natural sweetness.

Whatever the season, simply prepared vegetables are almost always your best choice following the above principles.

Grilled Asparagus

Asparagus is very high in vitamin K and folate, which is a water-soluble B-vitamin that is needed for the production and maintenance of new cells. Therefore, it's very important during pregnancy and infancy. If fresh salmon is available to you in the spring, grill it alongside the asparagus and serve with a fresh baby spinach salad. Simple and elegant.

SERVES 4

1 pound asparagus

3 tablespoons extra-virgin olive oil, divided

½ teaspoon sea salt

2 teaspoons fresh lemon juice

Freshly ground black pepper, to taste

¼ cup Parmesan cheese (optional), shaved with a potato peeler

Wash the asparagus and discard the tough ends (sometimes up to 2–3" of the bottom of the stalk must be cut or snapped away).

Heat coals or grill to medium-high, or you may also use the broiler. Brush the asparagus with 1 tablespoon of the oil and sprinkle with salt. Grill, turning asparagus until they have a bit of color on all sides.

Place on a platter, mix the remaining 2 tablespoons oil with the lemon juice, and sprinkle on the asparagus. Top with freshly pepper and cheese, if desired.

PER SERVING: 127 CALORIES; 12G FAT (80.2% CALORIES FROM FAT); 3G PROTEIN; 3G CARBOHYDRATE; 1G DIETARY FIBER; 4MG CHOLESTEROL; 329MG SODIUM.

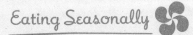

Eating Seasonally

Summer: THIS DISH IS ALSO WONDERFUL IN THE SUMMER MONTHS USING GREEN BEANS.

Kids in the Kitchen

HAVE YOUR KIDS LEARN ABOUT THE FRESHNESS OF VEGETABLES BY ALLOWING THEM TO 'SNAP' THE TOUGHER ENDS OFF OF THE ASPARAGUS.

Green Beans, Leeks, and Hazelnuts

Try this recipe instead of reaching for the canned green beans, canned soup, and jarred onions. Your family will love this side dish anytime, as the toasted nuts add the crunch and flavor that you might otherwise miss in the less-than-healthy original recipe.

SERVES 8

2 pounds fresh green beans

4 leeks, rinsed well

4 tablespoons unsalted butter or extra-virgin olive oil

½ cup hazelnuts or almonds, toasted and chopped

1 teaspoon lemon juice

Sea salt to taste

Black pepper to taste

Trim off the stem end of the beans and slice diagonally into 2" pieces. Place about 2" of water in a medium saucepan, add beans, and bring to a boil. Trim outer leaves off of leeks and slice into 2" diagonal pieces. Cook in separate pans 5–8 minutes or until al dente. Drain and rinse with cold water to stop the cooking. (You can save the water the vegetables were cooked in and use as a base for a soup.)

Melt the butter in a large frying pan and add the beans, leeks, and hazelnuts. Sauté until heated through, sprinkle with lemon juice, and season with salt and pepper if desired.

PER SERVING: 164 CALORIES; 11G FAT (58.2% CALORIES FROM FAT); 4G PROTEIN; 15G CARBOHYDRATE; 5G DIETARY FIBER; 16MG CHOLESTEROL; 74MG SODIUM.

Variations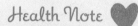

YOU MAY USE RED ONIONS INSTEAD OF LEEKS IF YOU LIKE. YOU MAY ALSO SAUTÉ THE LEEKS OR RED ONIONS IN A LITTLE OLIVE OIL INSTEAD OF COOKING THEM IN THE BOILING WATER. IN THE FALL AND WINTER, SUBSTITUTE BRUSSELS SPROUTS FOR THE GREEN BEANS. CUT THE SPROUTS IN HALF BEFORE COOKING; THEY TAKE ABOUT 5 MINUTES, DEPENDING ON SIZE.

Health Note

GREEN BEANS ARE AN EXCELLENT SOURCE OF VITAMINS K AND C, BESIDES BEING DELICIOUS! KEEP THEM A LITTLE CRUNCHY WITH YOUR COOKING SO THEY DON'T BECOME LIFELESS. YOU MAY STEAM THEM INSTEAD OF ADDING THEM TO BOILING WATER.

Corn and Cilantro Fritters

Compliments of A La Heart Catering in Santa Rosa, California, this dish is a little richer than our usual recipes, but it's wonderful nevertheless. Top the fritters with fresh salsa (page 75) or chipotle aioli. For the aioli, use the recipe on page 71 and add chopped chipotle in adobo sauce; play with these ingredients until you get the taste you desire. Go easy with the chipotles at first. Remember: You can always add more but you can't take them away. For dinner, serve these fritters on a bed of spinach leaves with a piece of grilled fish.

SERVES 12

2½ pounds corn, fresh or frozen

2 teaspoons chili powder, or to taste

1 teaspoon ground cumin, or to taste

3½ teaspoons sea salt, or to taste, divided

4 tablespoons sugar

4 tablespoons unsalted butter

¼ cup finely chopped red bell pepper

½ cup flour

½ cup matzo meal

2½ teaspoons baking powder

Pinch cayenne pepper

½ teaspoon freshly ground black pepper

4 large eggs

⅓ cup milk

½ bunch cilantro, finely chopped

Extra-virgin olive oil for sautéing

In a large skillet over medium-high heat sauté corn with the chili powder, cumin, 1 teaspoon of the salt, and sugar in the butter and then let cool. You can sauté the red bell pepper with the corn now or add it uncooked at the end of the recipe with the cilantro.

In a medium bowl, mix flour, matzo meal, the remaining 2½ teaspoons of the salt, baking powder, cayenne pepper, and black pepper.

In a small bowl mix the eggs and the milk. Stir into dry ingredients. Add corn, cilantro, and bell pepper (if you haven't done so already) and mix. Form into small patties. You may store in the refrigerator in single layers until you are ready to sauté them.

Sauté in a small amount of oil.

PER SERVING: 148 CALORIES; 6G FAT (35.9% CALORIES FROM FAT); 4G PROTEIN; 20G CARBOHYDRATE; 1G DIETARY FIBER; 74MG CHOLESTEROL; 678MG SODIUM.

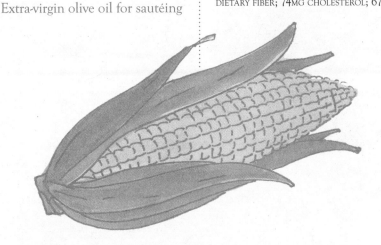

Broccoli with Lemon and Gomasio

We don't know of any child who doesn't like this simple recipe. They love the taste and enjoy using the mortar and pestle to make the gomasio.

SERVES 4

2 pounds broccoli, tough stems removed

1 teaspoon sesame oil

1 tablespoon fresh lemon juice

2 teaspoons gomasio (page 63)

Steam the broccoli until al dente. Drain and toss with oil, lemon juice, and gomasio.

PER SERVING: 199 CALORIES; 6G FAT (23.7% CALORIES FROM FAT); 17G PROTEIN; 30G CARBOHYDRATE; 17G DIETARY FIBER; 0MG CHOLESTEROL; 150MG SODIUM.

Cooking Tip

JUST ABOUT ANY VEGETABLE IS A BIT PERKIER WITH A LITTLE LEMON JUICE ON THE TOP. SO WHENEVER POSSIBLE, KEEP A STOCK OF FRESH LEMONS ON HAND. GOMASIO IS ALSO WONDERFUL ON CABBAGE AND OTHER CRUCIFEROUS VEGETABLES.

Variations

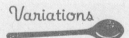

YOU CAN CERTAINLY ADD A VEGETABLE MIXTURE TO THIS RECIPE, SUCH AS ASPARAGUS, BELL PEPPERS, OR WHATEVER THE FAMILY LIKES. AND OF COURSE, THE KIDS MAY LIKE IT BETTER WITH SOME SHREDDED CHEESE ON THE BROCCOLI.

Sautéed Broccoli and Red Peppers

We chop up the stems of the broccoli too, which are just as tasty! Add some capers if you like for a Mediterranean flavor.

SERVES 6

1 bunch broccoli, cut into bite-size pieces

2 tablespoons extra-virgin olive oil, coconut oil, or unsalted butter

2 tablespoons unsalted butter (optional)

1 medium red bell pepper, sliced into thin strips

3 cloves garlic, minced

2 tablespoons pine nuts, toasted

In a large skillet, sauté broccoli in oil and butter 3–4 minutes. Add bell peppers, garlic, and pine nuts. Sauté 2–3 minutes or until vegetables are al dente.

PER SERVING: 126 CALORIES; 10G FAT (66.6% CALORIES FROM FAT); 4G PROTEIN; 7G CARBOHYDRATE; 4G DIETARY FIBER; 10MG CHOLESTEROL; 67MG SODIUM.

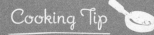

Cooking Tip

TO TOAST THE PINE NUTS, SIMPLY PLACE THEM IN A FRYING PAN OVER MEDIUM-LOW HEAT ON YOUR STOVE. BE VERY CAREFUL, AS THEY ONLY TAKE A MOMENT! THEY TURN FROM A NICE SLIGHTLY GOLDEN BROWN TO BURNT QUICKLY.

Health Note

CRUCIFEROUS VEGETABLES INCLUDE BROCCOLI, CAULIFLOWER, CABBAGE, BRUSSELS SPROUTS, BOK CHOY, AND KALE. THERE ARE STUDIES THAT SHOW THAT THESE TYPES OF VEGETABLES PROTECT US FROM CERTAIN CANCERS, INCLUDING CANCERS OF THE MOUTH, ESOPHAGUS, AND STOMACH.

Variations

TO CHANGE THINGS UP A BIT, TRY OTHER CRUCIFEROUS VEGETABLES IN THIS RECIPE, LIKE CAULIFLOWER, CABBAGE, BRUSSELS SPROUTS, BOK CHOY, OR KALE. OR EXPERIMENT WITH A COMBINATION. IF YOU USE BRUSSELS SPROUTS, CUT THEM IN HALF AND LIGHTLY STEAM THEM FIRST.

Garlicky Beans and Greens

If you like, garnish this flavorful side dish with a sprinkling of Parmesan cheese.
Serve these veggies with sautéed tofu or chicken for a terrific meal.

SERVES 4

· 1 tablespoon sea salt, plus more to taste

1½ pounds kale, chard, or mustard greens, trimmed and cut into 1" pieces

1 tablespoon extra-virgin olive oil

3 cloves garlic, crushed

One 15-ounce can cannellini beans, drained

6 dried tomato halves, rehydrated and chopped

½ cup vegetable broth (page 117) or chicken broth (page 119)

1 teaspoon chopped fresh rosemary

¼ teaspoon red pepper flakes, or to taste

Black pepper or cayenne pepper to taste

In a large saucepan, bring 2 quarts water to a boil. Add 1 tablespoon of the salt to boiling water. Toss the greens into the boiling water and cook until they are almost tender but still bright green, about 3-5 minutes. Kale takes a little longer to cook. Drain well and rinse with cold water. Set aside.

Heat oil in large skillet and sauté garlic until tender, but not browned, over medium heat. Stir in the beans and cook and stir for 8 minutes, heating beans gently. Stir in reserved greens and remaining ingredients and heat through, about 3-5 minutes. Serve hot.

PER SERVING: 174 CALORIES; 5G FAT (22.9% CALORIES FROM FAT); 8G PROTEIN; 27G CARBOHYDRATE; 8G DIETARY FIBER; TRACE CHOLESTEROL; 732MG SODIUM.

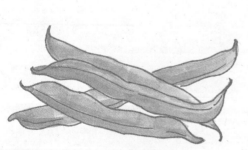

Health Note ♥

LEAFY GREENS ARE SOME OF THE HEALTHIEST FOODS YOU CAN EAT. (WE KNOW, WE'VE ALREADY SAID THIS A FEW TIMES, BUT IT'S TRUE!) SWISS CHARD IS HIGH IN VITAMINS K, A, AND C, AS WELL AS MAGNESIUM, MANGANESE, AND MANY OTHERS. BECAUSE IT'S HIGH IN DIETARY FIBER, CHARD AND OTHER LEAFY GREENS ARE VERY GOOD FOR MAINTAINING DIGESTIVE TRACT HEALTH. EAT YOUR GREENS!

Yam Casserole

Yams are naturally sweet, so we've been hard pressed to find anyone who doesn't love this recipe. A bonus is that your children can make this entire recipe; all you need to do is remove the hot yams from the oven and be sure that they are sufficiently cool before the kids begin to peel the yams. Yams are high in vitamin C, potassium, and fiber.

SERVES 8

4 large yams

2 tablespoons apple cider

1 tablespoon peeled and grated fresh ginger

¼ teaspoon cinnamon

½ teaspoon sea salt

½ teaspoon black pepper

½ cup sour cream or plain yogurt

Preheat the oven to 375°F.

Wash the yams and prick on either side with a knife. Place on a piece of foil or a baking sheet (only to prevent them from dripping all over your clean oven!) and bake for about 50 minutes. Let cool until you can handle. Peel the baked yams and place in a bowl.

In a small saucepan, place the apple cider, ginger, cinnamon, salt, and pepper. Sauté for 1 minute.

Add ginger mixture and sour cream to yams and purée using an electric mixture or potato masher. Place in a buttered casserole dish and heat through, uncovered, in the oven. Depending on the warmth of the yams during preparation, the cooking time can be 20–35 minutes.

PER SERVING: 166 CALORIES; 3G FAT (17.2% CALORIES FROM FAT); 2G PROTEIN; 33G CARBOHYDRATE; 5G DIETARY FIBER; 6MG CHOLESTEROL; 136MG SODIUM.

Variations

TO ADD MVP TO THIS DISH, FEEL FREE TO STIR IN ½ CUP SAUTÉED CHOPPED ONIONS AND ½ CUP SAUTÉED SLICED CELERY BEFORE PLACING THE CASSEROLE IN THE OVEN. SIMPLY SAUTÉ THE ONIONS AND CELERY TOGETHER IN ABOUT 1 TABLESPOON OF EXTRA-VIRGIN OLIVE OIL, BUTTER, OR GHEE (SEE PAGE 64).

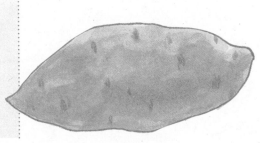

Roasted Winter Squash and Mixed Mushrooms

When you take these veggies out of the oven, stir in some washed and thoroughly dried spinach leaves for a splash of color and nutrition. You can also steam some tempeh and then sauté it in a bit of olive oil (or bake it), tossing the tempeh with a bit of Italian dressing the last couple minutes of sautéing and serving it alongside the roasted winter squash. Delicious!

SERVES 4–6

12 ounces crimini or portobello mushrooms

5 medium yams (about 2 pounds) or other winter squash

2 medium yellow or red onions

¼ cup extra-virgin olive oil

1 tablespoon chopped fresh rosemary (or 1½ teaspoons crushed dried rosemary)

1 teaspoon sea salt

½ teaspoon freshly ground black pepper

4 ounces shiitake mushrooms, tough stems removed

10 large cloves garlic, halved

Preheat oven to 425°F.

Trim mushrooms. Peel and cut yams in half lengthwise, then into ½" slices. Cut onions into 1" wedges. In a large bowl, combine oil, rosemary, salt, and pepper. Add crimini and shiitake mushrooms, yams, onions, and garlic; toss to coat. In two shallow roasting pans, arrange vegetables in a single layer. Roast, stirring once, until tender, about 25 minutes.

PER SERVING: 287 CALORIES; 10G FAT (29.0% CALORIES FROM FAT); 6G PROTEIN; 48G CARBOHYDRATE; 7G DIETARY FIBER; 0MG CHOLESTEROL; 334MG SODIUM.

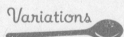

Variations

DON'T FORGET ABOUT STUFFING SQUASH, ALTHOUGH IT BECOMES MORE LIKE A MAIN DISH THEN, RATHER THAN A SIDE DISH. CUT YOUR SQUASH (ACORN, BUTTERNUT, AND SO ON) IN HALF, PLACE CUT SIDE DOWN ON A BAKING SHEET, AND BAKE UNTIL TENDER BUT NOT MUSHY. REMOVE SEEDS, STUFF WITH WHATEVER YOU LIKE, AND HEAT THROUGH. I HAVE STUFFED THEM WITH LEFTOVER HEALTH NUT BROWN RICE SALAD (PAGE 105) AND TOPPED WITH A BIT OF SALSA (PAGE 75). REALLY, ANY RICE AND VEGGIE COMBINATION IS DOABLE. USE YOUR IMAGINATION!

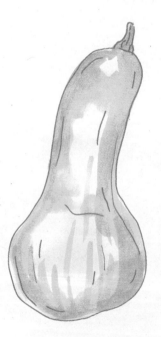

Roasted Roots with Garlic

This beautiful autumn and winter side dish is adapted from a recipe from The Candle Café in New York. Serve it with salmon for an unforgettable dinner. Want to roast fresh veggies in the spring and summer? No problem—see below for tips.

SERVES 4

2 medium carrots, peeled and cut into 1" pieces

2 medium parsnips, peeled and cut into small chunks

2 medium beets, peeled and cut into small chunks

1 medium yam, peeled and cut into small chunks

3 cloves garlic, chopped

2 tablespoons extra-virgin olive oil

2 tablespoons tamari or other soy sauce

1 pinch dried basil

1 pinch dried oregano

1 pinch dried thyme

½ teaspoon sea salt

½ teaspoon freshly ground black pepper

Preheat oven to 350°F.

In a large bowl, place all the veggies. Add the oil, tamari, dried herbs, salt, and pepper and toss to combine. Transfer to a shallow baking dish and bake for 35–45 minutes, or until tender but not mushy. Serve warm or at room temperature.

PER SERVING: 231 CALORIES; 7G FAT (27.3% CALORIES FROM FAT); 4G PROTEIN; 40G CARBOHYDRATE; 10G DIETARY FIBER; 0MG CHOLESTEROL; 809MG SODIUM.

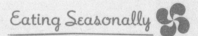

Eating Seasonally

ROOTS ARE PRIMARILY AUTUMN AND WINTER VEGETABLES. IN THE SPRING AND SUMMER, TRY THE ALTERNATIVES BELOW AND JUST CALL THIS RECIPE ROASTED VEGETABLES WITH GARLIC!

Spring: ASPARAGUS, GREEN GARLIC, GREEN ONIONS

Summer: ZUCCHINI, EGGPLANT, RED BELL PEPPERS, ONIONS, CARROTS, CELERY

Autumn: (OTHER THAN ROOTS!) BROCCOLI, CAULIFLOWER, BRUSSELS SPROUTS, ONIONS

Winter: (OTHER THAN ROOTS!) RUTABAGA, CELERIAC, TURNIPS

Mashed Rutabagas

Closely related to the turnip, the rutabaga is a root that's too often—in our opinion—overlooked. Here we use it instead of potatoes to create an all-American side dish. You can try grating fresh nutmeg as a garnish, but not too much or the flavor will take over. Or try peeling and grating the raw rutabaga and adding it to coleslaw or your next green salad. Note that rutabagas can be hard to peel, so many people remove the skin with a sharp knife rather than with a potato peeler.

SERVES 6

4 large rutabagas

2 tablespoons extra-virgin olive oil or butter

½ teaspoon sea salt, or to taste

Black pepper to taste

2 teaspoons minced fresh sage or fresh parsley

Using a potato peeler or a sharp knife, peel the rutabagas. Cut into 1" chunks (approximately). Place into a large (4-quart) saucepan and cover with cold water. Cover pan, bring to a boil, then reduce heat and simmer until soft, but not mushy, about 15 minutes.

Drain, reserving the cooking water. Use a potato masher or immersion blender to coarsely mash, adding some cooking liquid if necessary.

Stir in the oil, salt, and pepper and garnish with sage. Serve hot.

PER SERVING: 74 CALORIES; 5G FAT (54.7% CALORIES FROM FAT); 1G PROTEIN; 8G CARBOHYDRATE; 2G DIETARY FIBER; 0MG CHOLESTEROL; 175MG SODIUM.

Chinese Cabbage Sauté

This simple dish has a real depth of flavor due to the combination of coconut oil, jalapeños, and toasted seeds. If you don't think you like cabbage, this recipe might change your mind! Use either one or two jalapeño peppers depending on your taste buds.

SERVES 4

1½ teaspoons mustard seeds

1 teaspoon cumin seeds

1 teaspoon fennel seeds

½ head cabbage, cut into 1" slices

1 to 2 jalapeño peppers, seeded and diced

¼ cup coconut oil

1 teaspoon turmeric

¼ teaspoon sea salt

Heat a skillet over medium heat and add the mustard seeds, shaking the pan. Add the cumin and fennel seeds and cook until the seeds begin to pop, about 3–4 minutes. Watch that they do not burn. Remove from pan and set aside to cool.

Blanche the cabbage in boiling water for about a minute, then drain. Heat a large sauté pan over medium-high heat and add the jalapeños. Cook for 1 minute and then add the cabbage and cook, stirring often. Add the toasted mustard, cumin, and fennel seeds, oil, turmeric, and salt and sauté for about 5 minutes (the cabbage should retain its crunch). Taste and adjust the seasonings and serve at once.

PER SERVING: 126 CALORIES; 14G FAT (93.9% CALORIES FROM FAT); TRACE PROTEIN; 2G CARBOHYDRATE; 1G DIETARY FIBER; 0MG CHOLESTEROL; 32MG SODIUM.

Variations

WHEN PATTY WAS A LITTLE GIRL, HER MOM WOULD CUT UP A WHOLE CABBAGE INTO WEDGES (ENOUGH FOR A FAMILY OF EIGHT) AND PLACE THE WEDGES IN A PAN WITH A LITTLE WATER TO LIGHTLY STEAM. HER MOM WOULD THEN PLACE THE WEDGES ON THE PLATES WITH A LITTLE MELTED BUTTER ON THE TOP. THAT'S IT, YUM! YOU CAN EMBELLISH PATTY'S MOM'S RECIPE WITH CHOPPED CARROTS, RED BELL PEPPER, AND/OR ANY OTHER SEASONAL VEGGIE YOU LIKE.

Kids in the Kitchen

BE SURE TO HAVE YOUR KIDS MEASURE ALL OF THE DRIED HERBS. IT'S A GREAT WAY FOR THEM TO LEARN MATH, AND IT'S FUN TO MISE EN PLACE THE HERBS INTO A LITTLE BOWL OR RAMEKIN. THEY'LL FEEL LIKE CHEFS.

Carmelized Cauliflower

Who says cauliflower is boring? This wonderful side dish is delightful served with a spinach salad tossed with a lemony vinaigrette. If you use garbanzo beans in your salad (or toss them with the cauliflower toward the end of the cooking time) and have a little quinoa, you have a complete protein and a delicious meal!

SERVES 8

1 head cauliflower (about 3 pounds)

4 tablespoons melted unsalted butter or coconut oil

1 teaspoon honey or agave nectar

1 teaspoon paprika

½ teaspoon sea salt

½ teaspoon freshly ground black pepper

¼ teaspoon cinnamon

½ teaspoon cumin seeds

Preheat oven to 475°F.

Cut the cauliflower into florets, discarding the thicker stalk. In a large bowl, toss the cauliflower with the melted butter and honey. In a small bowl combine the remaining ingredients and toss with the cauliflower. Spread the cauliflower on a baking sheet in a single layer (use 2 pans if need be) and bake 20–25 minutes, or until al dente and carmelized, stirring only once.

PER SERVING: 58 CALORIES; 6G FAT (86.4% CALORIES FROM FAT); TRACE PROTEIN; 2G CARBOHYDRATE; TRACE DIETARY FIBER; 16MG CHOLESTEROL; 122MG SODIUM.

Basic Grains

Here is a handy guide for cooking grains common in this book. Everyone should know how to cook grains and beans. Be sure to have your children help you. It's a great way for them to exercise basic math skills. Get out measuring cups; clear ones are ideal for liquid ingredients. They can measure out the grains and then the liquid.

Basic Millet

1 CUP MILLET

2½ cups water or stock

Place the millet and water in a small (1½ quart) pan and bring to a boil. Reduce the heat, cover, and simmer 25–30 minutes, or until the liquid is absorbed. The millet should be tender but not mushy. Remove the pot from the heat and let it stand, covered, for 10 minutes. Fluff with a fork and serve. Like kasha, you can toast millet before cooking if you wish. To do this, place a dry frying pan on a medium-hot burner, add the millet, and stir for 2–3 minutes or until the grains begin to brown lightly and pop. Remove from the heat, add to the water, and cook as directed above. Yields 3 cups cooked millet.

Basic Wild Rice

1 cup wild rice

Sea salt to taste

3 cups water

Wash rice thoroughly. Add to salted (to taste) boiling water, in a heavy saucepan. Return water to boil and stir. Reduce heat and simmer, covered, 50–60 minutes, or just until kernels puff open. Uncover and fluff with table fork. Simmer 5 additional minutes. Drain any excess liquid. For chewier texture, cook for less time. For additional flavor, use vegetable or chicken broth instead of water. Yields 3–4 cups of cooked wild rice.

Quinoa

1 cup quinoa

2 cups water

½ teaspoon sea salt

Rinse quinoa very well in a fine-mesh strainer at least twice, or it will be bitter. Drain excess water. Bring water and salt to a boil in a 1½-quart saucepan. Add quinoa, reduce to a simmer, cover, and cook until all of the water is absorbed (about 15 minutes). You will know that the quinoa is done when all the grains have turned from white to transparent, and the spiral-like germ has separated. Turn off heat and let stand, covered, for 5 minutes. Fluff with a fork. Yields 3 cups cooked quinoa.

Basic Brown Rice

1 tablespoon extra-virgin olive oil

1 cup brown rice (long grain, short grain, or basmati)

2 cups warm water or stock

Sea salt to taste

Black pepper to taste

Place olive oil in a small (1½ quart) pan and turn heat to medium. Add brown rice and stir for a minute or two to coat rice. Add warm water or stock. Bring to a boil, reduce heat to low, and cover. Let cook undisturbed until done, about 40–50 minutes. Season with salt and pepper, if desired, and serve. Note that long-grain rice cooks to a fluffier texture and short grain to a stickier texture. Yields 3 cups cooked brown rice.

Farro

Sometimes referred to as emmer wheat, farro should be soaked 3–8 hours and then rinsed to drain any remaining chaff or other impurities before it is cooked. You can cook farro more like wild rice. Bring a pot of water to a boil and add the farro, then reduce heat to simmer. Cover and simmer 20–30 minutes or until al dente. A little "toothiness" is appropriate for farro.

Quinoa Tabbouleh

Quinoa, a South American seed once a staple of the Incans, is more protein-rich than other grains and is related to Swiss chard and spinach. (See page 196 for cooking instructions.) Its mild flavor allows the traditional Middle Eastern salad flavors to shine. Try stuffing this salad into a whole-wheat pita with extra lettuce for a healthy lunch.

SERVES 4

2 cups cooked quinoa (page 196)

½ cup diced red bell pepper

½ cup diced tomato

¼ cup finely chopped radishes

¼ cup diced red onions

2 tablespoons minced fresh mint, stems removed

2 tablespoons minced fresh parsley, stems removed

1½ tablespoons extra-virgin olive oil

2 tablespoons fresh lemon or lime juice

Sea salt to taste

Freshly ground black pepper to taste

Lettuce leaves, for serving

In a large bowl, combine the cooked quinoa with the vegetables, mint, and parsley and mix well. Toss with the oil, lemon juice, salt, and pepper. Serve on a lettuce leaf.

PER SERVING: 382 CALORIES; 10G FAT (23.5% CALORIES FROM FAT); 12G PROTEIN; 63G CARBOHYDRATE; 6G DIETARY FIBER; 0MG CHOLESTEROL; 24MG SODIUM.

Kids in the Kitchen

SHOW YOUR KIDS THE QUINOA AND EXPLAIN TO THEM THAT THEY ARE VERY SMALL SEEDS, BUT WHEN THEY ARE COOKED THEY EXPAND AND REVEAL THEIR LITTLE "SQUIGGLES."

Quinoa Pilaf with Fennel

If you use homemade vegetable broth without salt, the sodium content will be much less and the flavor so much nicer. This pilaf is lovely molded in a ramekin and inverted onto a plate with a sprig of fennel leaf. Serve it with baked chicken coated with Dijon mustard and some lightly steamed broccoli. This dish can also be made with brown rice (cooking time is 45–50 minutes) or millet (cooking time is 25–30 minutes).

SERVES 8

1 cup quinoa

1 tablespoon extra-virgin olive oil

½ small onion, finely chopped

1 small stalk celery, diced

1 small carrot, shredded

1 small fennel bulb, trimmed, cored, and diced

2 cups vegetable broth (page 117) or water

Sea salt to taste

Black pepper to taste

Rinse quinoa in a fine-mesh strainer under cold water.

Place the oil in a 3-quart saucepan and heat until warm. Add the onion, celery, carrot, and fennel and cook over medium heat, stirring occasionally, until onion is softened, about 5–6 minutes. Add the quinoa and sauté, stirring, until lightly toasted, 2–3 minutes. Add the broth, salt, and pepper to taste and cook over low heat, covered, until quinoa is tender and liquid is absorbed, approximately 15–20 minutes. The quinoa develops little spirals when done.

PER SERVING: 151 CALORIES; 4G FAT (23.0% CALORIES FROM FAT); 5G PROTEIN; 25G CARBOHYDRATE; 3G DIETARY FIBER; 1MG CHOLESTEROL; 434MG SODIUM.

Wild and Brown Rice with Seasonal Vegetables

Did you know that wild rice is not rice at all, but a grass? Wild rice is high in protein, manganese, some B-vitamins, and dietary fiber. The addition of veggies gives this side dish a delicious complexity. Serve it with a turkey or tofu cutlet that has been sautéed in a bit of olive oil, parsley, and sage.

SERVES 6

1½ tablespoons extra-virgin olive oil

2 cups sliced leeks

3 cloves garlic, minced

½ teaspoon turmeric

4 cups water

1½ cups long-grain brown rice

½ cup wild rice

2 medium carrots, diced

1 cup peas, frozen

2 tablespoons minced fresh parsley, stems removed

½ teaspoon dried thyme

½ teaspoon black pepper

½ teaspoon sea salt

12 asparagus, tough ends removed

Preheat oven to 375°F.

In a large cast-iron skillet or Dutch oven, heat oil. Add leeks and garlic and cook over medium heat about 7 minutes, stirring occasionally. Add the turmeric and cook 1 minute more.

Stir in water, brown rice, wild rice, carrots, peas, parsley, thyme, pepper, and salt. Cover and bake 45 minutes. Remove from the oven and fluff with a fork.

Arrange asparagus on top, cover, and bake until liquid is absorbed, about 10–15 minutes more. Remove from oven and let stand for 10 minutes before serving.

PER SERVING: 308 CALORIES; 5G FAT (14.9% CALORIES FROM FAT); 9G PROTEIN; 58G CARBOHYDRATE; 6G DIETARY FIBER; 0MG CHOLESTEROL; 183MG SODIUM.

Eating Seasonally

PRACTICE EATING SEASONALLY BY ADDING ANY OF THE VEGETABLES BELOW, OR SUBSTITUTING THEM FOR THE MAIN VEGGIES IN THIS RECIPE, DEPENDING ON THE TIME OF YEAR.

Spring: GREEN ONIONS, ASPARAGUS

Summer: LEEKS, GREEN BEANS, SLICED ZUCCHINI

Autumn and Winter: RED ONIONS, WINTER SQUASHES

Asian Rice Pilaf

Bring the wonderful aroma of toasted sesame seeds into your home with this Asian-inspired pilaf dish. It's wonderful served with steamed broccoli and prawns.

SERVES 6

½ cup chopped onion

1 tablespoon sesame oil

2 cloves garlic, minced

1 cup brown rice

2 cups vegetable broth (page 117)

1 tablespoon reduced-sodium soy sauce

⅛ teaspoon red pepper flakes, or to taste

½ cup thinly sliced green onions

½ cup diced red bell pepper

2 tablespoons sesame seeds, toasted (see Cooking Tip)

Cook the onion in the oil in a 2- to 3-quart saucepan over medium heat until the onion is tender, about 6–8 minutes. Add the garlic and sauté for another 2 minutes. Add rice and cook, stirring, for 1 minute. Add broth, soy sauce, and pepper flakes. Bring to a boil, stirring once or twice. Cover and simmer for about 45 minutes or until rice is tender and liquid is absorbed.

Stir in green onions, bell pepper, and sesame seeds into cooked rice. Cover and let stand 5 minutes. Fluff with fork.

PER SERVING: 214 CALORIES; 5G FAT (21.4% CALORIES FROM FAT); 5G PROTEIN; 37G CARBOHYDRATE; 3G DIETARY FIBER; 1MG CHOLESTEROL; 646MG SODIUM.

Cooking Tip

TO TOAST THE SESAME SEEDS, SIMPLY PLACE THEM IN A FRYING PAN OVER MEDIUM-LOW HEAT ON YOUR STOVE. BE VERY CAREFUL, AS THEY ONLY TAKE A MOMENT! THEY TURN FROM A NICE SLIGHTLY GOLDEN BROWN TO BURNT QUICKLY.

Carrot-Bulgur Pilaf

This side dish goes with just about anything. Or serve it on a bed of warm lentils to make it a complete protein and your main course.

SERVES 4

2 tablespoons extra-virgin olive oil

2 medium carrots, grated

1 cup bulgur

2 cups vegetable broth (page 117) or chicken broth (page 119)

1 teaspoon black pepper

⅓ cup chopped fresh cilantro or parsley, stems removed

In a medium saucepan heat the oil. Add carrots and bulgur and cook 2–3 minutes, stirring constantly. Add broth and pepper, cover, and simmer 15–20 minutes or until broth is absorbed and bulgur is tender.

Stir in cilantro and serve.

PER SERVING: 284 CALORIES; 9G FAT (28.3% CALORIES FROM FAT); 8G PROTEIN; 45G CARBOHYDRATE; 9G DIETARY FIBER; 1MG CHOLESTEROL; 837MG SODIUM.

White Beans with Shiitake Mushrooms and Roasted Garlic

This simple side dish is great served on steamed kale with half a baked chicken breast...or not! Beans have a lot of protein and are high in dietary fiber—something that most Americans are woefully shy of consuming yet is imperative for health.

SERVES 4

1½ cups sliced shiitake mushrooms

2 tablespoons extra-virgin olive oil

1 head roasted garlic (see Cooking Tip)

2 cups cooked cannellini beans (or one 15-ounce can, drained and rinsed)

½ cup chopped fresh parsley, stems removed

Sea salt to taste

Black pepper to taste

In a medium sauté pan, sauté mushrooms in the warm olive oil for 1–2 minutes. Add the garlic and the beans. Sauté for a few moments until heated through and then add the parsley and salt and pepper to taste.

PER SERVING: 188 CALORIES; 7G FAT (33.3% CALORIES FROM FAT); 9G PROTEIN; 23G CARBOHYDRATE; 8G DIETARY FIBER; 0MG CHOLESTEROL; 10MG SODIUM.

Cooking Tip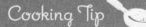

TO ROAST GARLIC, TAKE ONE WHOLE HEAD OF GARLIC AND CUT OFF THE TIPS OF THE HEAD WITH A SHARP KNIFE. PLACE IN A PAN AND DRIZZLE WITH OLIVE OIL. COVER AND LET BAKE AT 350°F UNTIL SOFT, ABOUT 45 MINUTES. COOL AND THEN SQUEEZE THE GARLIC "BUTTER" OUT OF THE CLOVES.

Lentil and Yam Curry with Broccoli

This is wonderful as a side dish to a simple broiled piece of fish. Or serve with a salad and fresh, warmed pita bread. You may use curry powder instead of the other spices if you like; start with 2 teaspoons of curry and go from there.

SERVES 4

⅔ cup lentils

2 tablespoons extra-virgin olive oil

1 medium onion, chopped

3 cloves garlic, minced

1" fresh ginger, grated

½ green chile, seeded and chopped

1 teaspoon cumin seed

1 teaspoon coriander seed

1 teaspoon turmeric

2 medium yams, or winter squash, cut into small chunks

½ teaspoon sea salt

Two 14-ounce cans chopped tomatoes

1 cup small broccoli florets, lightly steamed

Wash lentils, put them in a pan, and cover with cold water. Bring to a boil, reduce heat, and simmer until tender, about 15–20 minutes. Drain and set aside.

Heat the oil in large pan and sauté onion, garlic, ginger, and chile over low heat until softened but not brown, about 5–8 minutes. Add the cumin, coriander, and turmeric and cook for another 3–5 minutes until aromatic. Add the yams and the salt and stir. Then add the tomatoes and their juice, bring to a boil, cover, and simmer for 20 minutes or until yams are tender.

Add the reserved lentils and the broccoli. Cover again and cook until lentils and broccoli are warmed through. Stir well and serve.

PER SERVING: 324 CALORIES; 8G FAT (21.6% CALORIES FROM FAT); 13G PROTEIN; 54G CARBOHYDRATE; 16G DIETARY FIBER; 0MG CHOLESTEROL; 269MG SODIUM.

Chapter 10
Desserts

I f you have read this entire book before you turned to the dessert section, you know that our focus is adding more vegetables to everything. That goes for desserts, too!

Desserts can be a bit more challenging than adding veggies to, say, macaroni and cheese. When most of us think about desserts made with vegetables, we think of pumpkin pie or zucchini bread. We are quite sure you all have recipes for carrot cake and pumpkin bread, but have you ever thought about adding zucchini to brownies or beets to a chocolate cake? How about shredded carrots to cookies or cubed winter squash to rice or bread pudding? Upside down cake can be made with sliced butternut squash instead of pineapple (can you believe it?). When you come to realize that many vegetables have a primarily sweet flavor, it makes sense. After all, the sugar beet has been a common source of sugar for decades.

So start shredding those veggies and stir them into your desserts!

A couple of other things to reconsider are the sweeteners that you use as well as the flour. For sugar, sweeteners we prefer are Sucanat or Rapadura, which are, in essence, pure nonrefined cane sugar. They are both considered substitutes for brown sugar (which is white sugar with molasses added to it, and which should be avoided) and have a higher nutritional value and a smaller proportion of sucrose than white sugar. Let's not kid ourselves here, however—it's still sugar, and most people consume way too much of the stuff! We generally use much less than most recipes call for, and so our recipes are not too sweet.

Other sweetener choices are maple syrup, honey, and agave. Agave (sometimes called agave nectar, which works well in baked desserts) is the juice expressed from the center of the agave plant, which is filtered and then heated. Due to agave's higher fructose content, it is lower on the glycemic index (how quickly a sugar is absorbed and active in the bloodstream) than other sugars. You use less agave than sugar, as it's much sweeter.

We rarely use "white" flour and try to stay with whole-grain flours as much as possible. Whole-wheat pastry flour or whole-grain flour is a good choice for everyday baking. If a recipe calls for white flour and you choose to use a whole-grain flour like whole wheat, you need to use less flour, as whole-grain flour soaks up more liquid than white processed flours. A general rule is to use ⅞ cup whole-wheat flour for each cup of white flour in a recipe. We hope you find that our desserts are as delicious and innovative as our savory recipes. Don't be resistant to try these treats because they contain vegetables—you'll be pleasantly surprised at how versatile veggies can be!

Gluten-Free Flour Mix

If you are gluten-intolerant, you may use our nongluten flour mix as a substitute in any of our recipes, as well as in your own favorite recipes. Gluten is a protein found in wheat, rye, barley, and in some spelt, and some people are reactive to this substance, as they are to the milk proteins lactalbumin and casein. Here is our version of a nice baking flour mix that does not contain gluten flours.

YIELDS 12¾ CUPS

6¾ cups brown rice flour

¾ cup potato starch flour
(not potato flour)

2 cups tapioca starch flour

1 cup cornstarch or arrowroot

2 tablespoons xanthum or guar gum
(this is for "binding")

2¼ cups sweet rice flour

In a large bowl, whisk all ingredients well and store in the refrigerator in an airtight container (we use a 1-gallon glass jar) for up to three months. If you like, you can use teff, quinoa, amaranth, or buckwheat flour for half the required flour and use this mix for the other half.

PER SERVING: NUTRIENT DATA UNAVAILABLE.

Chocolate Beet Cake

What? You never had beets in a cake before? We know you're reading this book because you want to incorporate MVP into your meals, so don't back out now. Trust us, do not skip over this recipe because it's sounds...odd—your taste buds will never forgive you! You can't beet this chocolate cake! You can easily cut this cake into smaller pieces to serve more people. As Mary Poppins said, "Enough is as good as a feast."

SERVES 10

2 cups cooked and puréed beets (see Cooking Tip)

½ cup applesauce

1¼ cups sugar

½ cup unsalted butter, room temperature

½ cup plain yogurt

3 large eggs

2 teaspoons vanilla

½ cup cocoa powder

2½ cups whole-wheat pastry flour

1½ teaspoons baking soda

½ teaspoon sea salt

1 teaspoon cinnamon

½ cup chopped walnuts chopped (optional)

Preheat oven to 350°F. Grease and flour a 9" x 13" pan.

In a large mixing bowl, combine the beets, applesauce, sugar, butter, and yogurt. Using an electric mixer (or a whisk if you want the exercise!), mix well for 3 minutes. Add the eggs and mix well for 1 minute more.

In another bowl mix together the dry ingredients and add to wet ingredients. Stir until combined. Stir in the walnuts. Pour into prepared pan and bake 40–45 minutes or until toothpick comes out clean. Frost if you like, though we don't think it really needs it.

PER SERVING: 379 CALORIES; 16G FAT (35.1% CALORIES FROM FAT); 9G PROTEIN; 56G CARBOHYDRATE; 6G DIETARY FIBER; 82MG CHOLESTEROL; 331MG SODIUM.

Cooking Tip

TO MAKE BEET PURÉE, ROAST BEETS OR BOIL UNTIL SOFT BUT NOT MUSHY. REMOVE SKIN AND PURÉE IN FOOD PROCESSOR.

Sweet as Sugar

When it comes to processed, refined sugars, we like to "just say no." And we encourage you to make a healthier food choice by doing the same. We limit our sugar consumption whenever possible, but when we do need a sweetener that resembles granulated sugar, we reach for dried sugarcane juice. Evaporated cane juice is a healthier alternative to refined sugar, as it does not undergo the same degree of processing that refined sugar does. Remember however, that it is still sugar and to limit your intake of any type of sweetener. Rapadura and Sucanat are two brand-name cane-sugar products that have been minimally processed, if at all. If you don't find these brands at your market, you can use any evaporated cane juice product that has been minimally processed. If that fails, you can always rely on granulated sugar.

In this book, anytime a recipe calls for "sugar," we encourage you to use evaporated cane juice—we do—and the result is no different than using granulated sugar, except that it's healthier for you.

Garden Cake

This moist, delicious dessert is similar to carrot cake, although not as "heavy," and it's full of vegetables. You may glaze it with a mixture of powdered sugar, a little lemon juice, and, if desired, either water or milk until it's the consistency you like—although the cake really doesn't need frosting. Patty's sister Margaret followed this recipe for a party with great success. You know people are close friends when you can experiment at a party!

SERVES 12

½ cup walnut oil

½ cup applesauce

3 eggs

1¼ cups sugar

2 teaspoons vanilla

2 cups whole-wheat flour

2 teaspoons nonaluminum baking powder (see Cooking Tip)

¼ teaspoon sea salt

1½ teaspoons cinnamon

1 cup unpeeled and grated carrots

1 cup unpeeled and grated zucchini

½ cup unpeeled and grated beets

1 cup chocolate chips (optional)

½ cup chopped walnuts

Preheat oven to 350°F. Grease and flour a 9" x 13" pan.

In a large bowl, mix the oil, applesauce, eggs, and sugar, beating well with a hand mixer or whisk for 3–4 minutes.

In a small bowl, combine flour, baking powder, salt, and cinnamon. Stir into wet ingredients. Add shredded carrots, zucchini, beets, chocolate chips (if desired), and walnuts. Stir until blended and pour into prepared pan. Bake 35–40 minutes or until toothpick comes out clean.

PER SERVING: 385 CALORIES; 19G FAT (42.1% CALORIES FROM FAT); 7G PROTEIN; 53G CARBOHYDRATE; 5G DIETARY FIBER; 47MG CHOLESTEROL; 146MG SODIUM.

Cooking Tip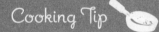

TO MAKE HOMEMADE BAKING POWDER, SIFT ¼ CUP CREAM OF TARTAR AND 2 TABLESPOONS BAKING SODA THROUGH A FINE-MESH STRAINER THREE TIMES. KEEP IN AIRTIGHT JAR AT ROOM TEMPERATURE. WILL KEEP FOR 4 WEEKS. BE SURE TO RESIFT BEFORE USING, AS IT TENDS TO CLUMP.

Pumpkin Cake

This recipe was the result of, as it turns out, a fortunate accident. Patty was preparing a similar pumpkin cake recipe and inadvertently doubled the eggs. She then kept going with the alterations and was very happy with the results. This cake is not too sweet yet very yummy. Serve as a healthier dessert or even for breakfast with a nice winter fruit salad.

SERVES 8

1 small sugar pumpkin

6 large eggs, separated

1 cup sugar

½ tablespoon nonaluminum baking powder

1½ cups finely chopped almonds

Pinch of freshly grated nutmeg, plus more for garnish (optional)

Grated zest of one lemon, plus more for garnish (optional)

6 tablespoons all-purpose flour, divided

Butter for greasing

Fresh mint leaves for garnish (optional)

Preheat the oven to 375°F. Bake a small sugar pumpkin in the oven until tender, about 50 minutes. Remove from oven, set aside to cool, and lower oven temperature to 350°F. When cool, remove skin and seeds and chop very finely.

In a bowl, beat the egg yolks with the sugar until fluffy. Add the baking powder, almonds, nutmeg, lemon zest, 5 tablespoons of the flour, and the pumpkin. Mix until well blended.

In a small bowl, beat the egg whites and fold them gently into the batter. Butter a 9" springform pan and dust with the remaining 1 tablespoon flour. Pour the batter into the pan and cook in the oven for about 1 hour (covering the top with foil after 40 minutes of cooking). Cool on a wire rack. Turn out onto a platter and garnish with lemon zest and grated nutmeg, or mint leaves, if desired. Serve at room temperature.

PER SERVING: 334 CALORIES; 17G FAT (44.5% CALORIES FROM FAT); 10G PROTEIN; 38G CARBOHYDRATE; 3G DIETARY FIBER; 140MG CHOLESTEROL; 137MG SODIUM.

Butternut Squash Upside-Down Cake

Patty was home trying to determine which vegetables instead of pineapple could be just as delectable in a pineapple-upside down cake, when a window cleaner and a UPS driver showed up. Both sampled this version and agreed it was a hit— and Patty could stop experimenting!

SERVES 8

1 medium butternut squash

⅓ cup unsalted butter, plus ½ cup more at room temperature

½ cup sugar

½ cup granulated sugar

1 large egg

1½ cups whole-wheat flour

1½ teaspoons nonaluminum baking powder

½ teaspoon sea salt

½ cup milk

Preheat oven to 375°F.

Peel the butternut squash and, starting with the large end (because there are no seeds in the larger end), slice into ¼" slices. You will need 6 slices; use the remainder for another purpose. Steam the slices over, not in, simmering water for about 5 minutes or until they are tender but not mushy; pat dry and set aside.

In a 9" cast-iron pan, melt 1/3 cup of the butter and add the sugar, stirring until it is melted. Arrange the squash in the pan on top of the melted butter and sugar mixture.

In a medium bowl, combine the remaining ½ cup softened butter with the granulated sugar and beat until light and fluffy. Add the egg and beat again.

Mix together the remaining dry ingredients in a small bowl and add it to the wet batter alternately with the milk. The batter will be thick. Pour over the warm squash mixture and bake for about 25 minutes.

Remove from oven and let cool for 5 minutes. Place a plate on top of the cast iron pan and invert the pan so that the cake is butternut squash side up. Best served warm.

PER SERVING: 354 CALORIES; 21G FAT (50.6% CALORIES FROM FAT); 5G PROTEIN; 41G CARBOHYDRATE; 3G DIETARY FIBER; 77MG CHOLESTEROL; 231MG SODIUM.

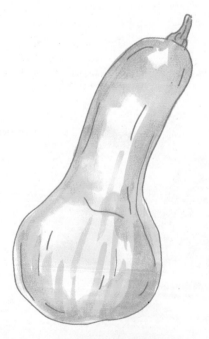

Zucchini Brownies

Zucchini and applesauce make these brownies a healthier version. With the addition of nuts and whole-grain flour, each brownie has 4 grams of dietary fiber—something you don't usually see in brownies! For an extra-special treat, make ice cream sandwiches—your kids will love them. After the brownies have cooled, cut them into squares and then cut them in half horizontally. Now spread them with slightly softened ice cream, wrap them up, and place them in the freezer. Fun!

SERVES 12

1¾ cups whole-wheat flour

1 teaspoon sea salt

1 teaspoon baking soda

½ cup cocoa

2 large eggs

2 cups grated zucchini

¾ cup maple syrup

½ cup applesauce

2 teaspoons vanilla

½ cup chopped walnuts (optional)

Preheat oven to 350°F. Grease and flour a 9" x 13" pan.

In a small bowl, whisk together the dry ingredients. In a medium bowl, mix together the remaining wet ingredients and beat well for 2–3 minutes. Slowly stir in the dry ingredients and stir until blended. Stir in walnuts, if you like.

Place into the prepared pan and bake for 25 minutes or until a toothpick comes out clean.

PER SERVING: 175 CALORIES; 5G FAT (21.8% CALORIES FROM FAT); 6G PROTEIN; 32G CARBOHYDRATE; 4G DIETARY FIBER; 31MG CHOLESTEROL; 275MG SODIUM.

Basic Cookies

This recipe is very adaptable to suit whatever you're craving—you'll hardly taste the veggies. Your children will love to help make these great cookies.

MAKES ABOUT 48 COOKIES.

½ cup unsalted butter, room temperature

1¼ cups sugar

2 eggs

½ cup applesauce

1 teaspoon vanilla

2¼ cups whole-wheat pastry flour

1 teaspoon sea salt

1 teaspoon baking soda

½ cup shredded carrots

½ cup shredded zucchini

½ cup chopped walnuts

Preheat oven to 350°F.

In a large bowl, beat together butter and sugar until light and fluffy. Add the eggs and vanilla. In a separate bowl whisk together the dry ingredients and then add to the wet ingredients. Next, stir in the carrots, zucchini, and walnuts. Using a spoon drop rounded spoonfuls of the batter onto a greased (or parchment paper-lined) cookie sheet. Bake 10–12 minutes depending on size.

PER SERVING: 109 CALORIES; 2G FAT (19.2% CALORIES FROM FAT); 3G PROTEIN; 20G CARBOHYDRATE; 1G DIETARY FIBER; 17MG CHOLESTEROL; 141MG SODIUM.

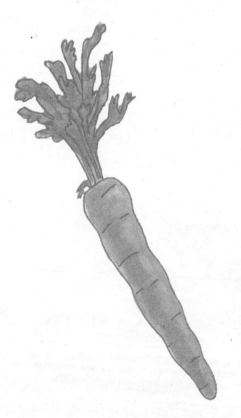

Variations

YOU CAN ADD CHOCOLATE CHIPS OR RAISINS OR GRANOLA OR...WHATEVER YOUR IMAGINATION TELLS YOU! IF YOU WANT TO MAKE OATMEAL COOKIES, USE ¼ CUP LESS FLOUR AND ADD 1½ CUPS OF OATS. PATTY ONCE HAD A STUDENT TELL HER THAT SHE ADDED CHOPPED FRESH BASIL AND ZUCCHINI AND THE COOKIES WERE WONDERFUL.

YOU MAY ALSO USE HALF UNBLEACHED FLOUR AND HALF WHOLE-WHEAT FLOUR OR A NONGLUTEN MIX IF YOU LIKE. THE POSSIBILITIES ARE ENDLESS....

Zucchini-Pineapple Bread

Try this bread for dessert or breakfast. It's easy to make and delicious. You can also make a spread for it by mixing some cream cheese or ricotta cheese with a little honey and chopped walnuts.

SERVES 24

5 eggs beaten until frothy

1 cup walnut oil

1½ cups sugar

1 tablespoon vanilla extract

3¼ cups flour

1 cup oat bran or wheat germ

1 teaspoon cinnamon

1 teaspoon nutmeg

1 tablespoon baking soda

½ teaspoon nonaluminum baking powder

3 cups shredded zucchini

1 cup crushed pineapple, drained

1 cup grated carrots

Preheat oven to 350°F. Grease and flour two 8" x 4" loaf pans and one 3 ¼" loaf pan.

Mix frothy eggs and oil. Blend in sugar and vanilla. Mix thoroughly. Add all remaining ingredients and mix well. Pour into 3 loaf pans. Bake smaller loaf for about 35 minutes, the larger loaves for about 1 hour, or until toothpick inserted in center comes out clean.

PER SERVING: 227 CALORIES; 11G FAT (40.4% CALORIES FROM FAT); 4G PROTEIN; 31G CARBOHYDRATE; 2G DIETARY FIBER; 39MG CHOLESTEROL; 182MG SODIUM.

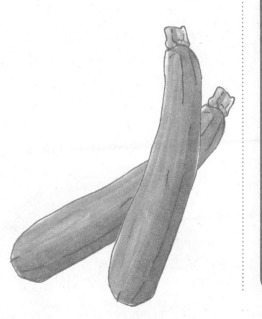

Cooking Tip

EVERYONE'S OVEN IS A LITTLE DIFFERENT, SO BE SURE TO CHECK THESE LOAVES WITH A TOOTHPICK ROUGHLY 10 MINUTES BEFORE THE TOTAL BAKING TIME TO SEE IF THEY ARE DONE. FOR THE BIGGER LOAF PANS, CHECK AFTER 50 MINUTES; FOR THE SMALLER PAN, CHECK AFTER 25 MINUTES. THE TOOTHPICK WILL COME OUT CLEAN AFTER BEING INSERTED INTO THE LARGER PART OF THE LOAF— THAT'S HOW YOU'LL KNOW WHEN THE BREAD IS DONE.

Brown Rice Pudding

Looking for some old-fashioned comfort food to fill your tummy as you sit by a fire with a good book? Search no further. Yams or other winter squash make this aromatic and delicious cold-weather dish more nutritious.

SERVES 6

3½ cups whole milk, divided

½ cup short-grain brown rice

¼ teaspoon sea salt

1½ cups peeled and diced yams

3 large eggs

¼ cup honey

1 tablespoon vanilla

½ teaspoon cinnamon

⅓ cup dried cranberries

In a medium saucepan, combine 3 cups of the milk, brown rice, and salt. Heat to almost boiling then reduce heat and simmer, covered, stirring occasionally for 1 hour. Stir in the yams and continue to cook, also covered, until yams are tender and rice is creamy and thick, about another 30 minutes.

In a medium bowl, whisk together the remaining ½ cup milk, eggs, honey, vanilla, and cinnamon. Stir in cranberries. Gradually stir this mixture into the hot rice mixture and cook until thickened, about 5 minutes. Serve warm or cold.

PER SERVING: 272 CALORIES; 7G FAT (24.7% CALORIES FROM FAT); 9G PROTEIN; 42G CARBOHYDRATE; 2G DIETARY FIBER; 113MG CHOLESTEROL; 180MG SODIUM.

Variations

MANY RECIPES FOR RICE PUDDING CALL FOR CREAM, BUT WE CHOOSE TO USE WHOLE MILK. IF YOU LIKE, USE 2% MILK, SOYMILK, OR ALMOND MILK. WE LIKE CRANBERRIES WITH THE YAMS, BUT IF YOU PREFER, YOU MAY USE RAISINS. ALSO, PUMPKIN OR BUTTERNUT SQUASH WORKS WELL. ALTHOUGH NOT YOUR TYPICAL DESSERT VEGETABLES, 1/3 CUP COOKED PEAS MAY BE STIRRED IN THE LAST 5 MINUTES OF COOKING. IT'S NOT FOR EVERYONE, BUT WE LIKE THE ADDITION. IF THE PEAS ARE FROZEN, JUST RUN THEM UNDER HOT WATER IN A STRAINER FIRST, THEN DRAIN BEFORE ADDING.

Rhubarb Compote

This is delectable for dessert served with frozen yogurt or for breakfast served with plain or vanilla yogurt. If you like, add some chopped apples when you cook the rhubarb for added flavor and nutrition.

SERVES 6

⅔ cup honey

1 cup water (for boiling), plus
3 tablespoons cold water (for cornstarch)

4 cups chopped rhubarb (cut into
½" pieces)

1 teaspoon vanilla

2 tablespoons cornstarch or arrowroot

Dissolve honey in 1 cup of the water in a large saucepan. Bring to a boil over medium-high heat. Add rhubarb. Reduce heat to low and simmer, uncovered, 15–25 minutes or until rhubarb is tender but not mushy. Stir in vanilla. Combine cornstarch with 3 tablespoons water and mix well. Gradually stir cornstarch mixture into rhubarb; cook and stir until mixture comes to a boil. Reduce heat and simmer 3–5 minutes or until mixture thickens. Pour into serving bowl and refrigerate until cold.

PER SERVING: 144 CALORIES; TRACE FAT (0.9% CALORIES FROM FAT); 1G PROTEIN; 37G CARBOHYDRATE; 2G DIETARY FIBER; 0MG CHOLESTEROL; 6MG SODIUM.

Health Note

RHUBARB IS HIGH IN VITAMINS C AND K AS WELL AS DIETARY FIBER.

Index